DOUBLE
WALKER™

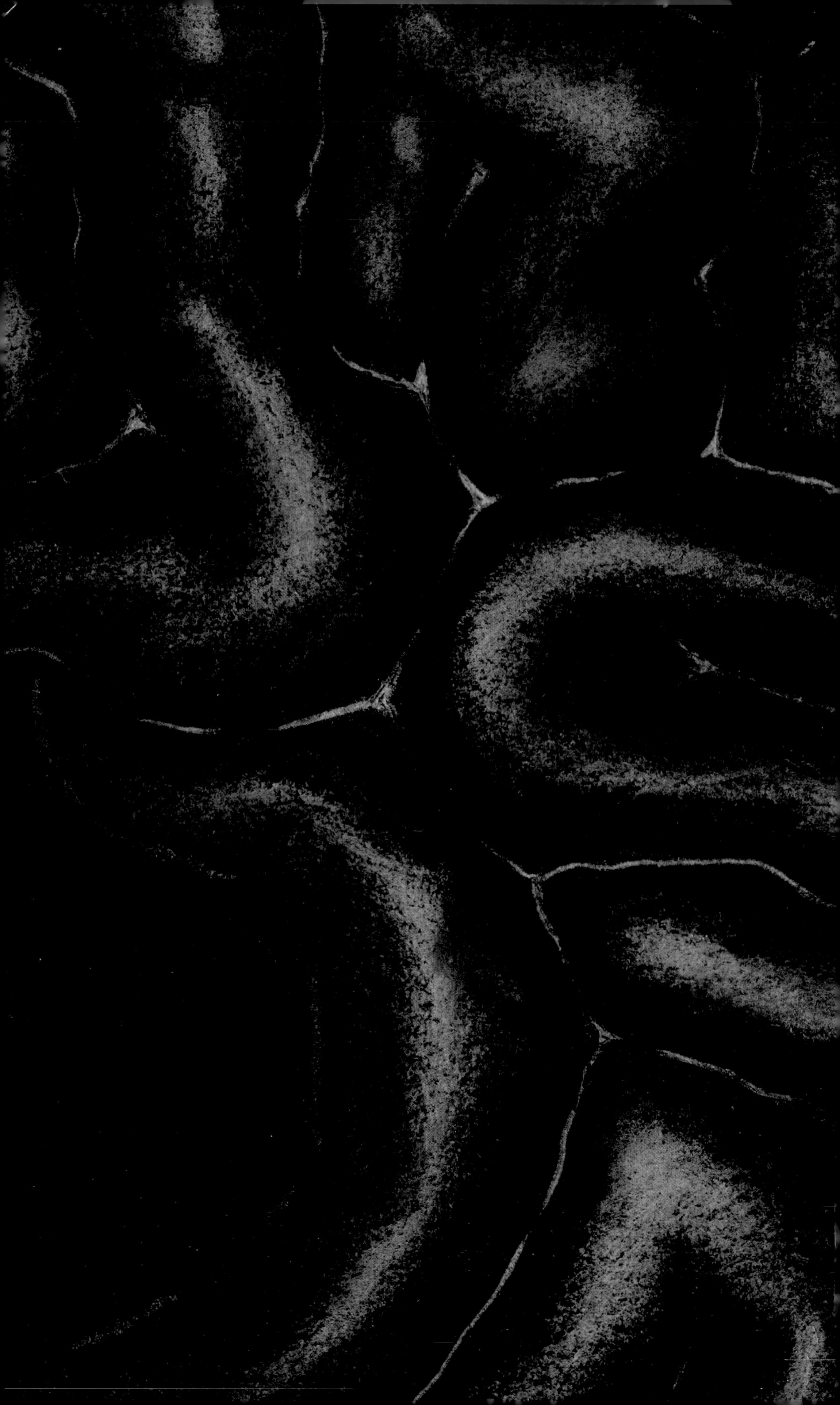

DOUBLE WALKER

Written by **MICHAEL W. CONRAD**

Illustrated by **NOAH BAILEY**

Lettering by **TAYLOR ESPOSITO**

Title Design by **KYLE ARENDS**

Cover by **NOAH BAILEY**

DARK HORSE BOOKS

DARK HORSE TEAM

President and Publisher **MIKE RICHARDSON**

Editor **DANIEL CHABON**

Assistant Editors **CHUCK HOWITT-LEASE and MISHA GEHR**

Designer **KATHLEEN BARNETT**

Digital Art Technician **JASON RICKERD**

Special thanks to David Steinberger, Chip Mosher, and Bryce Gold

Neil Hankerson Executive Vice President | Tom Weddle Chief Financial Officer | Dale LaFountain Chief Information Officer | Tim Wiesch Vice President of Licensing | Matt Parkinson Vice President of Marketing | Vanessa Todd-Holmes Vice President of Production and Scheduling | Mark Bernardi Vice President of Book Trade and Digital Sales | Randy Lahrman Vice President of Product Development and Sales | Ken Lizzi General Counsel | Dave Marshall Editor in Chief | Davey Estrada Editorial Director | Chris Warner Senior Books Editor | Cary Grazzini Director of Specialty Projects | Lia Ribacchi Art Director | Matt Dryer Director of Digital Art and Prepress | Michael Gombos Senior Director of Licensed Publications | Kari Yadro Director of Custom Programs | Kari Torson Director of International Licensing

Published by Dark Horse Books
A division of Dark Horse Comics LLC
10956 SE Main Street
Milwaukie, OR 97222

First edition: December 2022
ISBN 978-1-50673-089-9

10 9 8 7 6 5 4 3 2 1
Printed in China

FSC www.fsc.org MIX Paper from responsible sources FSC® C169962

Comic Shop Locator Service: comicshoplocator.com

Library of Congress Cataloging-in-Publication Data

Names: Conrad, Michael W., writer. | Bailey, Noah, illustrator. | Esposito, Taylor, letterer.
Title: Double walker / written by Michael W. Conrad ; illustrated by Noah Bailey ; lettering by Taylor Esposito.
Description: First edition. | Milwaukie, OR : Dark Horse Books, 2022. | Summary: "Cully and Gemma are watching their carefree, childless days come to an end and decide to take one last trip to the magical Scottish Highlands before the baby arrives. What was meant to be a romantic trip soon spirals into paranoia and violence as a bizarre string of murders follows them on their journey."-- Provided by publisher.
Identifiers: LCCN 2022020338 | ISBN 9781506730899 (trade paperback)
Subjects: LCGFT: Horror comics. | Graphic novels.
Classification: LCC PN6727.C5844 D68 2022 | DDC 741.5/973--dc23/eng/20220513
LC record available at https://lccn.loc.gov/2022020338

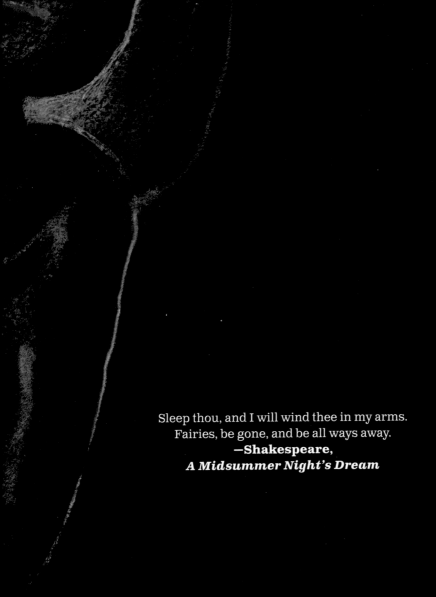

Sleep thou, and I will wind thee in my arms.
Fairies, be gone, and be all ways away.
—**Shakespeare,**
A Midsummer Night's Dream

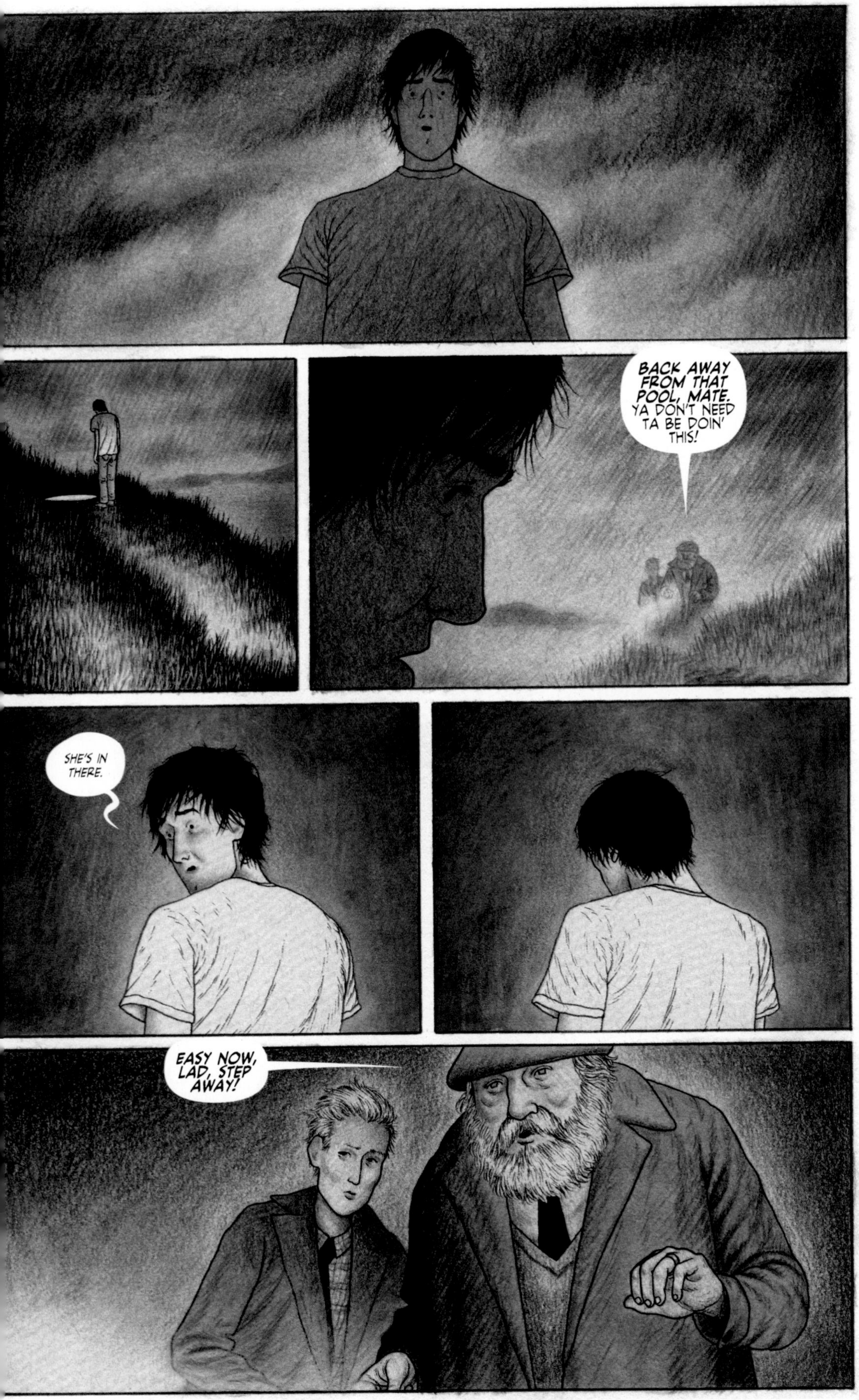
BACK AWAY FROM THAT POOL, MATE. YA DON'T NEED TA BE DOIN' THIS!
SHE'S IN THERE.
EASY NOW, LAD, STEP AWAY!

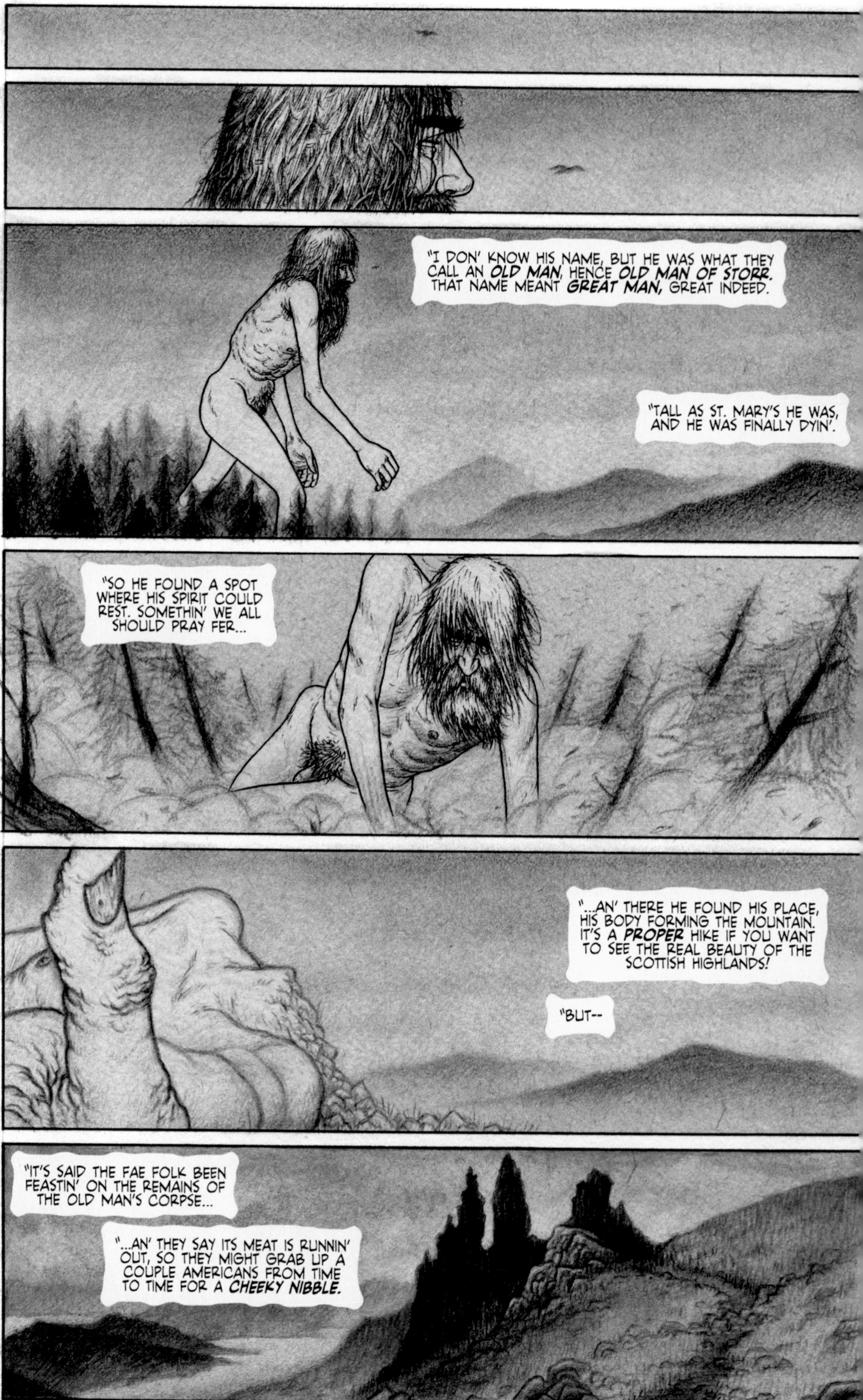
"I DON' KNOW HIS NAME, BUT HE WAS WHAT THEY CALL AN OLD MAN, HENCE OLD MAN OF STORR. THAT NAME MEANT GREAT MAN, GREAT INDEED.
"TALL AS ST. MARY'S HE WAS, AND HE WAS FINALLY DYIN'.
"SO HE FOUND A SPOT WHERE HIS SPIRIT COULD REST. SOMETHIN' WE ALL SHOULD PRAY FER...
"...AN' THERE HE FOUND HIS PLACE, HIS BODY FORMING THE MOUNTAIN. IT'S A PROPER HIKE IF YOU WANT TO SEE THE REAL BEAUTY OF THE SCOTTISH HIGHLANDS!
"BUT--
"IT'S SAID THE FAE FOLK BEEN FEASTIN' ON THE REMAINS OF THE OLD MAN'S CORPSE...
"...AN' THEY SAY ITS MEAT IS RUNNIN' OUT, SO THEY MIGHT GRAB UP A COUPLE AMERICANS FROM TIME TO TIME FOR A CHEEKY NIBBLE.

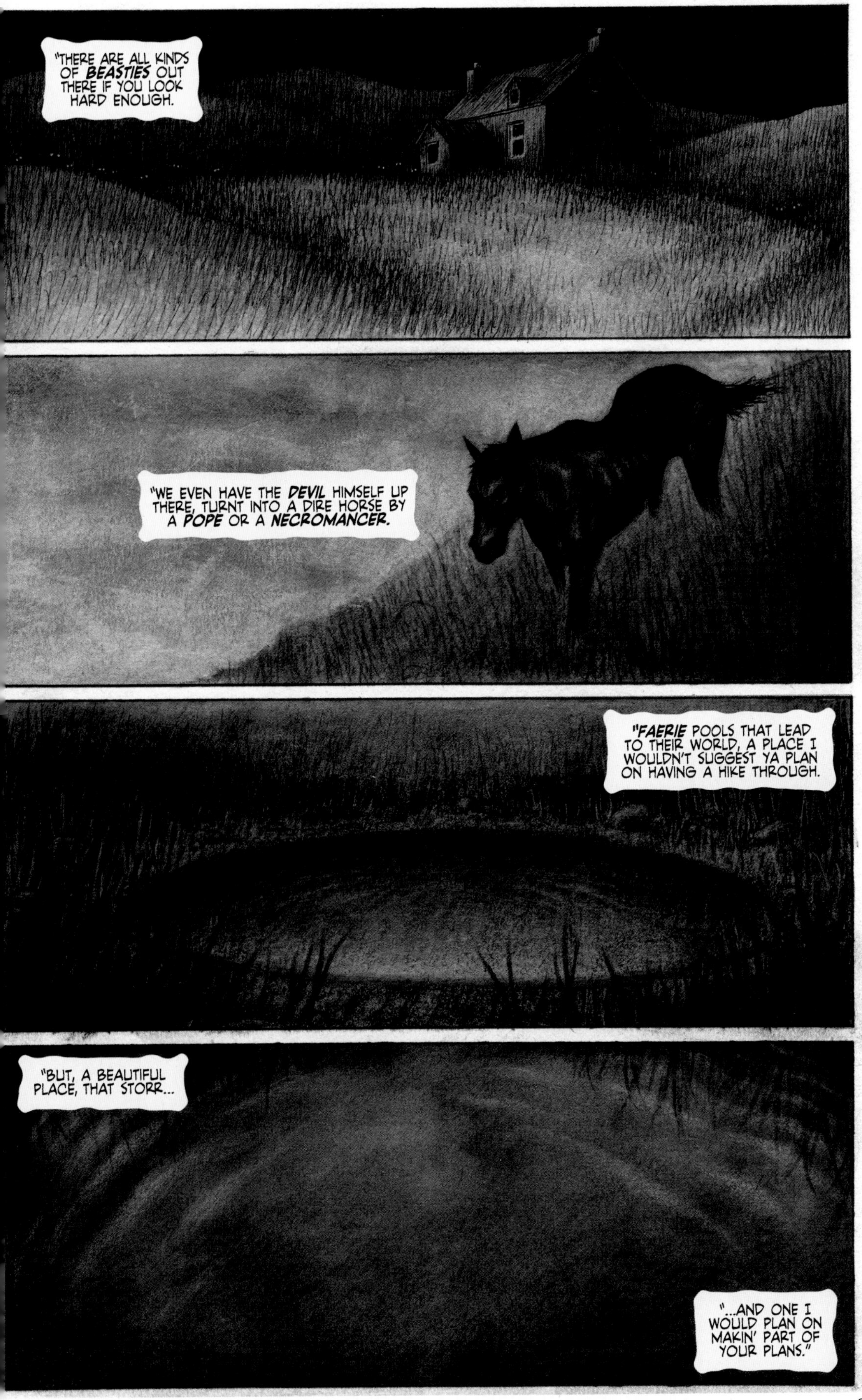
"THERE ARE ALL KINDS OF BEASTIES OUT THERE IF YOU LOOK HARD ENOUGH.
"WE EVEN HAVE THE DEVIL HIMSELF UP THERE, TURNT INTO A DIRE HORSE BY A POPE OR A NECROMANCER.
"FAERIE POOLS THAT LEAD TO THEIR WORLD, A PLACE I WOULDN'T SUGGEST YA PLAN ON HAVING A HIKE THROUGH.
"BUT, A BEAUTIFUL PLACE, THAT STORR...
"...AND ONE I WOULD PLAN ON MAKIN' PART OF YOUR PLANS."

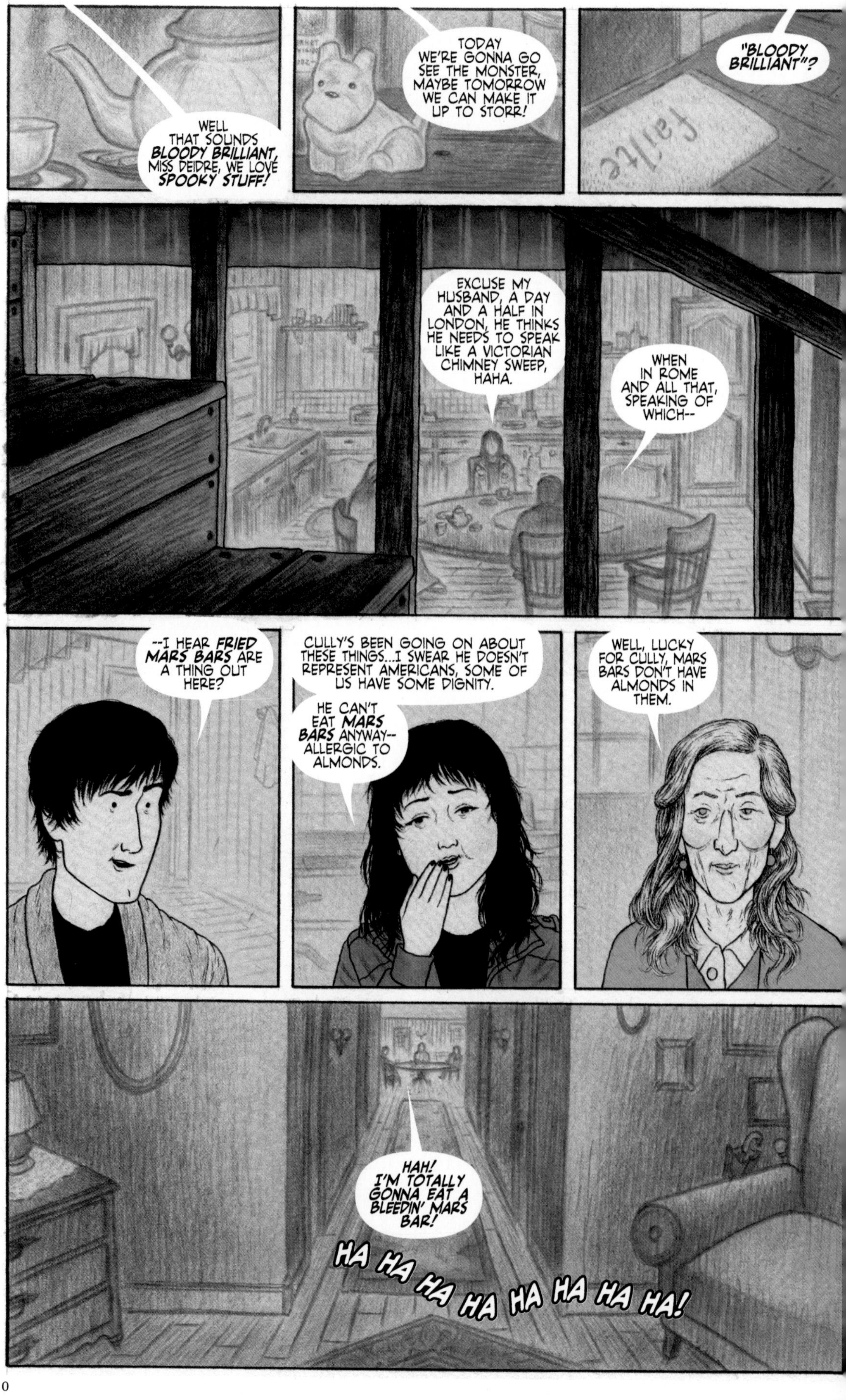
WELL THAT SOUNDS BLOODY BRILLIANT, MISS DEIDRE, WE LOVE SPOOKY STUFF!
TODAY WE'RE GONNA GO SEE THE MONSTER, MAYBE TOMORROW WE CAN MAKE IT UP TO STORR!
"BLOODY BRILLIANT"?
failte
EXCUSE MY HUSBAND, A DAY AND A HALF IN LONDON, HE THINKS HE NEEDS TO SPEAK LIKE A VICTORIAN CHIMNEY SWEEP, HAHA.
WHEN IN ROME AND ALL THAT, SPEAKING OF WHICH--
--I HEAR FRIED MARS BARS ARE A THING OUT HERE?
CULLY'S BEEN GOING ON ABOUT THESE THINGS...I SWEAR HE DOESN'T REPRESENT AMERICANS, SOME OF US HAVE SOME DIGNITY.
HE CAN'T EAT MARS BARS ANYWAY-- ALLERGIC TO ALMONDS.
WELL, LUCKY FOR CULLY, MARS BARS DON'T HAVE ALMONDS IN THEM.
HAH! I'M TOTALLY GONNA EAT A BLEEDIN' MARS BAR!
HA HA HA HA HA HA HA HA!

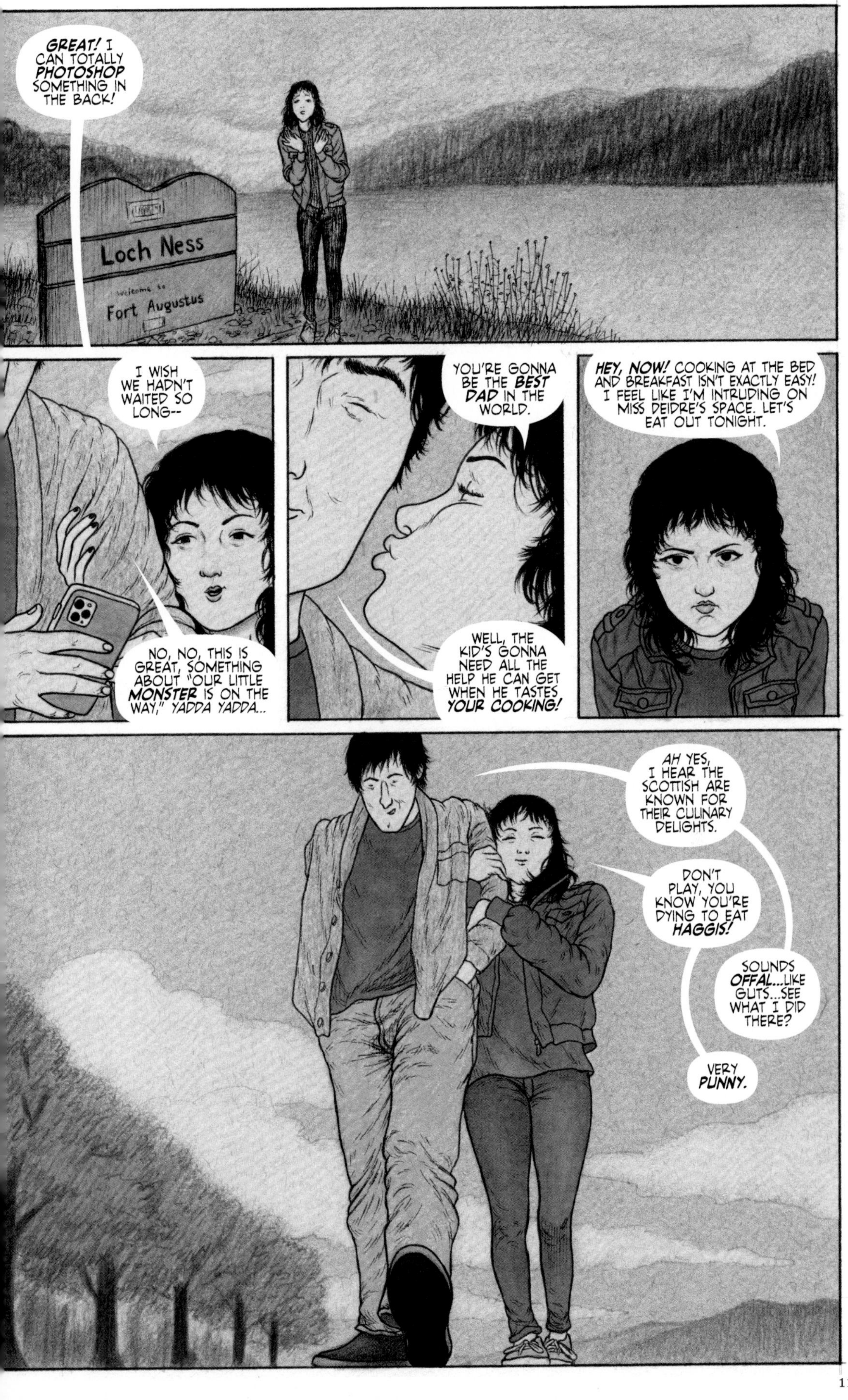
GREAT! I CAN TOTALLY PHOTOSHOP SOMETHING IN THE BACK!
Loch Ness
Welcome to
Fort Augustus
I WISH WE HADN'T WAITED SO LONG--
NO, NO, THIS IS GREAT, SOMETHING ABOUT "OUR LITTLE MONSTER IS ON THE WAY," YADDA YADDA...
YOU'RE GONNA BE THE BEST DAD IN THE WORLD.
WELL, THE KID'S GONNA NEED ALL THE HELP HE CAN GET WHEN HE TASTES YOUR COOKING!
HEY, NOW! COOKING AT THE BED AND BREAKFAST ISN'T EXACTLY EASY! I FEEL LIKE I'M INTRUDING ON MISS DEIDRE'S SPACE. LET'S EAT OUT TONIGHT.
AH YES, I HEAR THE SCOTTISH ARE KNOWN FOR THEIR CULINARY DELIGHTS.
DON'T PLAY, YOU KNOW YOU'RE DYING TO EAT HAGGIS!
SOUNDS OFFAL...LIKE GUTS...SEE WHAT I DID THERE?
VERY PUNNY.

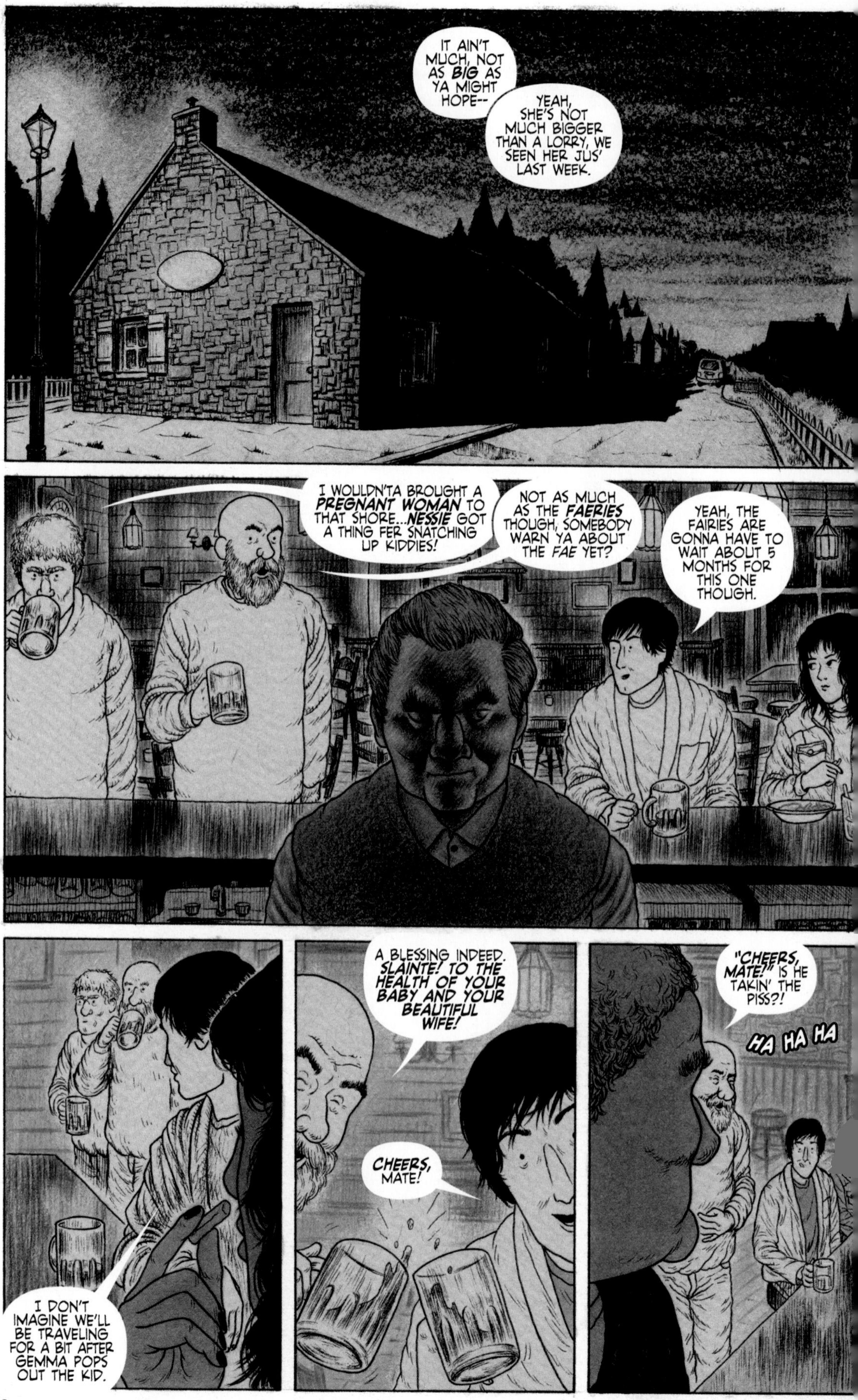
IT AIN'T MUCH, NOT AS BIG AS YA MIGHT HOPE--
YEAH, SHE'S NOT MUCH BIGGER THAN A LORRY, WE SEEN HER JUS' LAST WEEK.
I WOULDN'TA BROUGHT A PREGNANT WOMAN TO THAT SHORE...NESSIE GOT A THING FER SNATCHING UP KIDDIES!
NOT AS MUCH AS THE FAERIES THOUGH, SOMEBODY WARN YA ABOUT THE FAE YET?
YEAH, THE FAIRIES ARE GONNA HAVE TO WAIT ABOUT 5 MONTHS FOR THIS ONE THOUGH.
I DON'T IMAGINE WE'LL BE TRAVELING FOR A BIT AFTER GEMMA POPS OUT THE KID.
A BLESSING INDEED. SLAINTE! TO THE HEALTH OF YOUR BABY AND YOUR BEAUTIFUL WIFE!
CHEERS, MATE!
"CHEERS, MATE!" IS HE TAKIN' THE PISS?!
HA HA HA

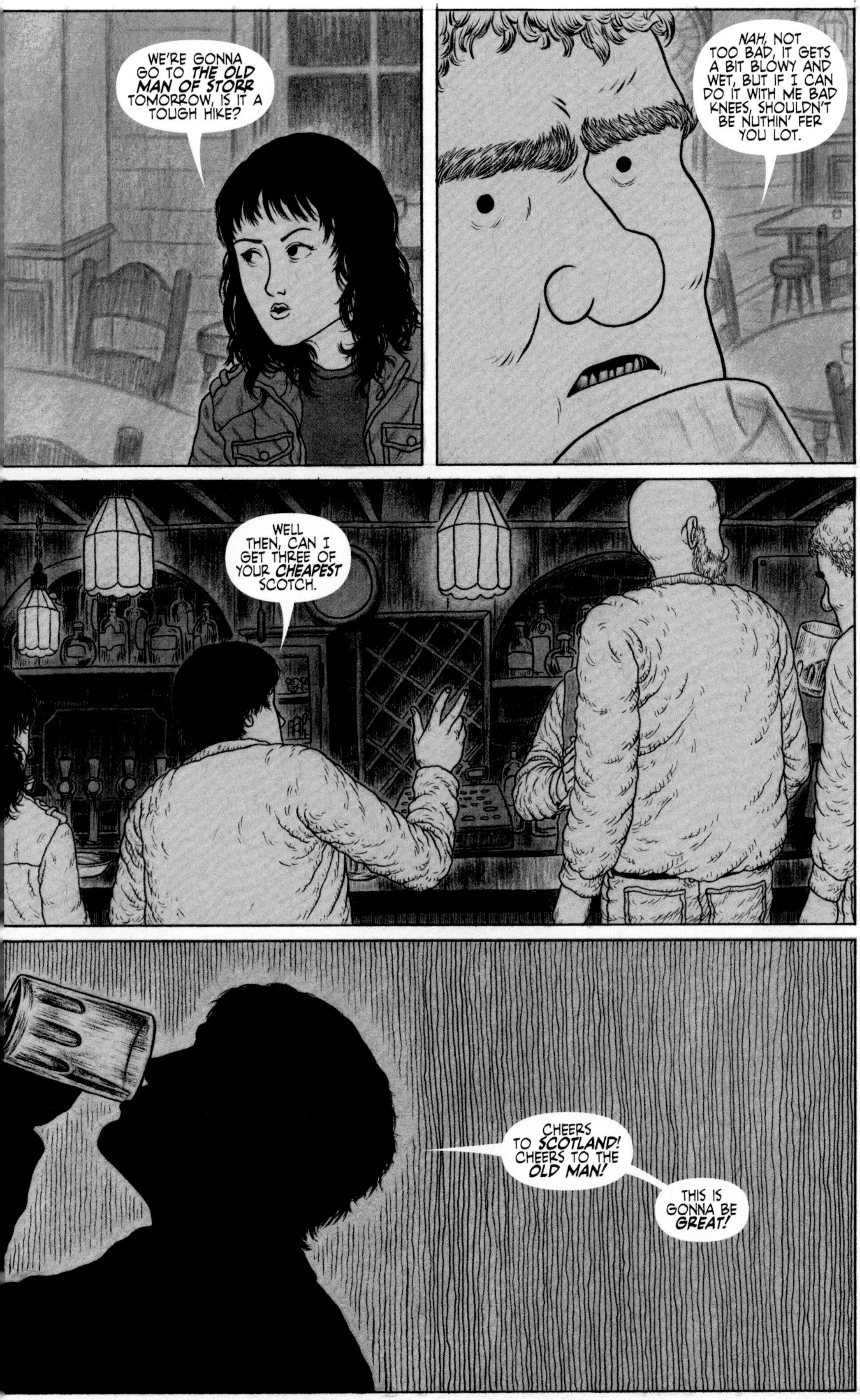
WE'RE GONNA GO TO THE OLD MAN OF STORR TOMORROW, IS IT A TOUGH HIKE?
NAH, NOT TOO BAD, IT GETS A BIT BLOWY AND WET, BUT IF I CAN DO IT WITH ME BAD KNEES, SHOULDN'T BE NUTHIN' FER YOU LOT.
WELL THEN, CAN I GET THREE OF YOUR CHEAPEST SCOTCH.
CHEERS TO SCOTLAND! CHEERS TO THE OLD MAN!
THIS IS GONNA BE GREAT!

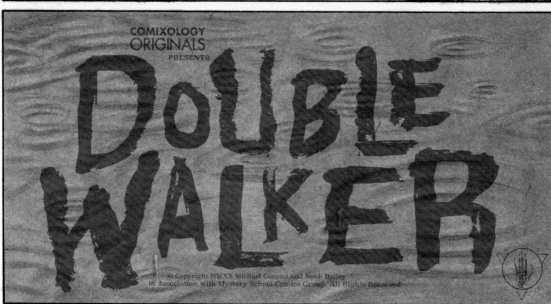

COMIXOLOGY
ORIGINALS
PRESENTS

DOUBLE WALKER

© Copyright MMXX Michael Conrad and Noah Bailey
in Association with Mystery School Comics Group. All Rights Reserved

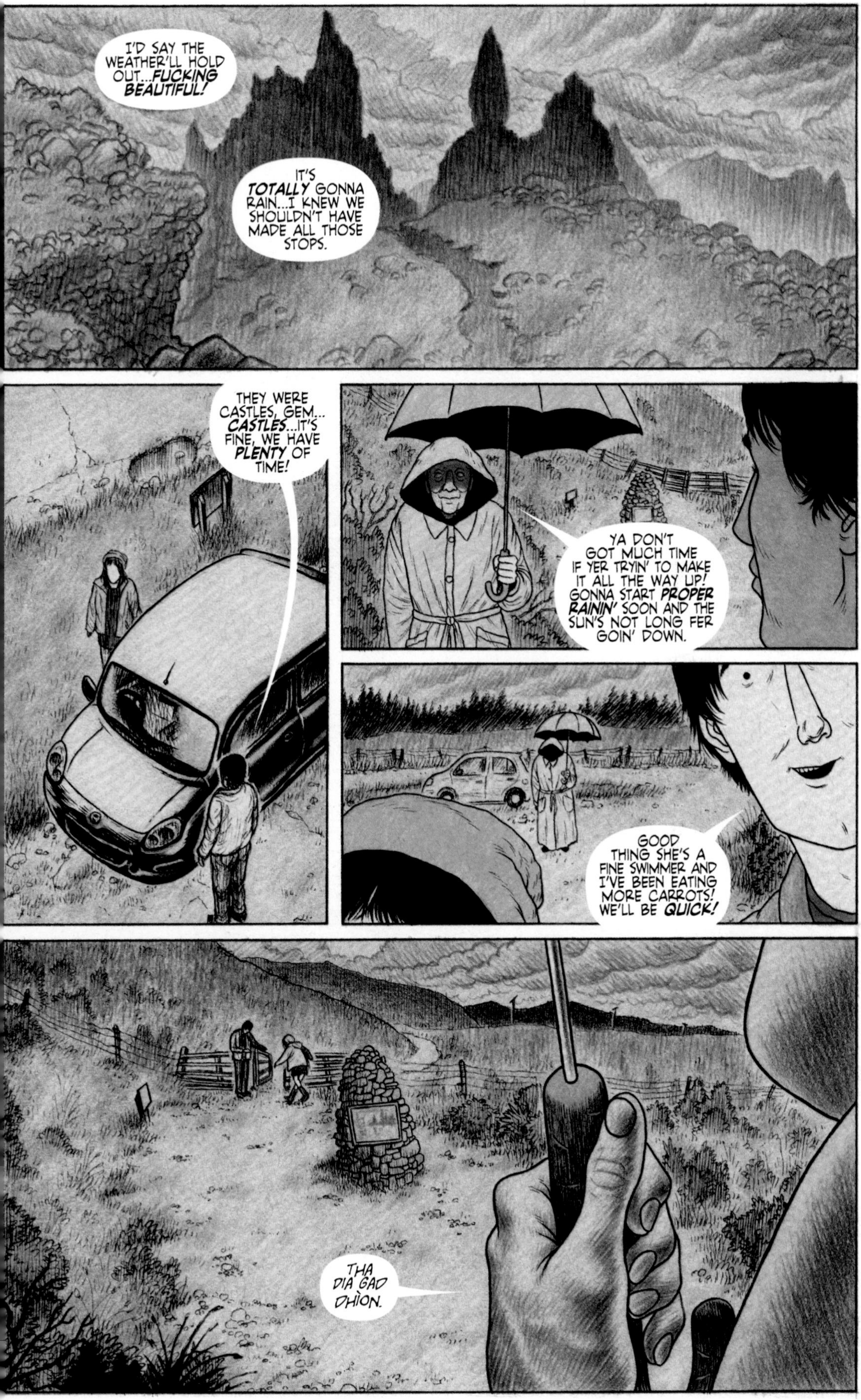
I'D SAY THE WEATHER'LL HOLD OUT...**FUCKING BEAUTIFUL!**
IT'S **TOTALLY** GONNA RAIN...I KNEW WE SHOULDN'T HAVE MADE ALL THOSE STOPS.
THEY WERE CASTLES, GEM... **CASTLES**...IT'S FINE, WE HAVE **PLENTY** OF TIME!
YA DON'T GOT MUCH TIME IF YER TRYIN' TO MAKE IT ALL THE WAY UP! GONNA START **PROPER RAININ'** SOON AND THE SUN'S NOT LONG FER GOIN' DOWN.
GOOD THING SHE'S A FINE SWIMMER AND I'VE BEEN EATING MORE CARROTS! WE'LL BE **QUICK!**
THA DIA GAD DHÌON.

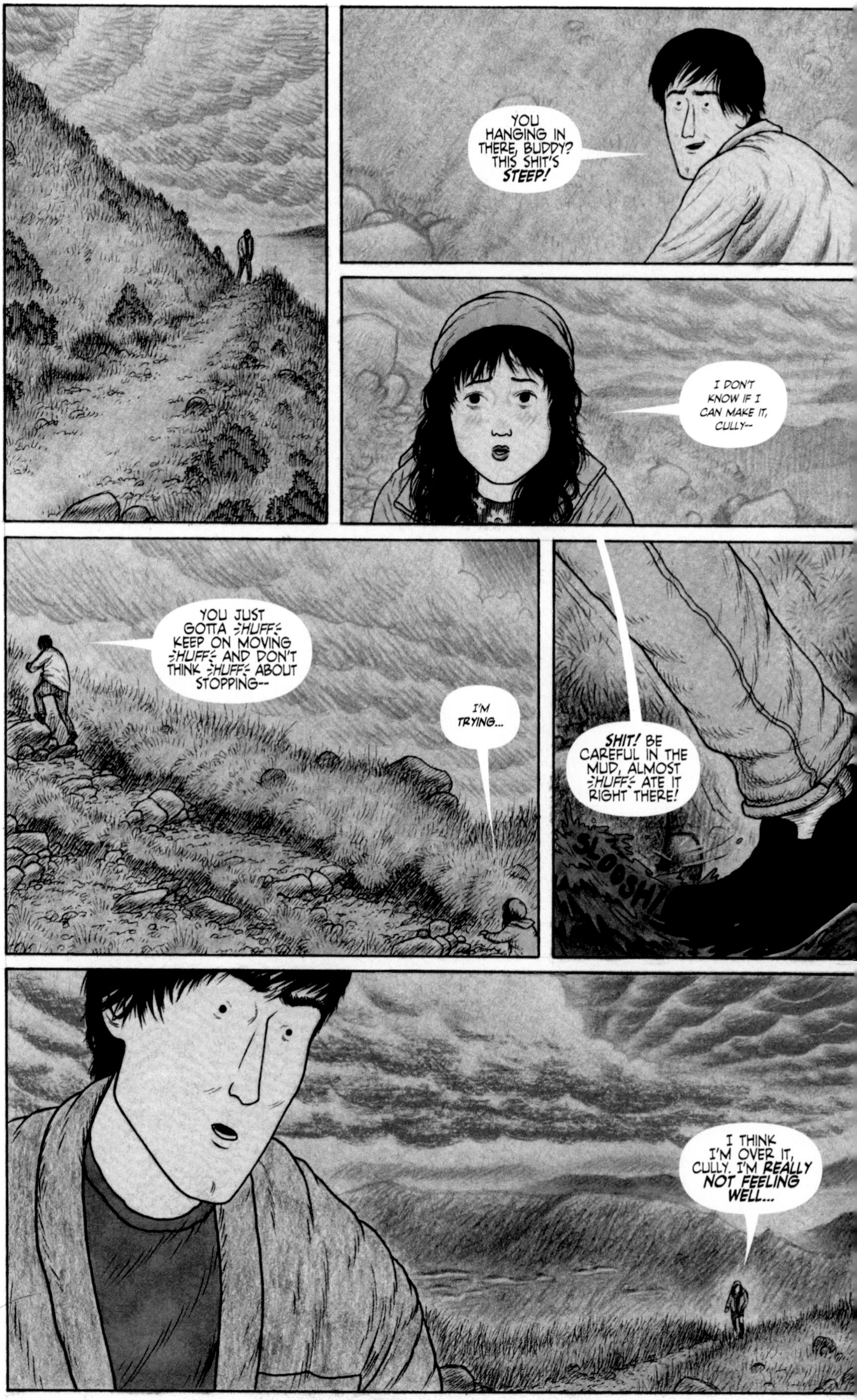
YOU HANGING IN THERE, BUDDY? THIS SHIT'S STEEP!
I DON'T KNOW IF I CAN MAKE IT, CULLY--
YOU JUST GOTTA *HUFF* KEEP ON MOVING *HUFF* AND DON'T THINK *HUFF* ABOUT STOPPING--
I'M TRYING...
SHIT! BE CAREFUL IN THE MUD, ALMOST *HUFF* ATE IT RIGHT THERE!
SLOOSH!
I THINK I'M OVER IT, CULLY. I'M REALLY NOT FEELING WELL...

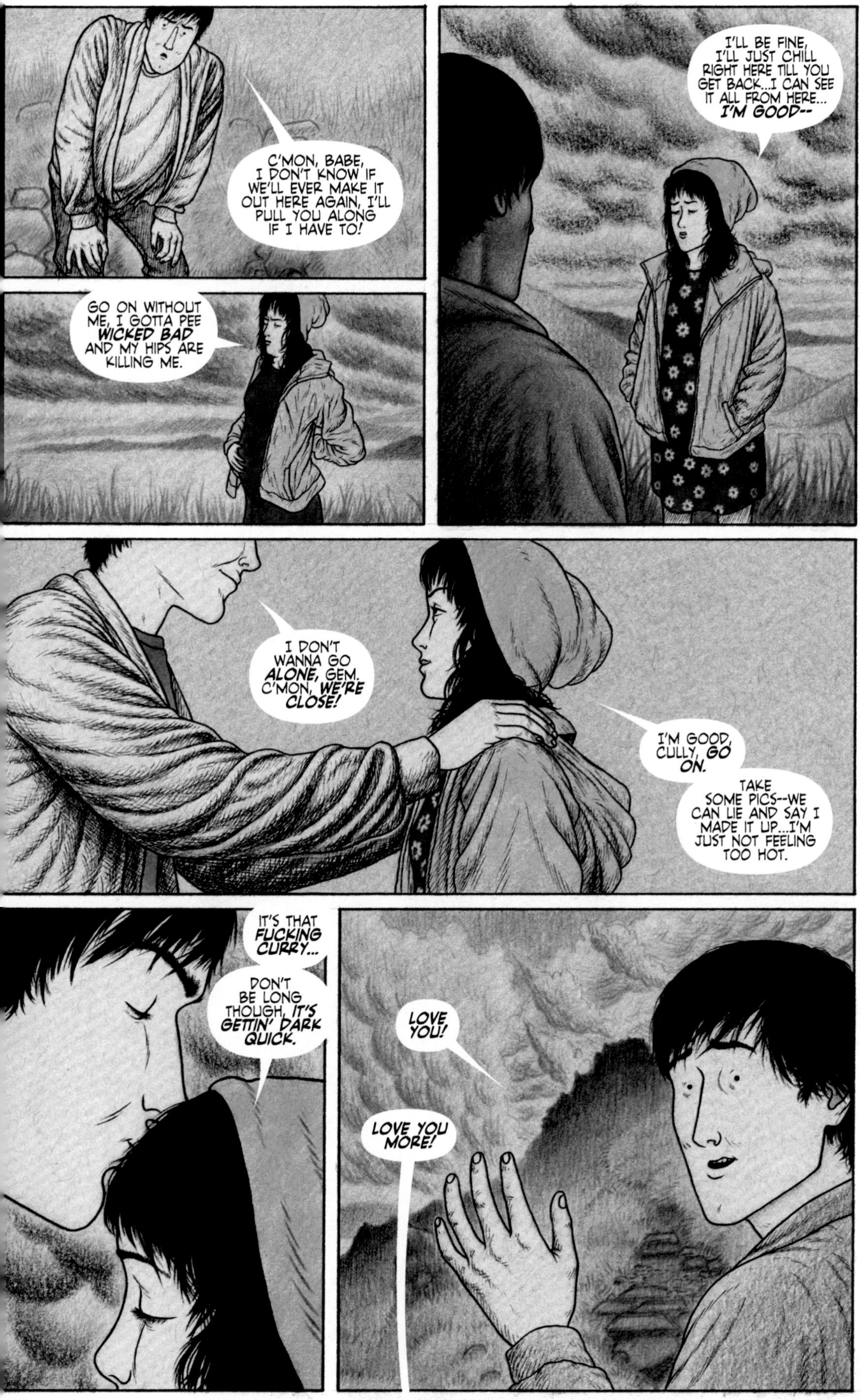
C'MON, BABE, I DON'T KNOW IF WE'LL EVER MAKE IT OUT HERE AGAIN, I'LL PULL YOU ALONG IF I HAVE TO!
GO ON WITHOUT ME, I GOTTA PEE WICKED BAD AND MY HIPS ARE KILLING ME.
I'LL BE FINE, I'LL JUST CHILL RIGHT HERE TILL YOU GET BACK...I CAN SEE IT ALL FROM HERE... I'M GOOD--
I DON'T WANNA GO ALONE, GEM. C'MON, WE'RE CLOSE!
I'M GOOD, CULLY, GO ON.
TAKE SOME PICS--WE CAN LIE AND SAY I MADE IT UP...I'M JUST NOT FEELING TOO HOT.
IT'S THAT FUCKING CURRY...
DON'T BE LONG THOUGH, IT'S GETTIN' DARK QUICK.
LOVE YOU!
LOVE YOU MORE!

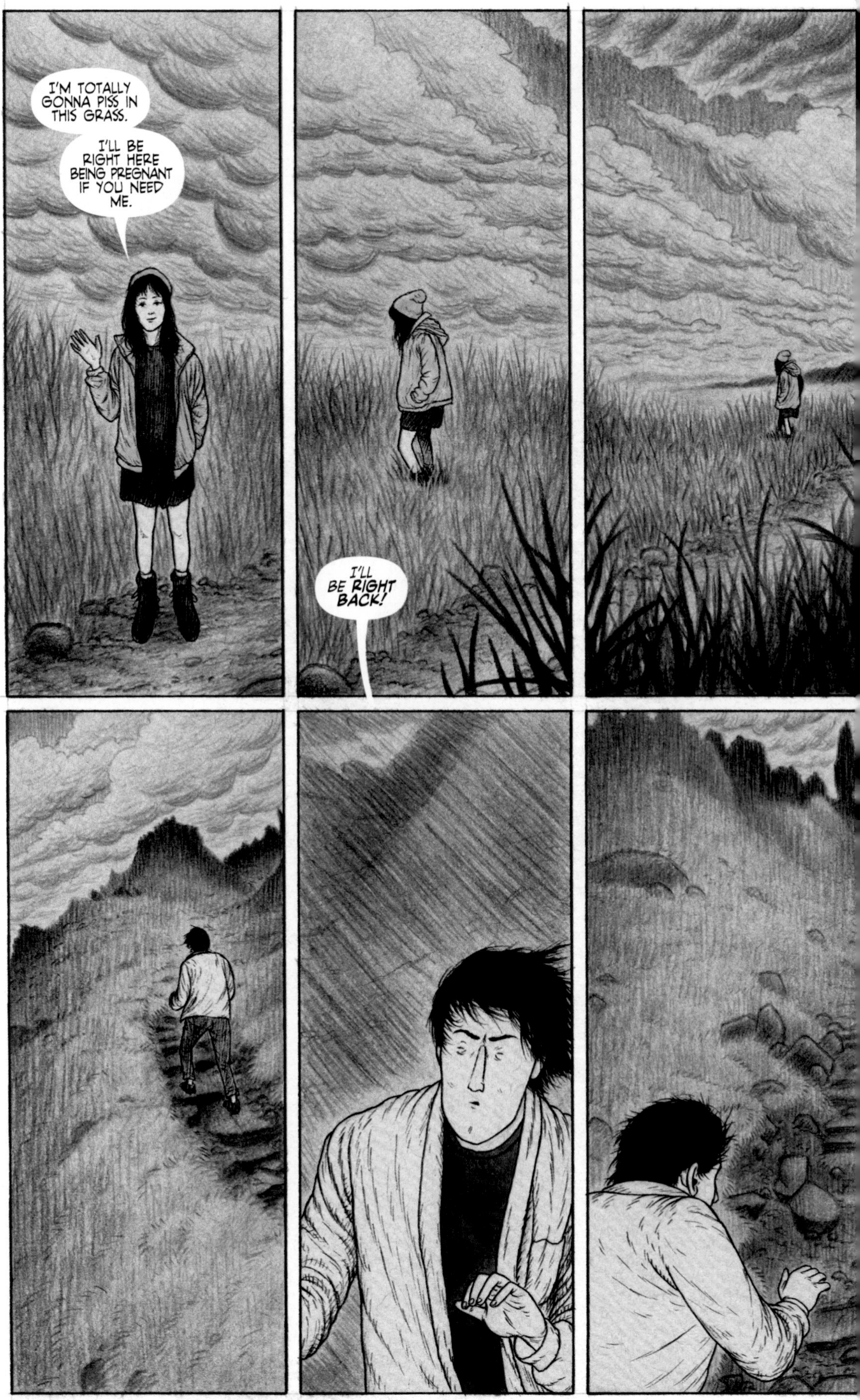

I'M TOTALLY GONNA PISS IN THIS GRASS.
I'LL BE RIGHT HERE BEING PREGNANT IF YOU NEED ME.
I'LL BE RIGHT BACK!

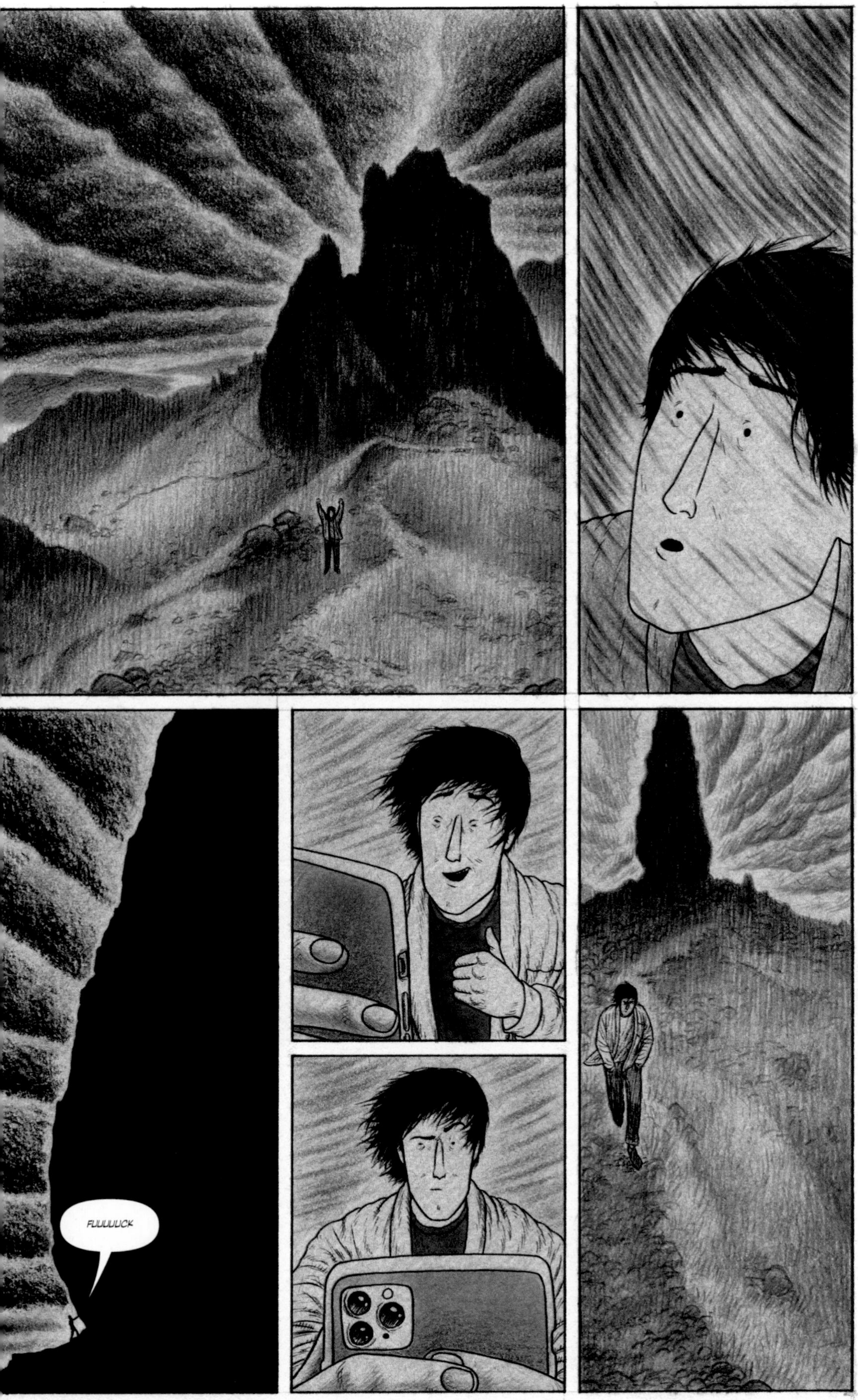
FUUUUUCK

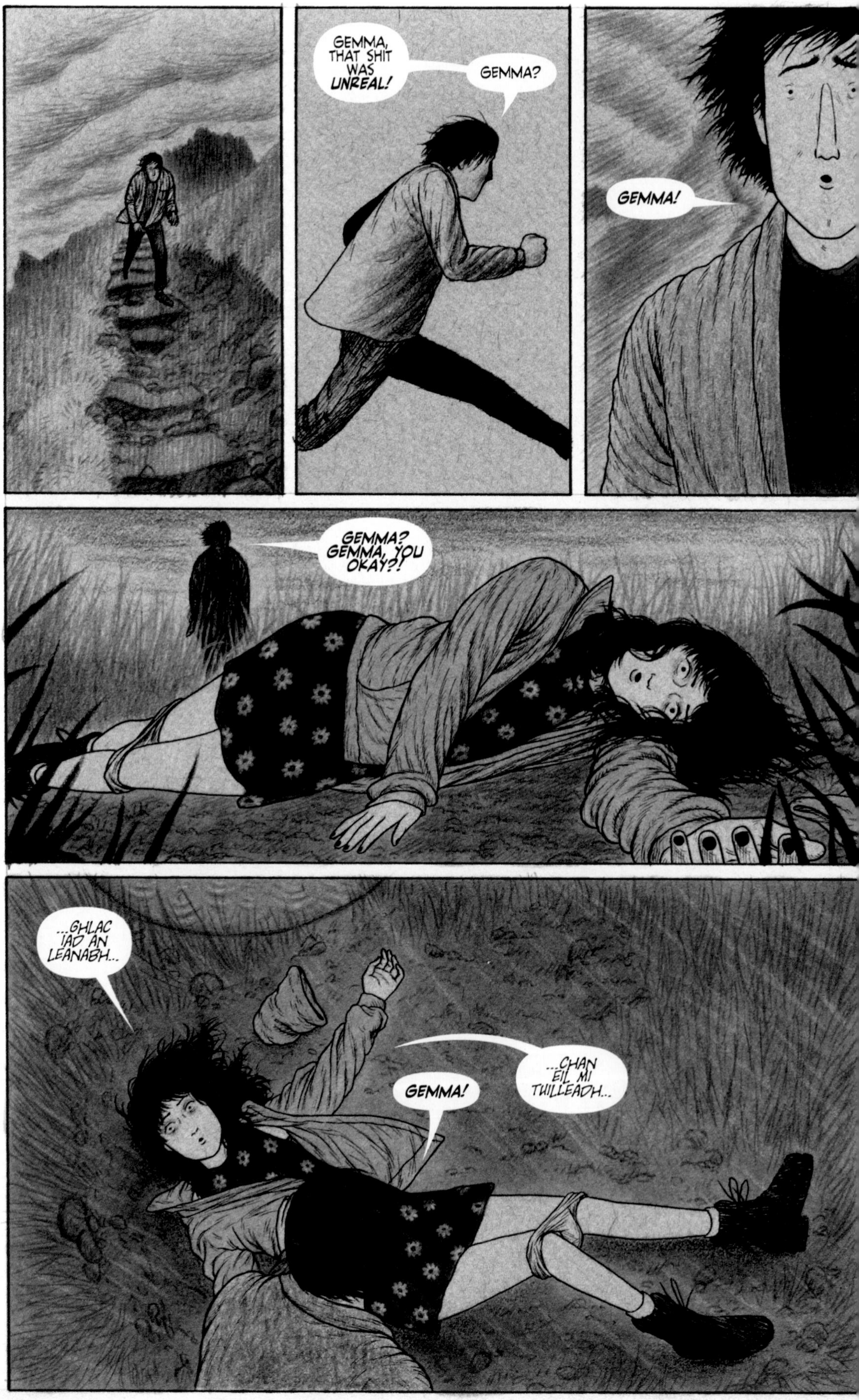
GEMMA, THAT SHIT WAS UNREAL!
GEMMA?
GEMMA!
GEMMA? GEMMA, YOU OKAY?!
...GHLAC IAD AN LEANABH...
...CHAN EIL MI TUILLEADH...
GEMMA!

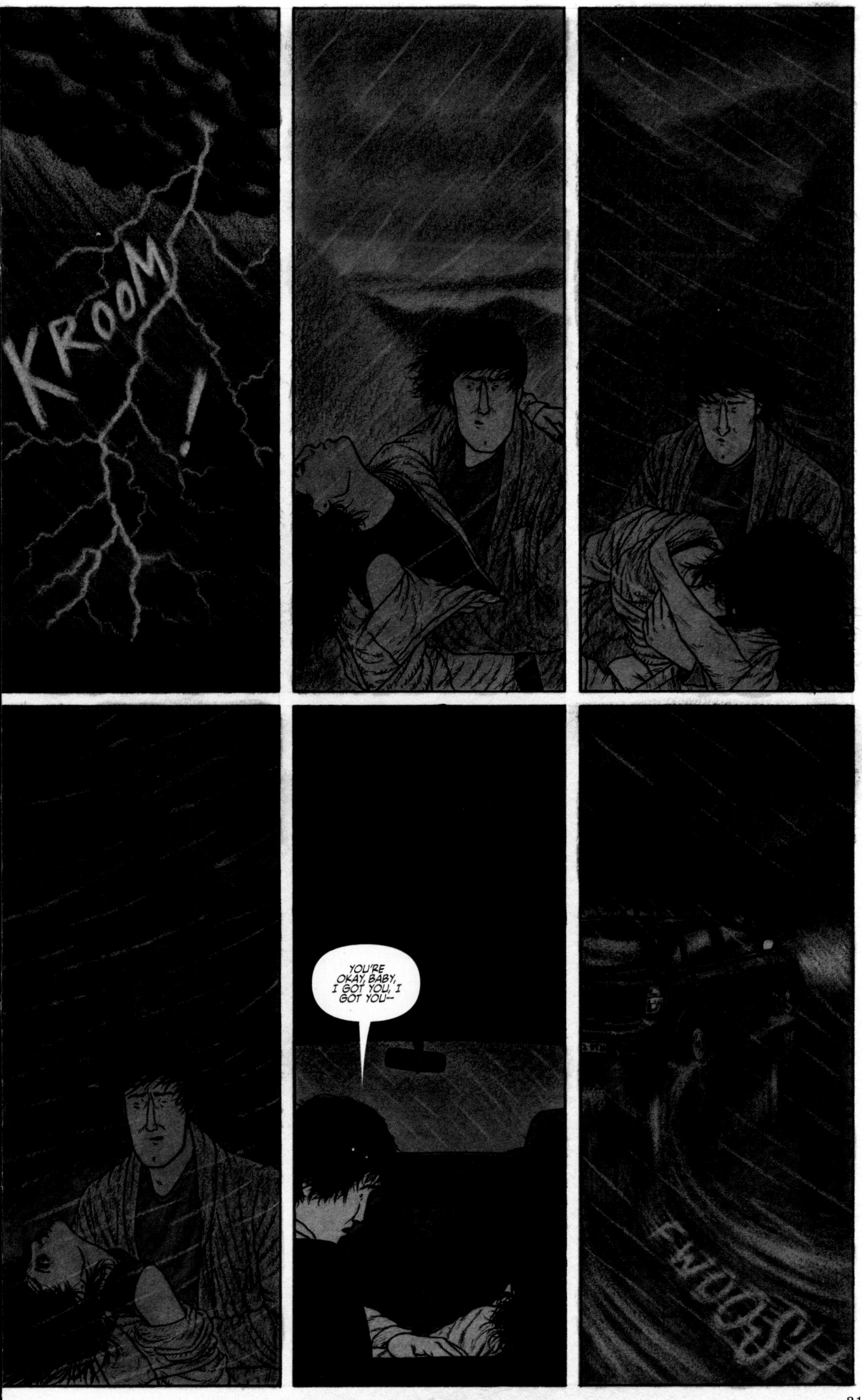
KROOM!
YOU'RE OKAY, BABY, I GOT YOU, I GOT YOU--
FWOOSH

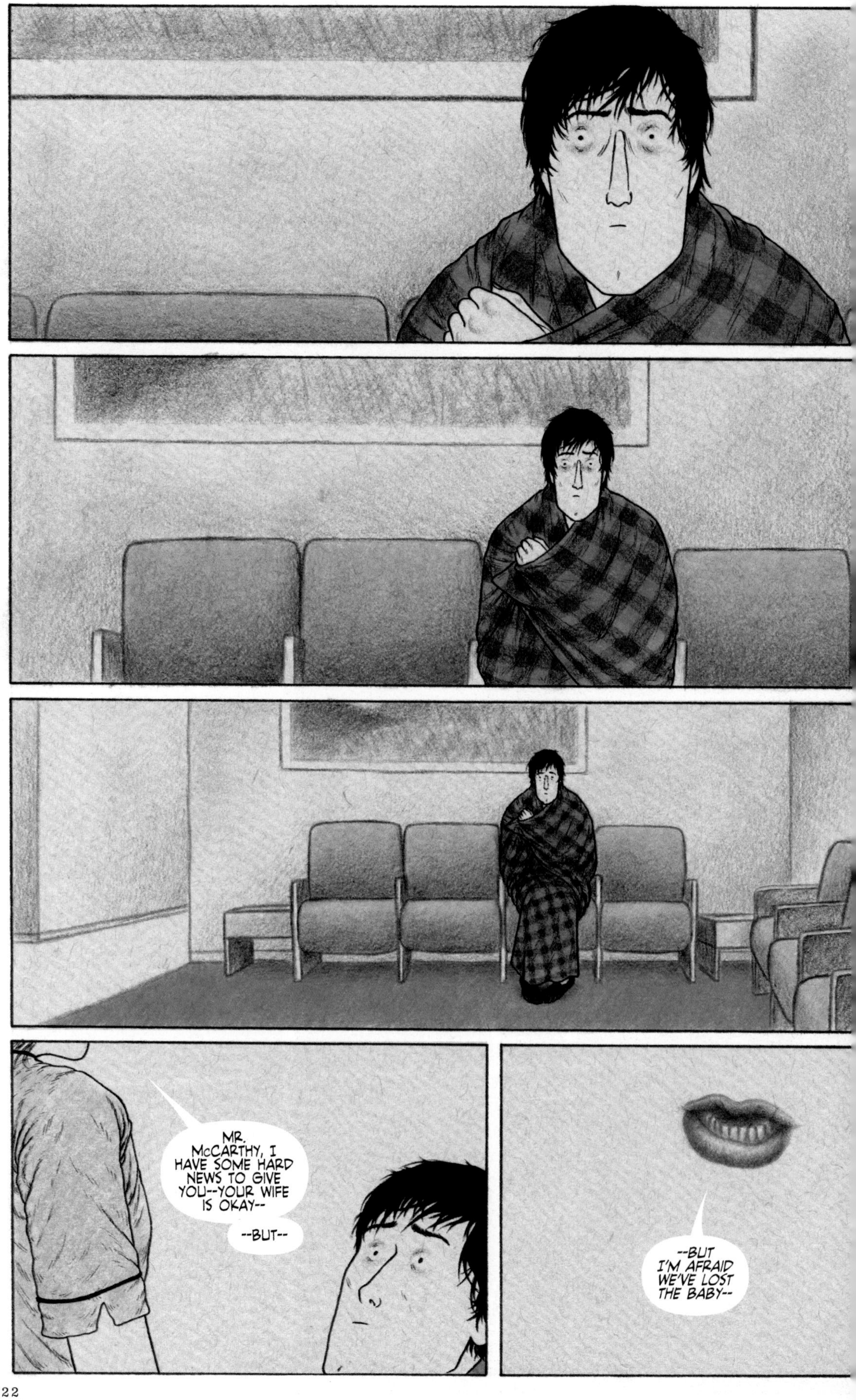
MR. McCARTHY, I HAVE SOME HARD NEWS TO GIVE YOU--YOUR WIFE IS OKAY--
--BUT--
--BUT I'M AFRAID WE'VE LOST THE BABY--

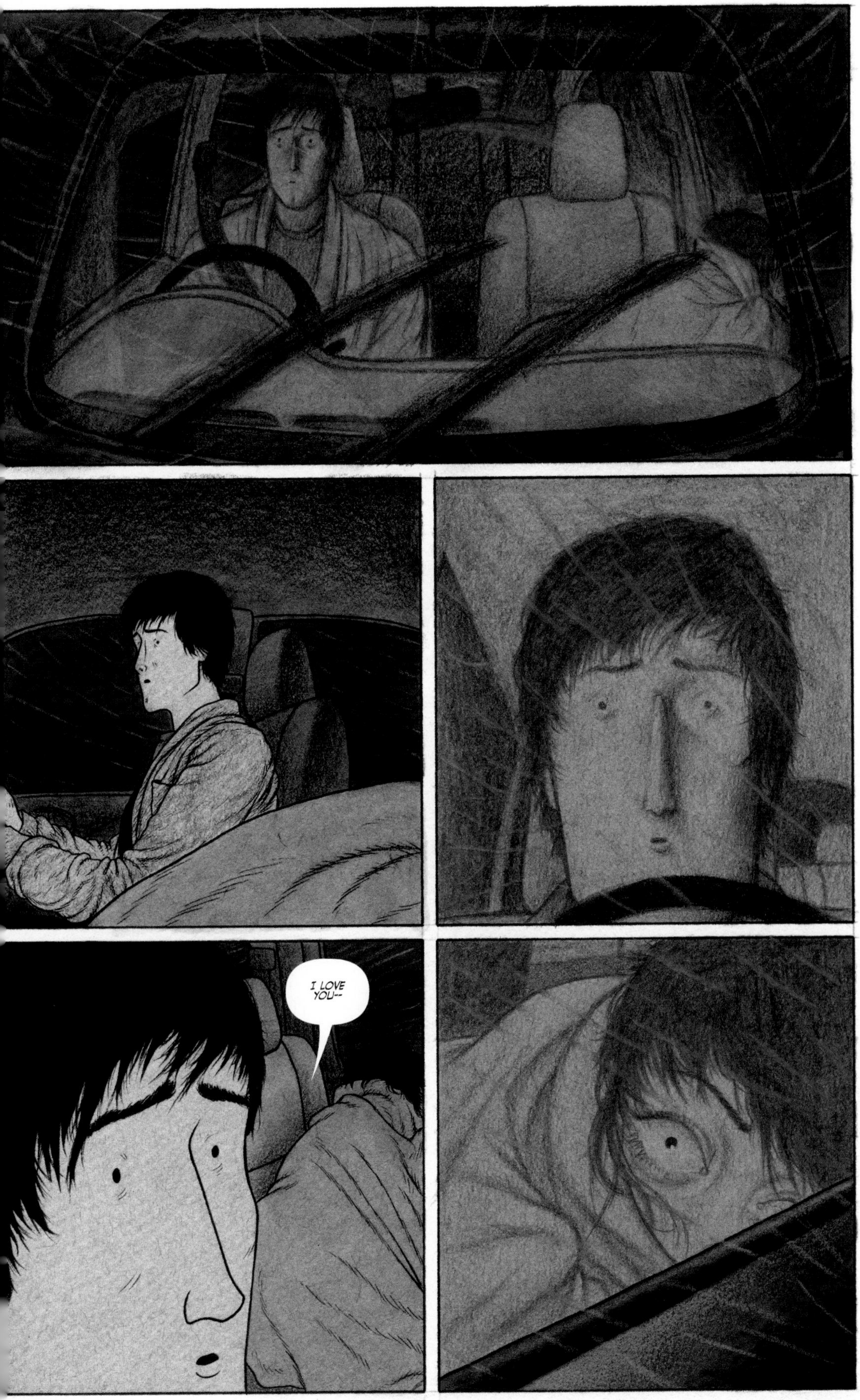
I LOVE YOU--

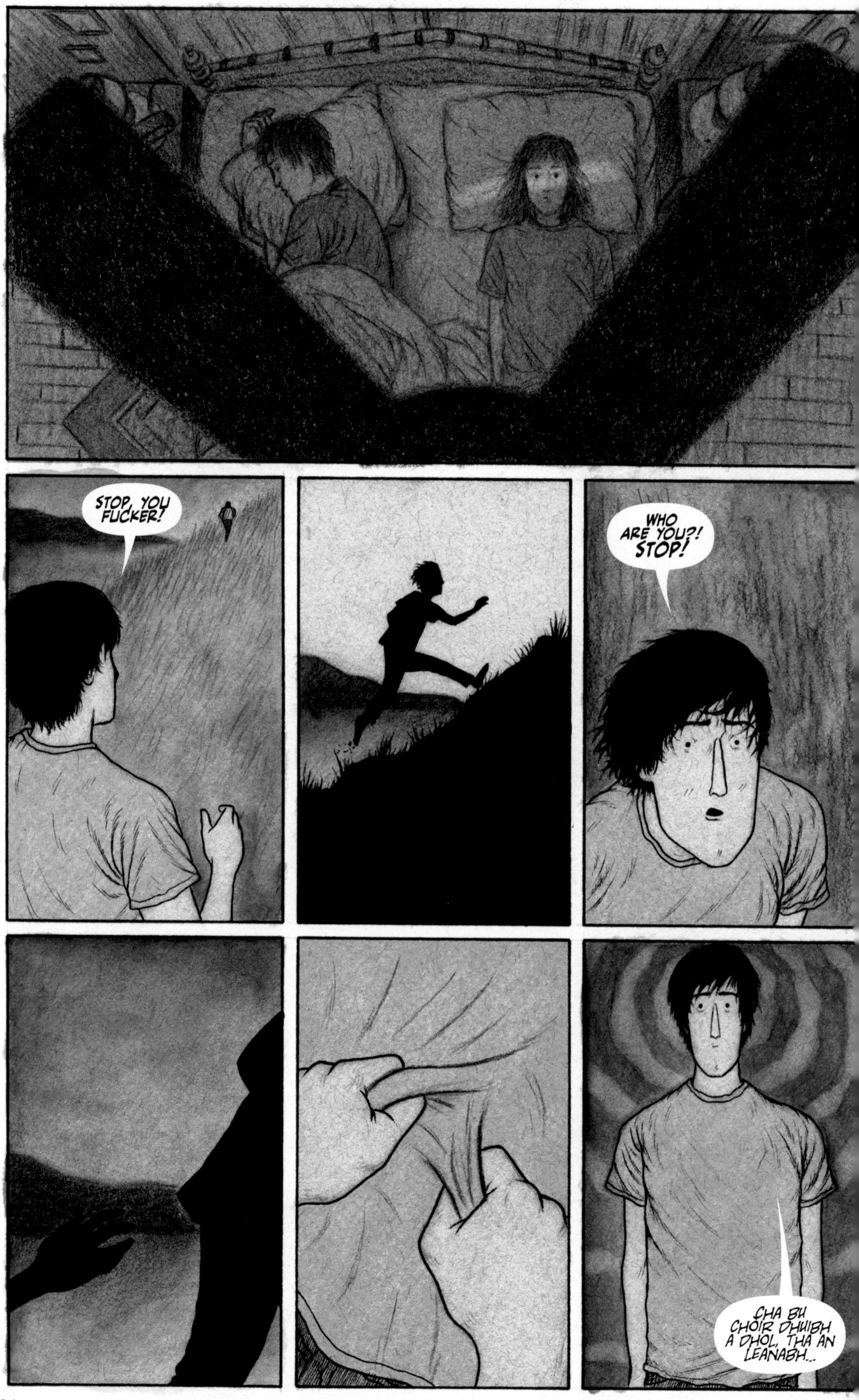
STOP, YOU FUCKER!
WHO ARE YOU?! STOP!
CHA BU CHOIR DHUIBH A DHOL, THA AN LEANABH...

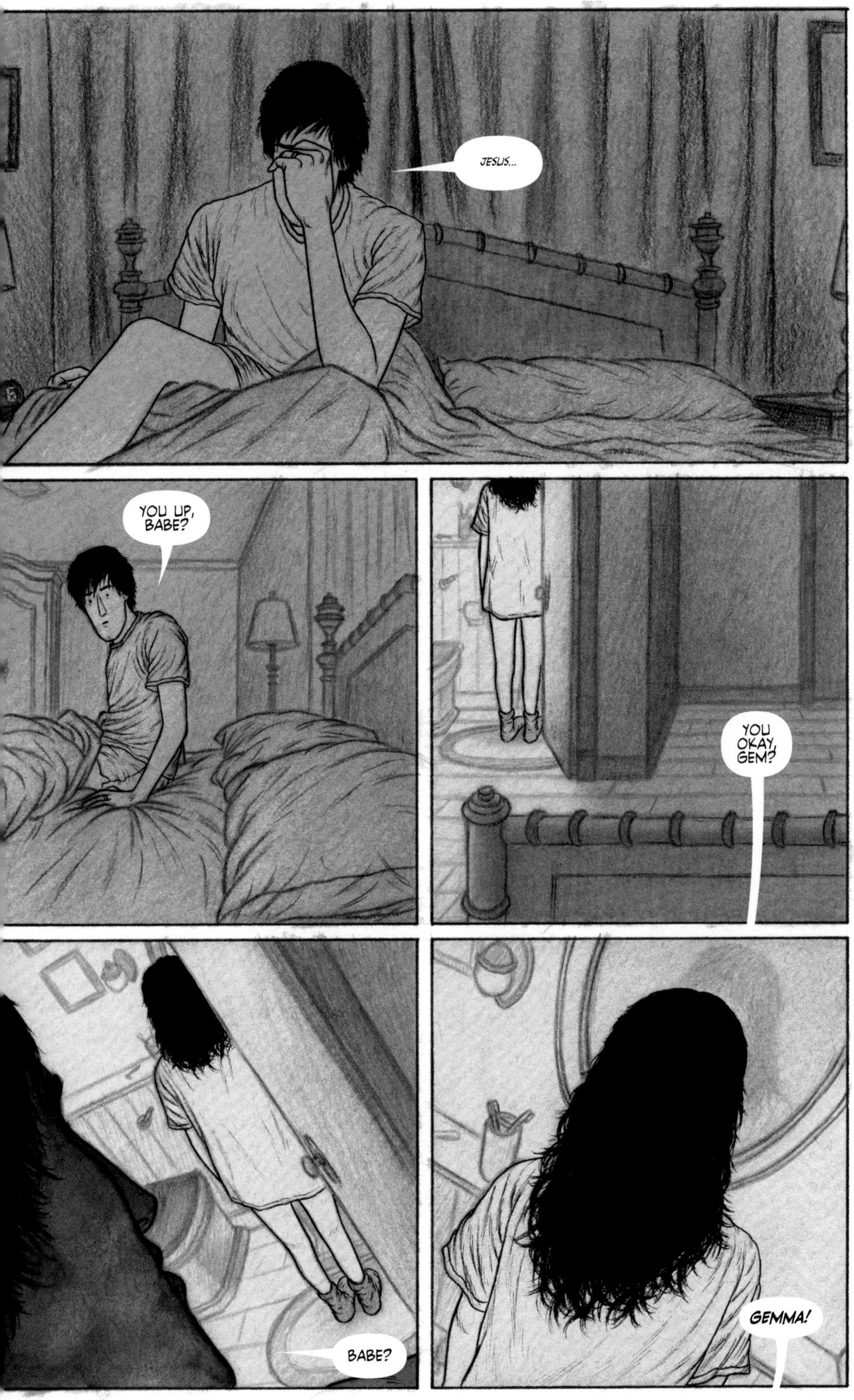
JESUS...
YOU UP, BABE?
YOU OKAY, GEM?
BABE?
GEMMA!

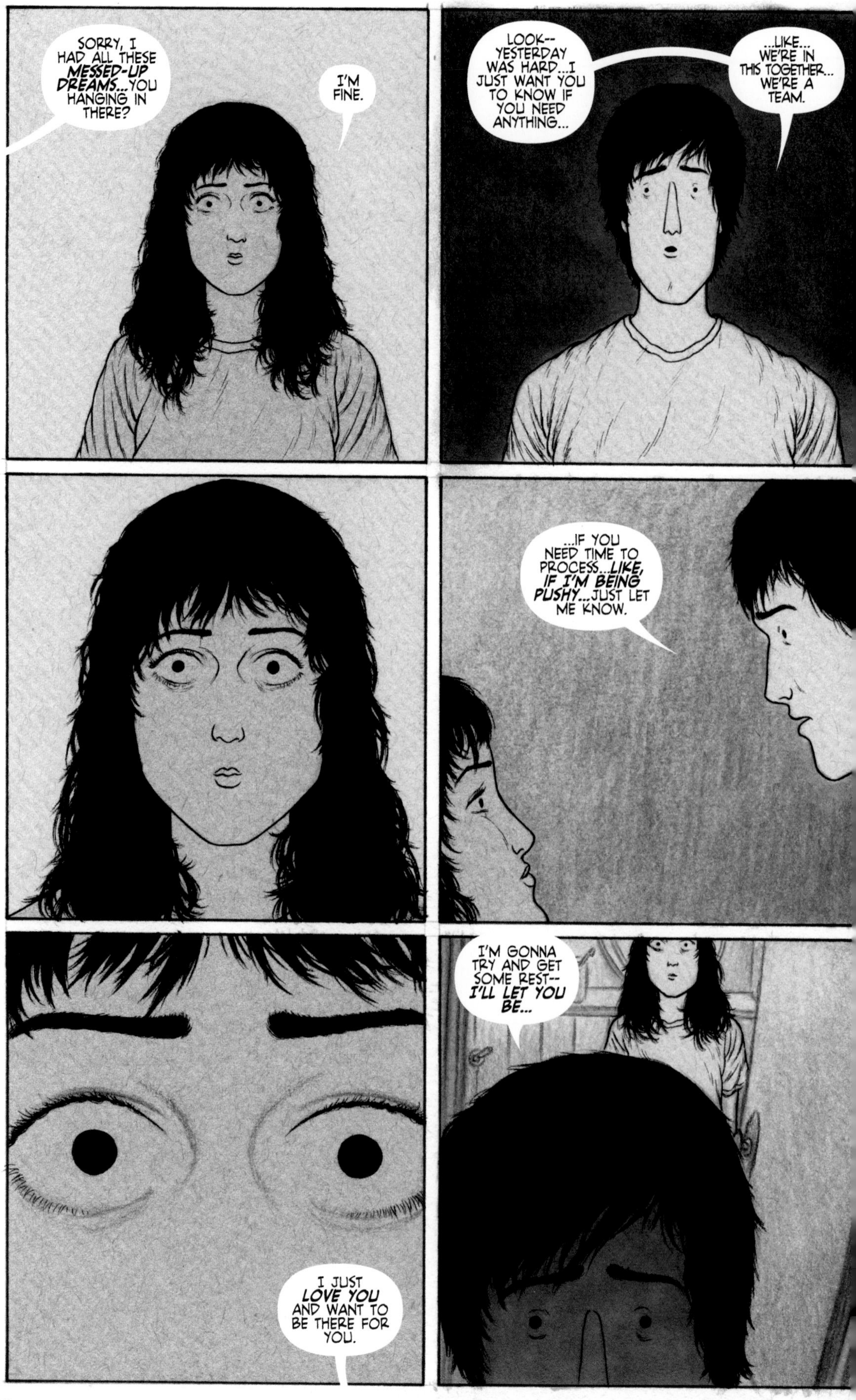
SORRY, I HAD ALL THESE MESSED-UP DREAMS...YOU HANGING IN THERE?
I'M FINE.
LOOK-- YESTERDAY WAS HARD...I JUST WANT YOU TO KNOW IF YOU NEED ANYTHING...
...LIKE... WE'RE IN THIS TOGETHER... WE'RE A TEAM.
...IF YOU NEED TIME TO PROCESS...LIKE, IF I'M BEING PUSHY...JUST LET ME KNOW.
I JUST LOVE YOU AND WANT TO BE THERE FOR YOU.
I'M GONNA TRY AND GET SOME REST-- I'LL LET YOU BE...

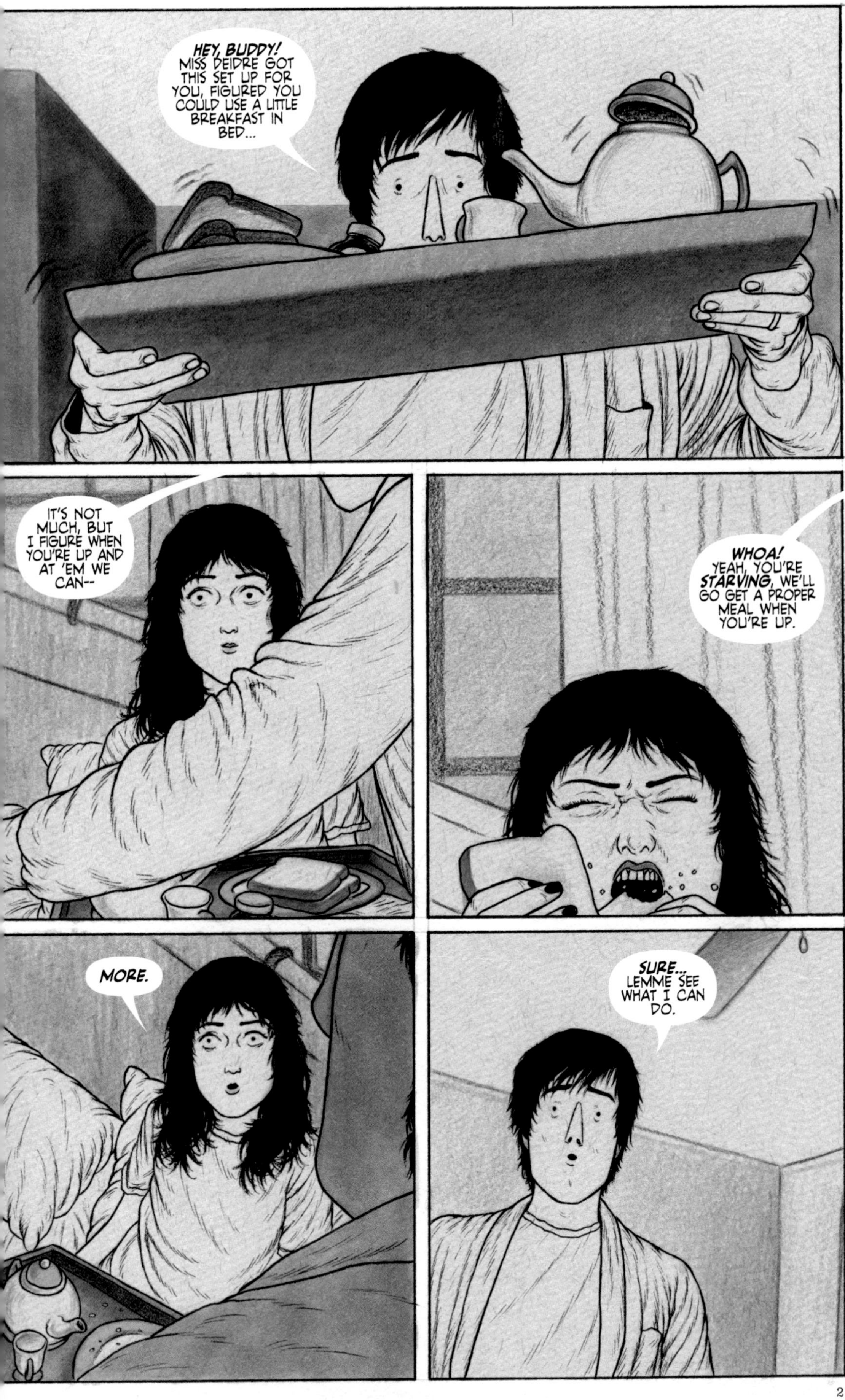
HEY, BUDDY! MISS DEIDRE GOT THIS SET UP FOR YOU, FIGURED YOU COULD USE A LITTLE BREAKFAST IN BED...
IT'S NOT MUCH, BUT I FIGURE WHEN YOU'RE UP AND AT 'EM WE CAN--
WHOA! YEAH, YOU'RE STARVING, WE'LL GO GET A PROPER MEAL WHEN YOU'RE UP.
MORE.
SURE... LEMME SEE WHAT I CAN DO.

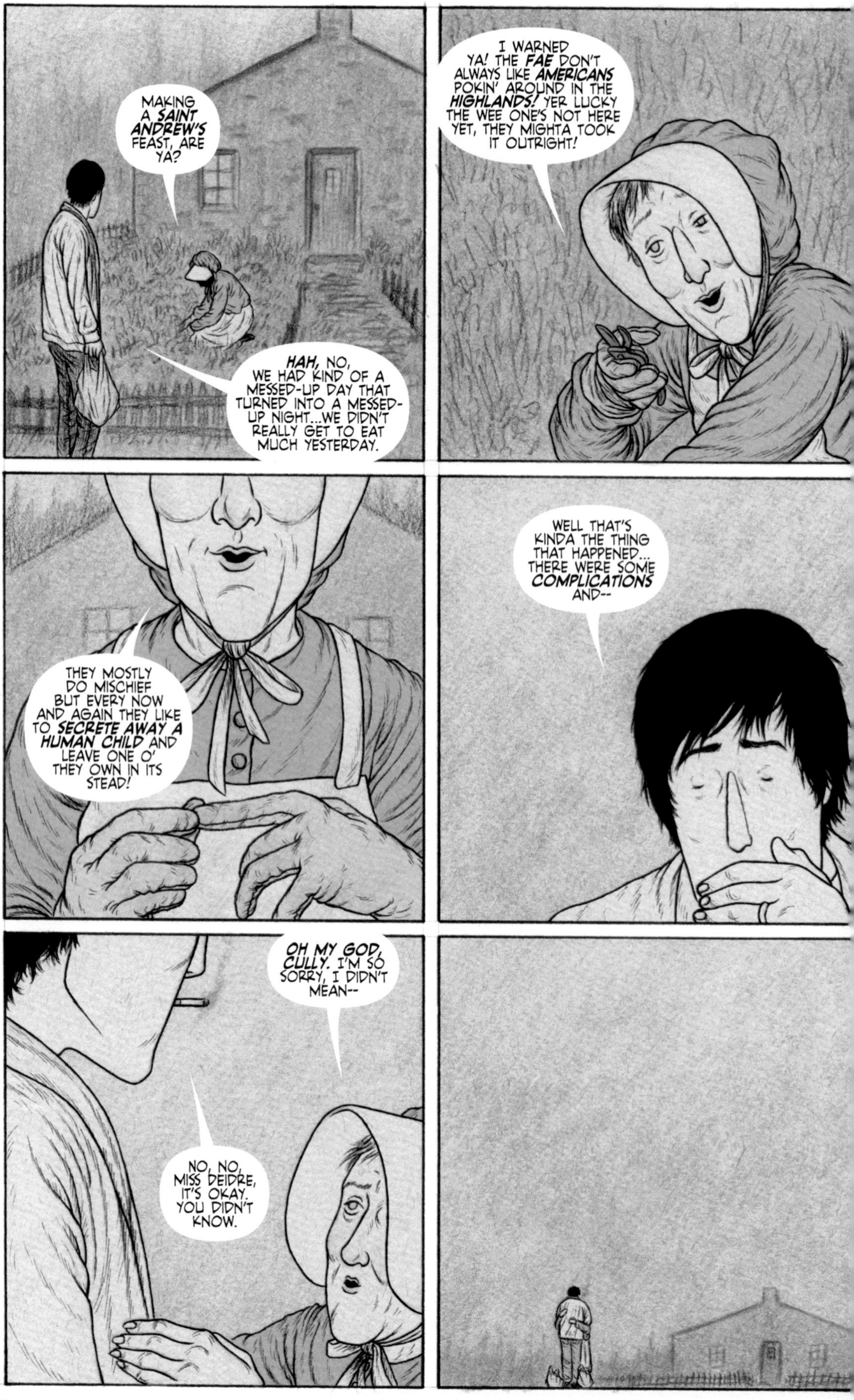
MAKING A SAINT ANDREW'S FEAST, ARE YA?
HAH, NO, WE HAD KIND OF A MESSED-UP DAY THAT TURNED INTO A MESSED-UP NIGHT...WE DIDN'T REALLY GET TO EAT MUCH YESTERDAY.
I WARNED YA! THE FAE DON'T ALWAYS LIKE AMERICANS POKIN' AROUND IN THE HIGHLANDS! YER LUCKY THE WEE ONE'S NOT HERE YET, THEY MIGHTA TOOK IT OUTRIGHT!
THEY MOSTLY DO MISCHIEF BUT EVERY NOW AND AGAIN THEY LIKE TO SECRETE AWAY A HUMAN CHILD AND LEAVE ONE O' THEY OWN IN ITS STEAD!
WELL THAT'S KINDA THE THING THAT HAPPENED... THERE WERE SOME COMPLICATIONS AND--
OH MY GOD, CULLY. I'M SO SORRY, I DIDN'T MEAN--
NO, NO, MISS DEIDRE, IT'S OKAY. YOU DIDN'T KNOW.

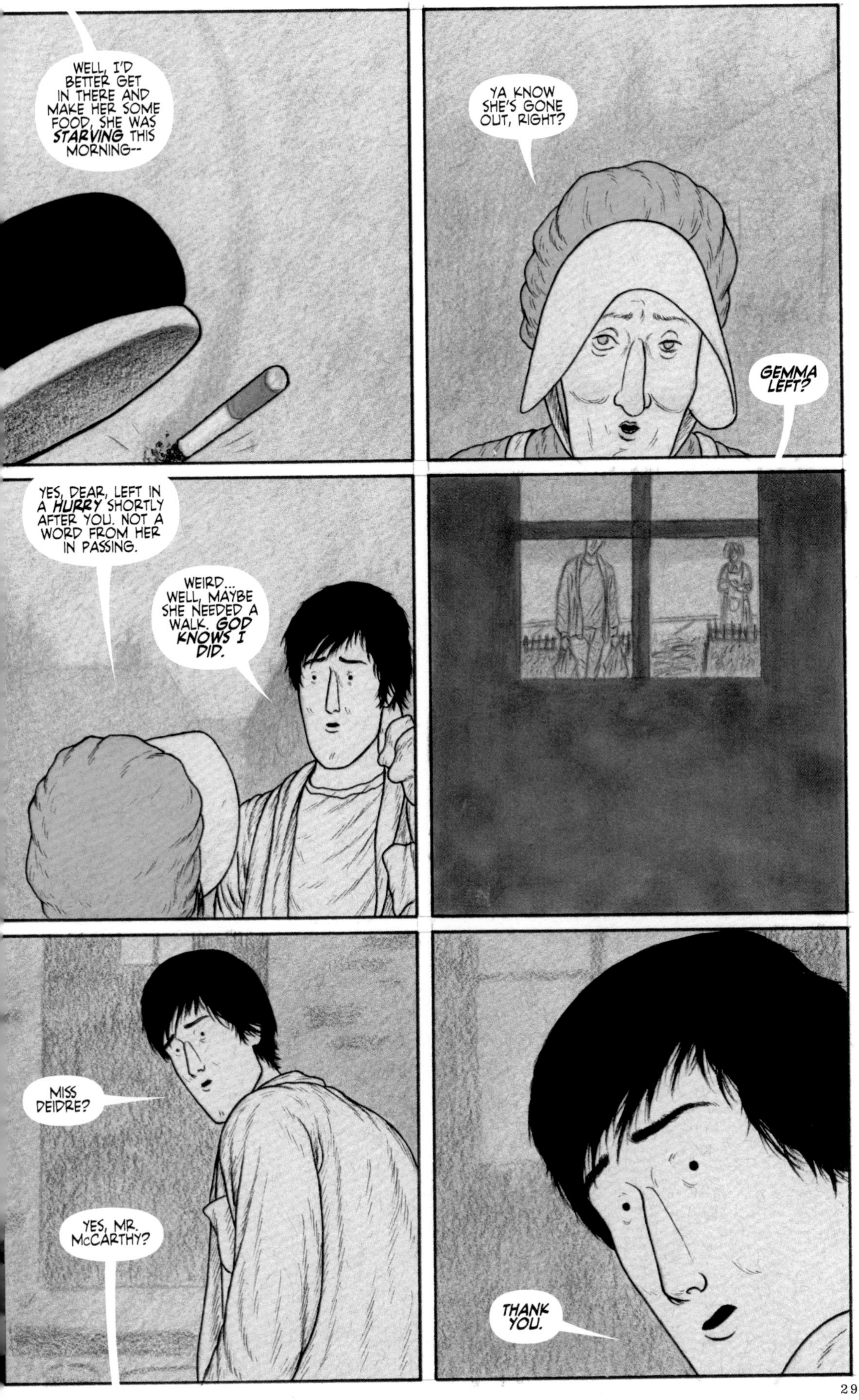
WELL, I'D BETTER GET IN THERE AND MAKE HER SOME FOOD, SHE WAS *STARVING* THIS MORNING--
YA KNOW SHE'S GONE OUT, RIGHT?
GEMMA LEFT?
YES, DEAR, LEFT IN A *HURRY* SHORTLY AFTER YOU. NOT A WORD FROM HER IN PASSING.
WEIRD... WELL, MAYBE SHE NEEDED A WALK. *GOD KNOWS I DID.*
MISS DEIDRE?
YES, MR. McCARTHY?
THANK YOU.

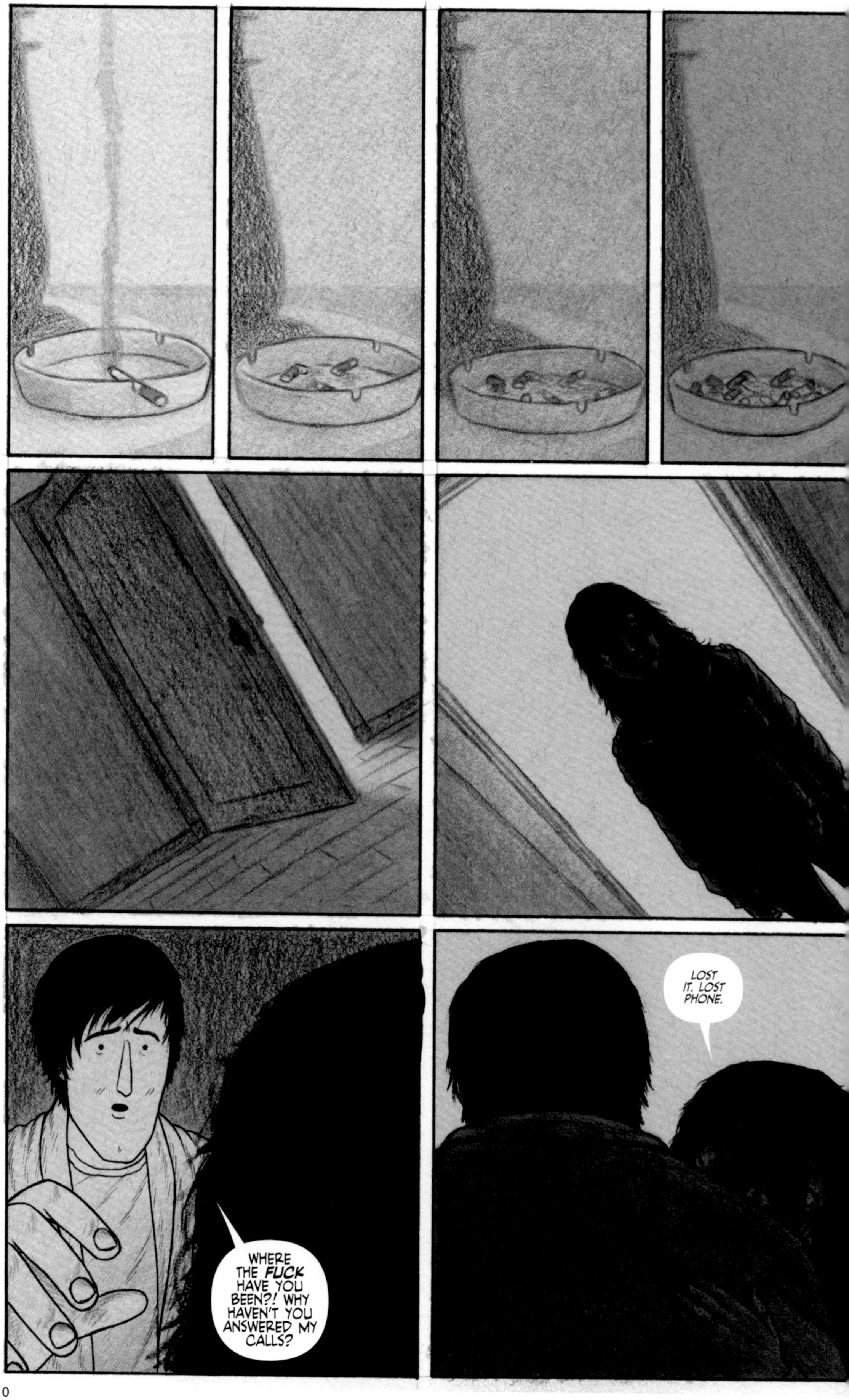
WHERE THE FUCK HAVE YOU BEEN?! WHY HAVEN'T YOU ANSWERED MY CALLS?
LOST IT. LOST PHONE.

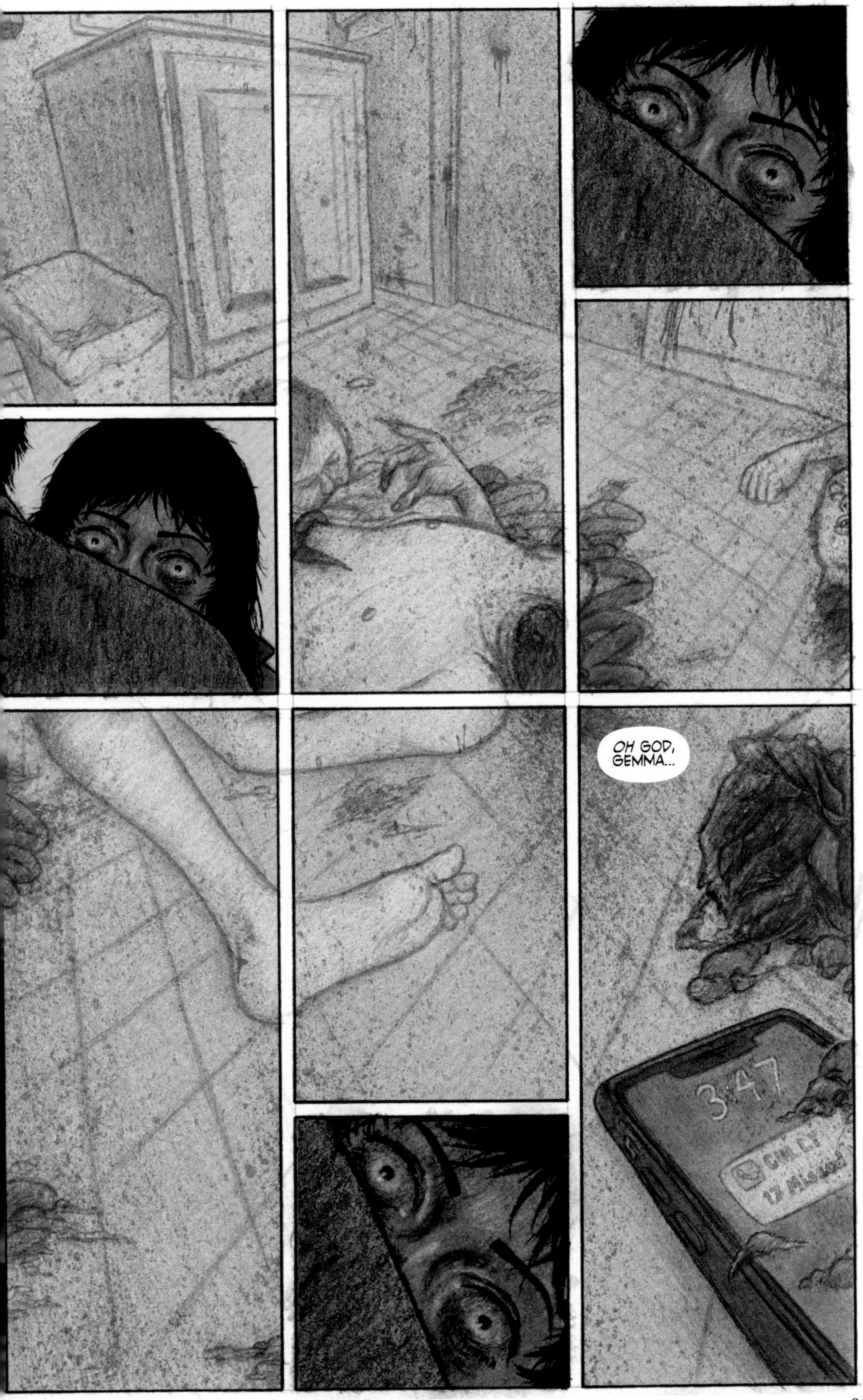
OH GOD, GEMMA...
3:47
17 Missed

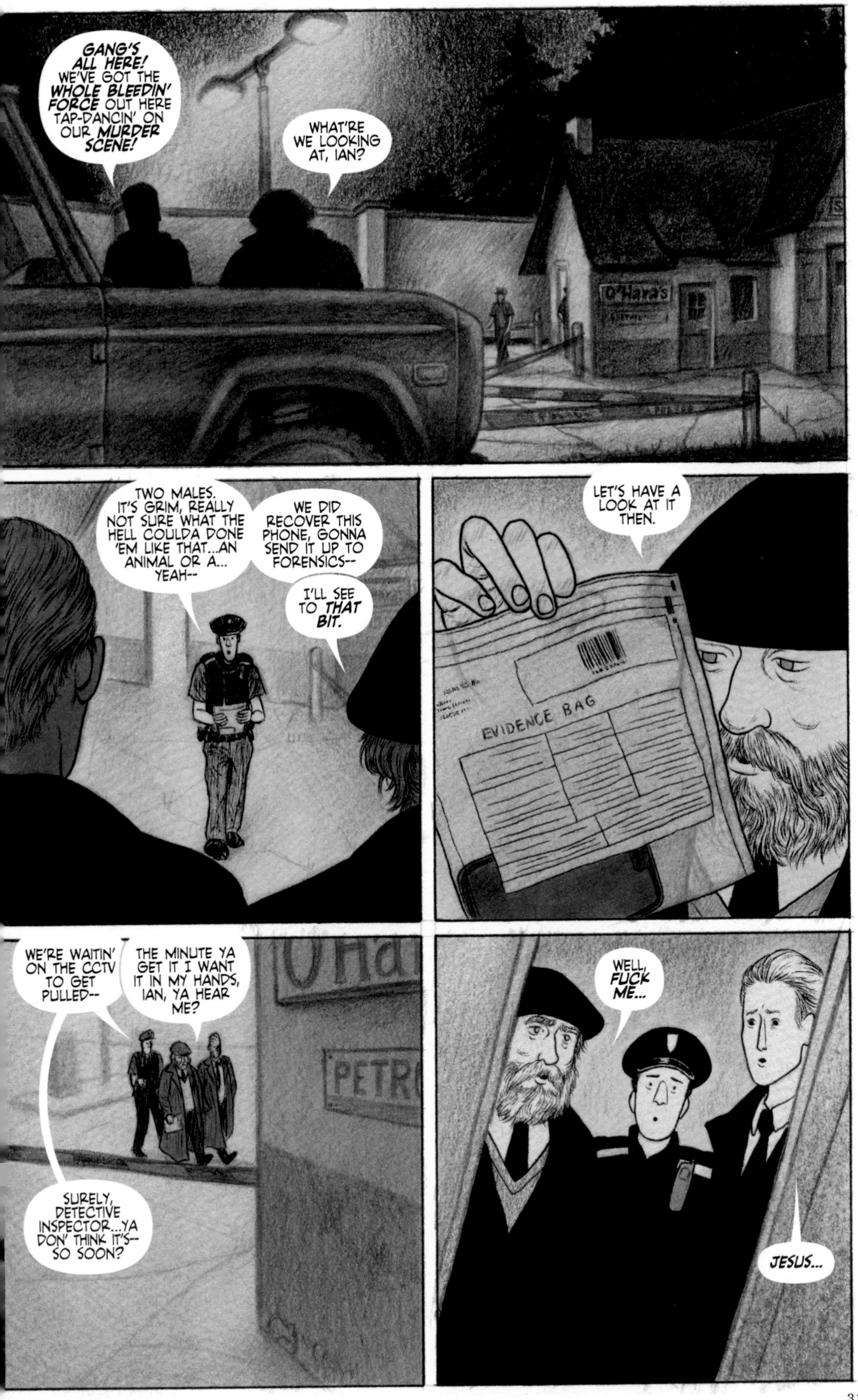
GANG'S ALL HERE! WE'VE GOT THE WHOLE BLEEDIN' FORCE OUT HERE TAP-DANCIN' ON OUR MURDER SCENE!
WHAT'RE WE LOOKING AT, IAN?
O'Hara's
TWO MALES. IT'S GRIM, REALLY NOT SURE WHAT THE HELL COULDA DONE 'EM LIKE THAT...AN ANIMAL OR A... YEAH--
WE DID RECOVER THIS PHONE, GONNA SEND IT UP TO FORENSICS--
I'LL SEE TO THAT BIT.
LET'S HAVE A LOOK AT IT THEN.
EVIDENCE BAG
WE'RE WAITIN' ON THE CCTV TO GET PULLED--
THE MINUTE YA GET IT I WANT IT IN MY HANDS, IAN, YA HEAR ME?
SURELY, DETECTIVE INSPECTOR...YA DON' THINK IT'S-- SO SOON?
PETRO
WELL, FUCK ME...
JESUS...

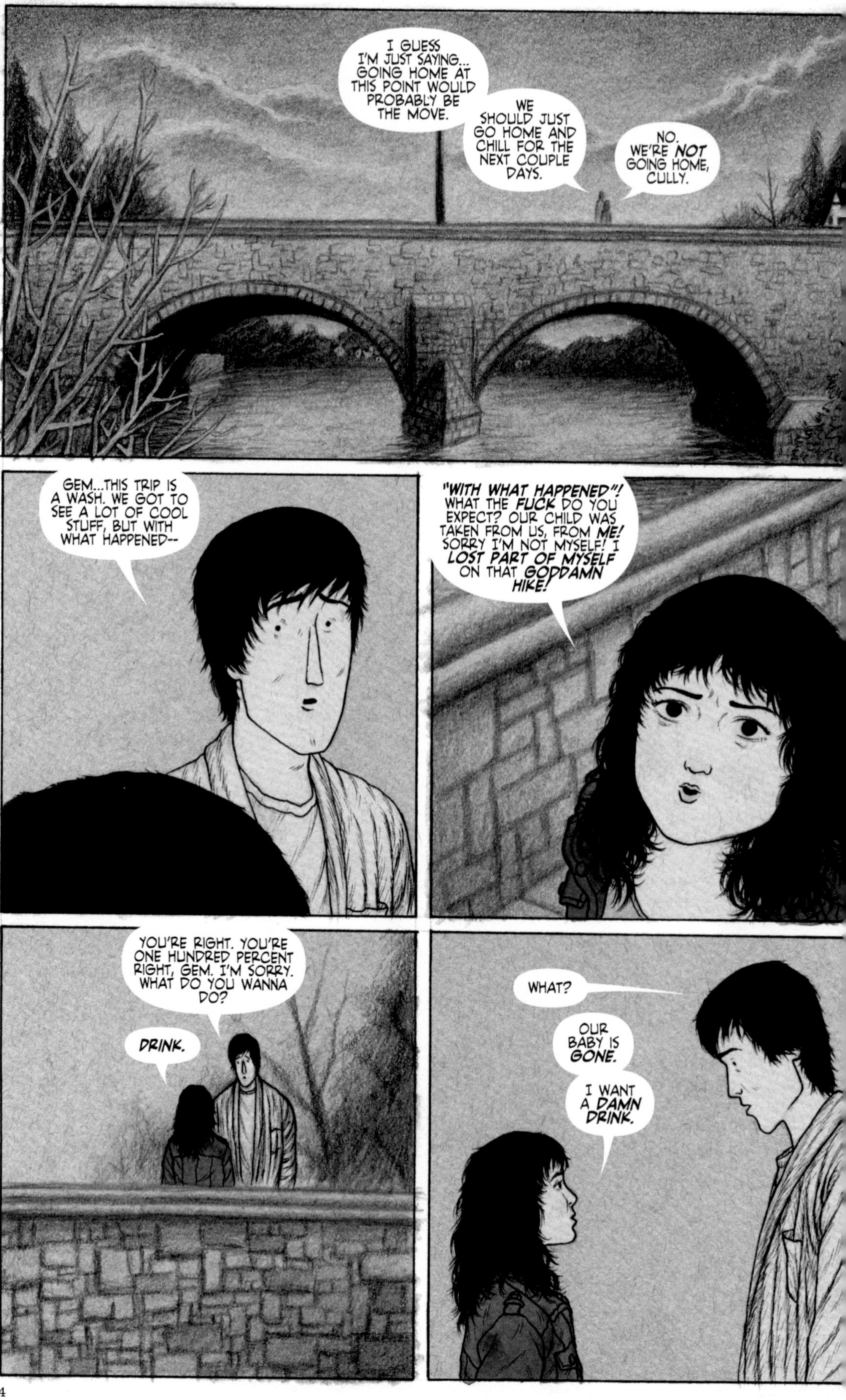
I GUESS I'M JUST SAYING... GOING HOME AT THIS POINT WOULD PROBABLY BE THE MOVE.
WE SHOULD JUST GO HOME AND CHILL FOR THE NEXT COUPLE DAYS.
NO. WE'RE NOT GOING HOME, CULLY.
GEM...THIS TRIP IS A WASH. WE GOT TO SEE A LOT OF COOL STUFF, BUT WITH WHAT HAPPENED--
"WITH WHAT HAPPENED"! WHAT THE FUCK DO YOU EXPECT? OUR CHILD WAS TAKEN FROM US, FROM ME! SORRY I'M NOT MYSELF! I LOST PART OF MYSELF ON THAT GODDAMN HIKE!
YOU'RE RIGHT. YOU'RE ONE HUNDRED PERCENT RIGHT, GEM. I'M SORRY. WHAT DO YOU WANNA DO?
DRINK.
WHAT?
OUR BABY IS GONE.
I WANT A DAMN DRINK.

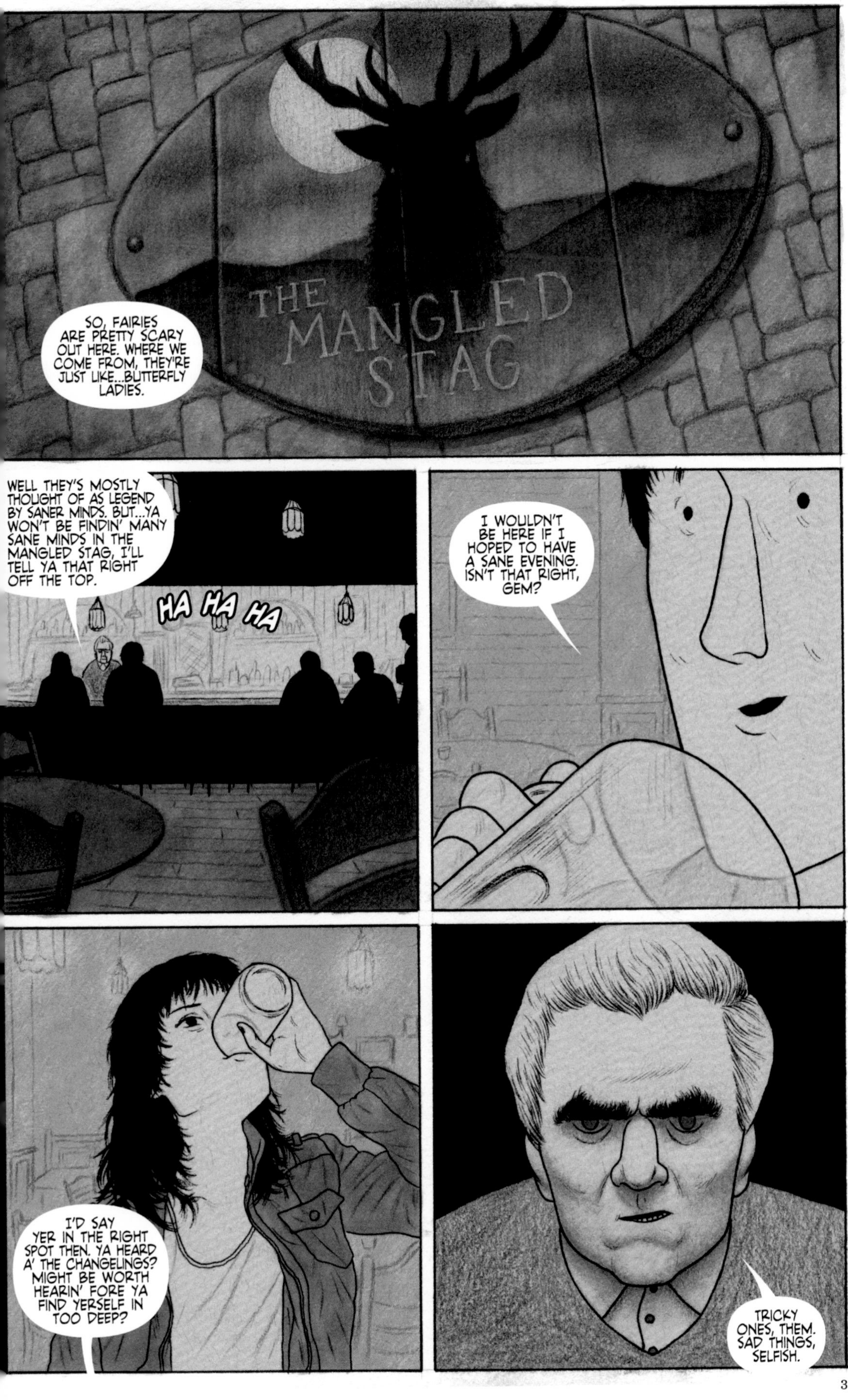
THE MANGLED STAG
SO, FAIRIES ARE PRETTY SCARY OUT HERE. WHERE WE COME FROM, THEY'RE JUST LIKE...BUTTERFLY LADIES.
WELL THEY'S MOSTLY THOUGHT OF AS LEGEND BY SANER MINDS. BUT...YA WON'T BE FINDIN' MANY SANE MINDS IN THE MANGLED STAG, I'LL TELL YA THAT RIGHT OFF THE TOP.
HA HA HA
I WOULDN'T BE HERE IF I HOPED TO HAVE A SANE EVENING. ISN'T THAT RIGHT, GEM?
I'D SAY YER IN THE RIGHT SPOT THEN. YA HEARD A' THE CHANGELINGS? MIGHT BE WORTH HEARIN' FORE YA FIND YERSELF IN TOO DEEP?
TRICKY ONES, THEM. SAD THINGS, SELFISH.

"THE FAE HAVE THEIR OWN RULES AND WAYS, LIVING ALONGSIDE US DOIN' THEIR FAERIE THING. NORMALLY THEY MIND THEIR OWN...

"BUT SOMETIMES THERE BE A DYIN' FAE CHILD. THEY MAKE THIS ONE A *CHANGELING.*

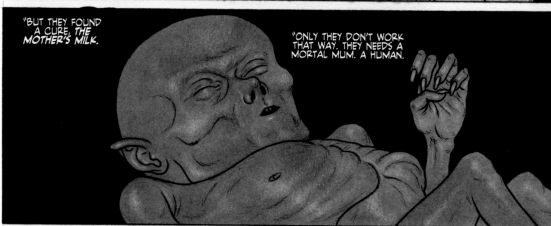

"BUT THEY FOUND A CURE, *THE MOTHER'S MILK.*

"ONLY THEY DON'T WORK THAT WAY. THEY NEEDS A MORTAL MUM. A HUMAN.

"SO THEY MAKES A DEAL WIT' THE MOON OR SOME OTHER, MAYBE A DARK FORCE.

"THEY MAKE AN UNHOLY THING, A MOCKERY OF LIFE, SOMETHING THAT CAN PASS FOR ANOTHER.

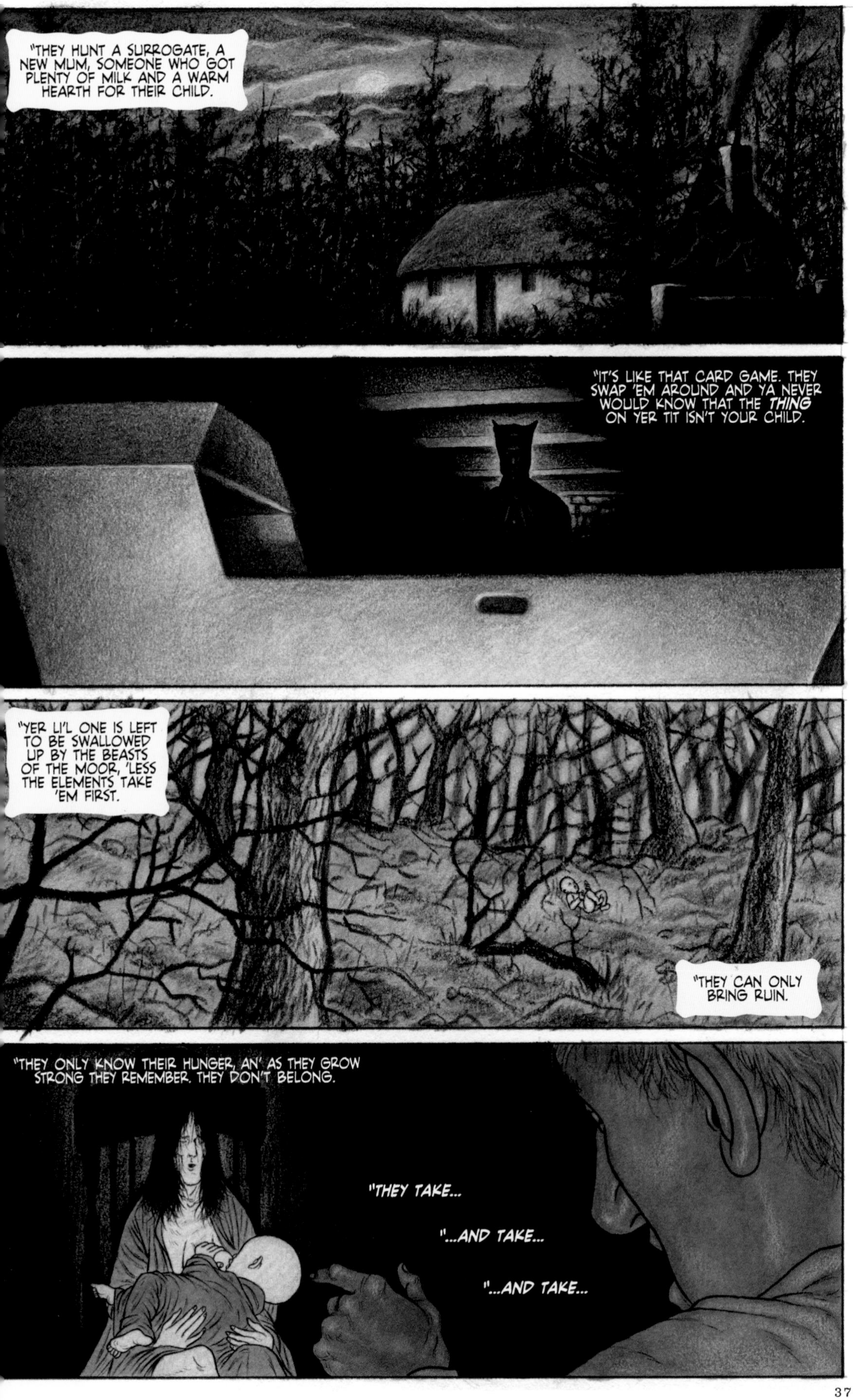
"THEY HUNT A SURROGATE, A NEW MUM, SOMEONE WHO GOT PLENTY OF MILK AND A WARM HEARTH FOR THEIR CHILD.
"IT'S LIKE THAT CARD GAME. THEY SWAP 'EM AROUND AND YA NEVER WOULD KNOW THAT THE *THING* ON YER TIT ISN'T YOUR CHILD.
"YER LI'L ONE IS LEFT TO BE SWALLOWED UP BY THE BEASTS OF THE MOOR, 'LESS THE ELEMENTS TAKE 'EM FIRST.
"THEY CAN ONLY BRING RUIN.
"THEY ONLY KNOW THEIR HUNGER, AN' AS THEY GROW STRONG THEY REMEMBER. THEY DON'T BELONG.
"THEY TAKE...
"...AND TAKE...
"...AND TAKE...

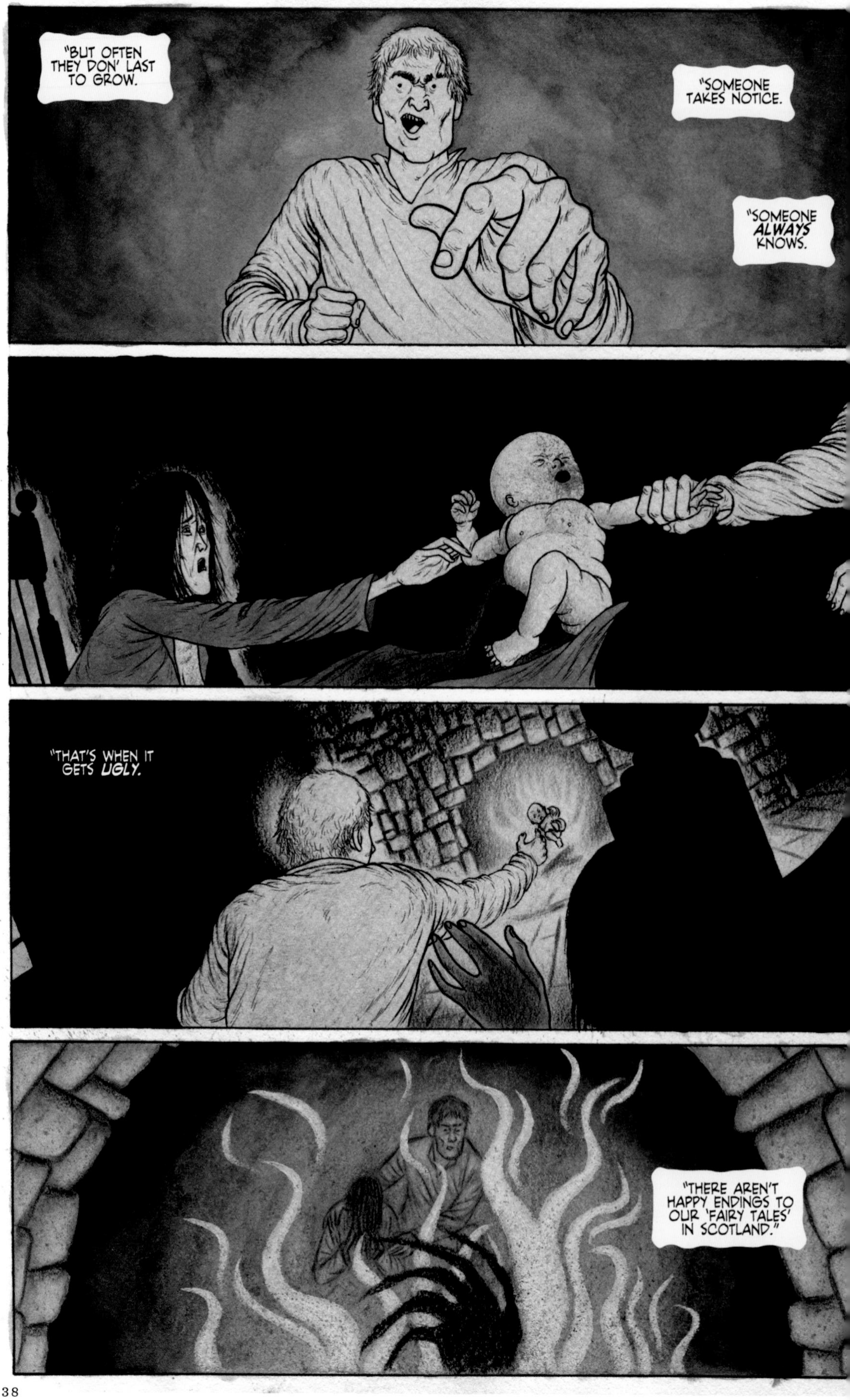
"BUT OFTEN THEY DON' LAST TO GROW.
"SOMEONE TAKES NOTICE.
"SOMEONE *ALWAYS* KNOWS.
"THAT'S WHEN IT GETS *UGLY*.
"THERE AREN'T HAPPY ENDINGS TO OUR 'FAIRY TALES' IN SCOTLAND."

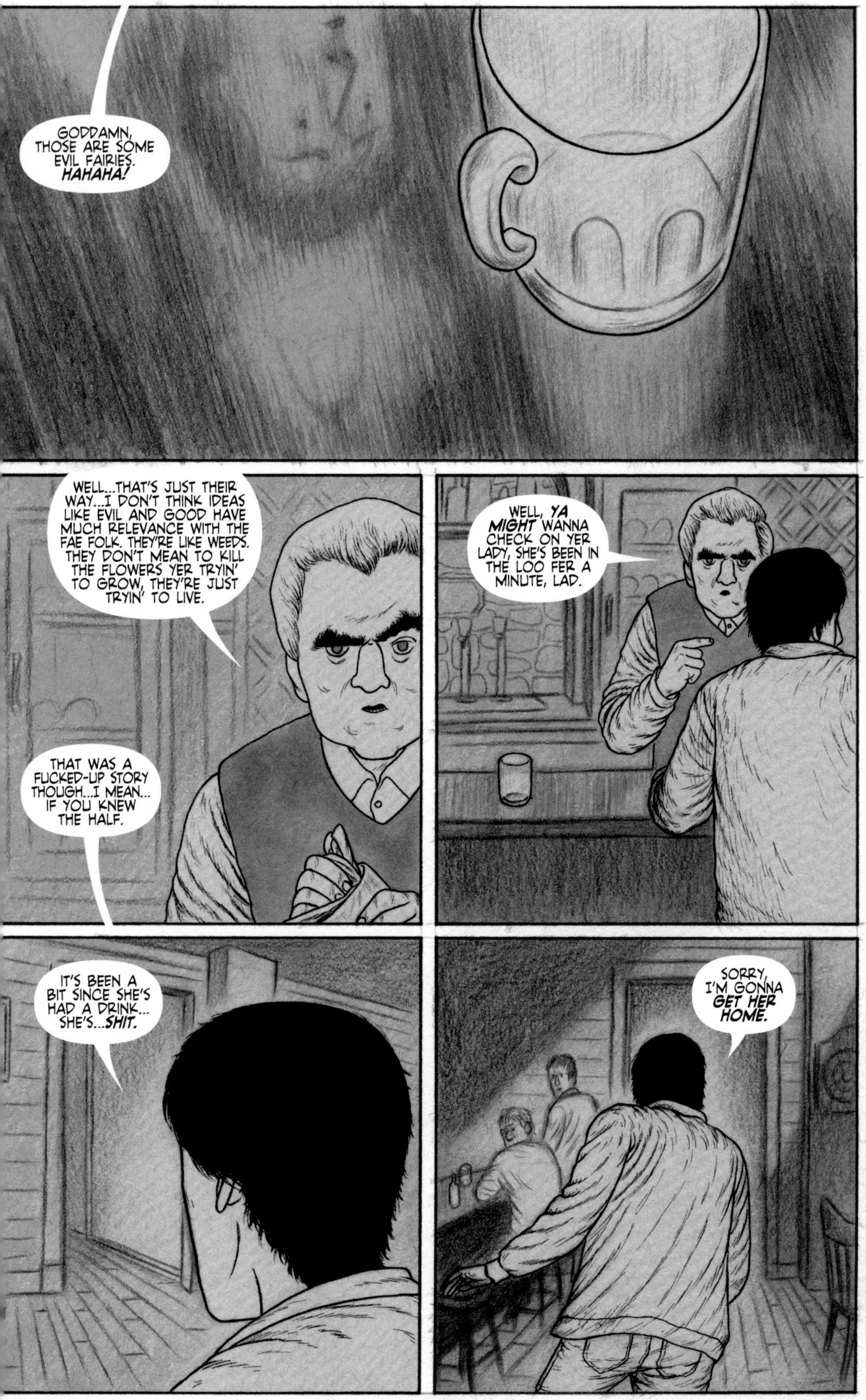
GODDAMN, THOSE ARE SOME EVIL FAIRIES. HAHAHA!
WELL...THAT'S JUST THEIR WAY...I DON'T THINK IDEAS LIKE EVIL AND GOOD HAVE MUCH RELEVANCE WITH THE FAE FOLK. THEY'RE LIKE WEEDS. THEY DON'T MEAN TO KILL THE FLOWERS YER TRYIN' TO GROW, THEY'RE JUST TRYIN' TO LIVE.
THAT WAS A FUCKED-UP STORY THOUGH...I MEAN... IF YOU KNEW THE HALF.
WELL, YA MIGHT WANNA CHECK ON YER LADY, SHE'S BEEN IN THE LOO FER A MINUTE, LAD.
IT'S BEEN A BIT SINCE SHE'S HAD A DRINK... SHE'S...SHIT.
SORRY, I'M GONNA GET HER HOME.

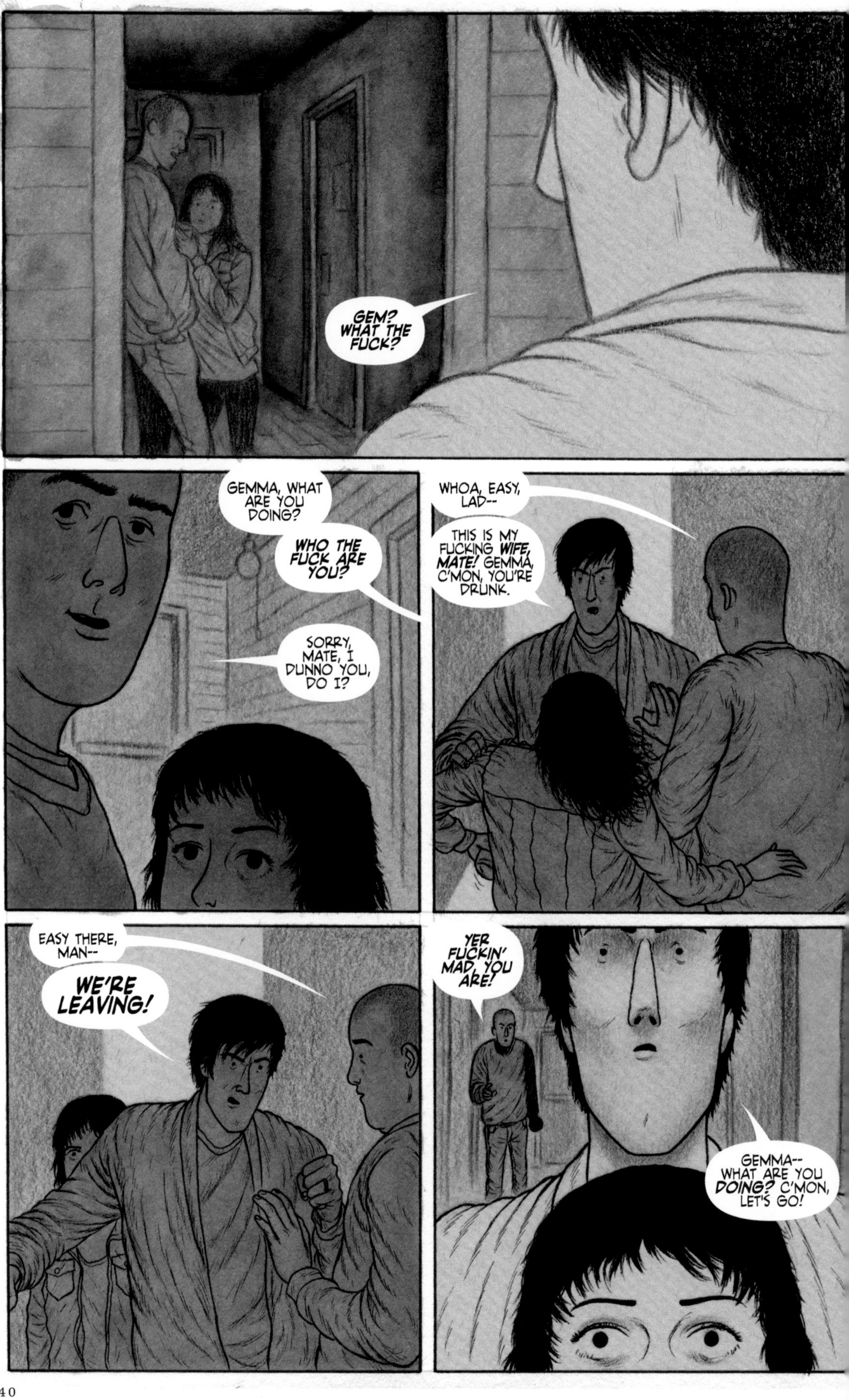
GEM? WHAT THE FUCK?
GEMMA, WHAT ARE YOU DOING?
WHO THE FUCK ARE YOU?
SORRY, MATE, I DUNNO YOU, DO I?
WHOA, EASY, LAD--
THIS IS MY FUCKING WIFE, MATE! GEMMA, C'MON, YOU'RE DRUNK.
EASY THERE, MAN--
WE'RE LEAVING!
YER FUCKIN' MAD, YOU ARE!
GEMMA-- WHAT ARE YOU DOING? C'MON, LET'S GO!

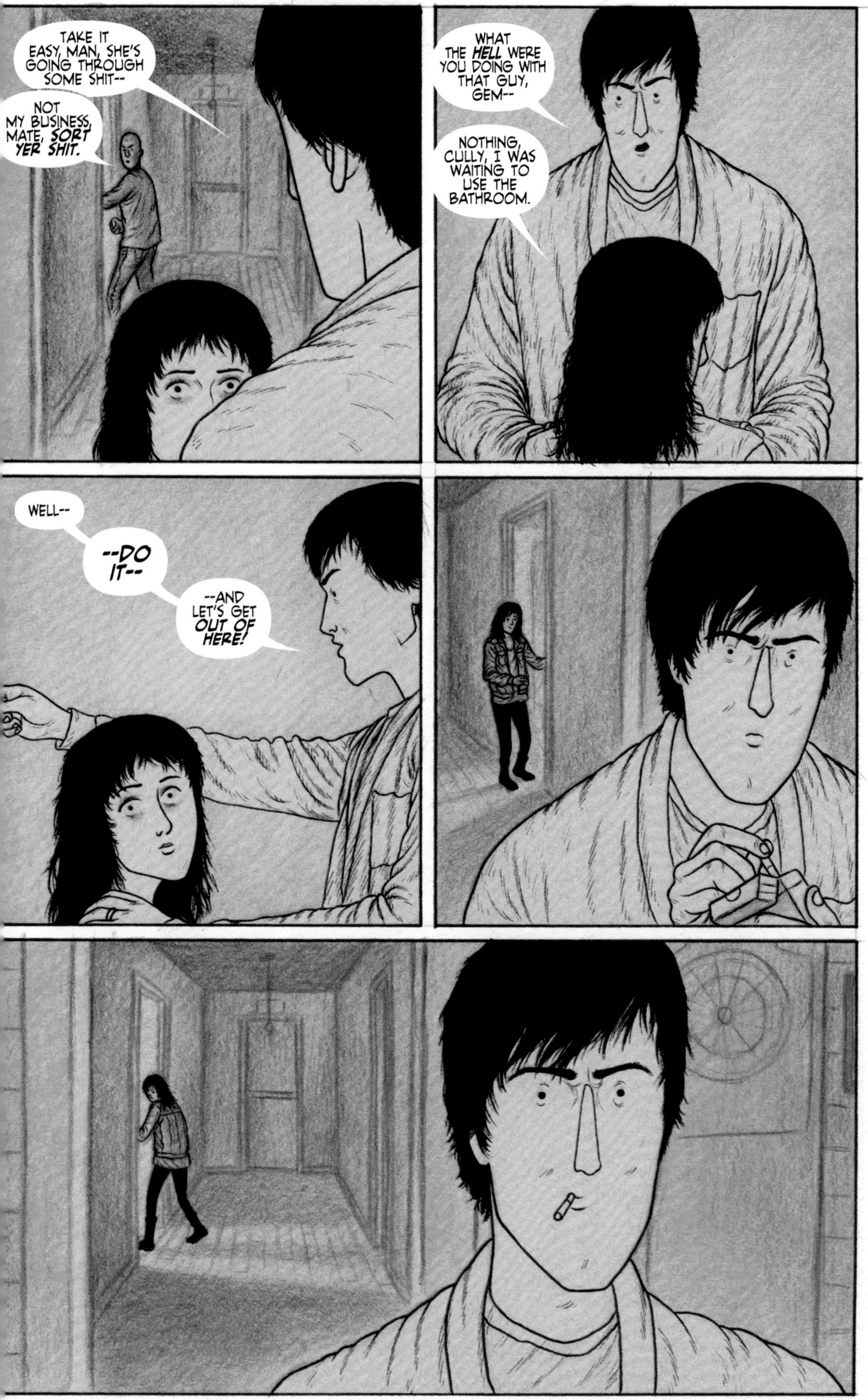
TAKE IT EASY, MAN, SHE'S GOING THROUGH SOME SHIT--
NOT MY BUSINESS, MATE, SORT YER SHIT.
WHAT THE HELL WERE YOU DOING WITH THAT GUY, GEM--
NOTHING, CULLY, I WAS WAITING TO USE THE BATHROOM.
WELL--
--DO IT--
--AND LET'S GET OUT OF HERE!

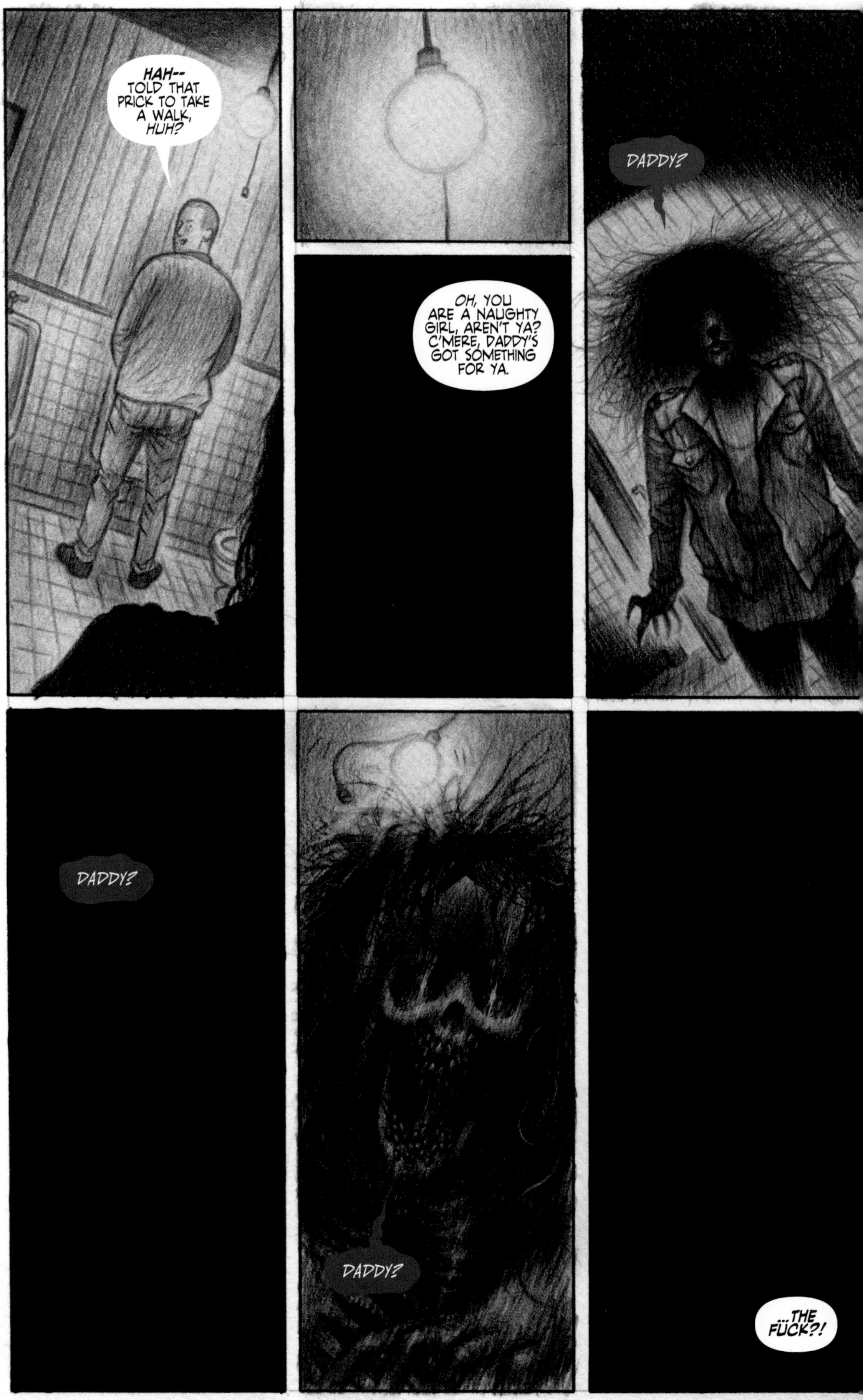
HAH-- TOLD THAT PRICK TO TAKE A WALK, HUH?
OH, YOU ARE A NAUGHTY GIRL, AREN'T YA? C'MERE, DADDY'S GOT SOMETHING FOR YA.
DADDY?
DADDY?
DADDY?
...THE FUCK?!

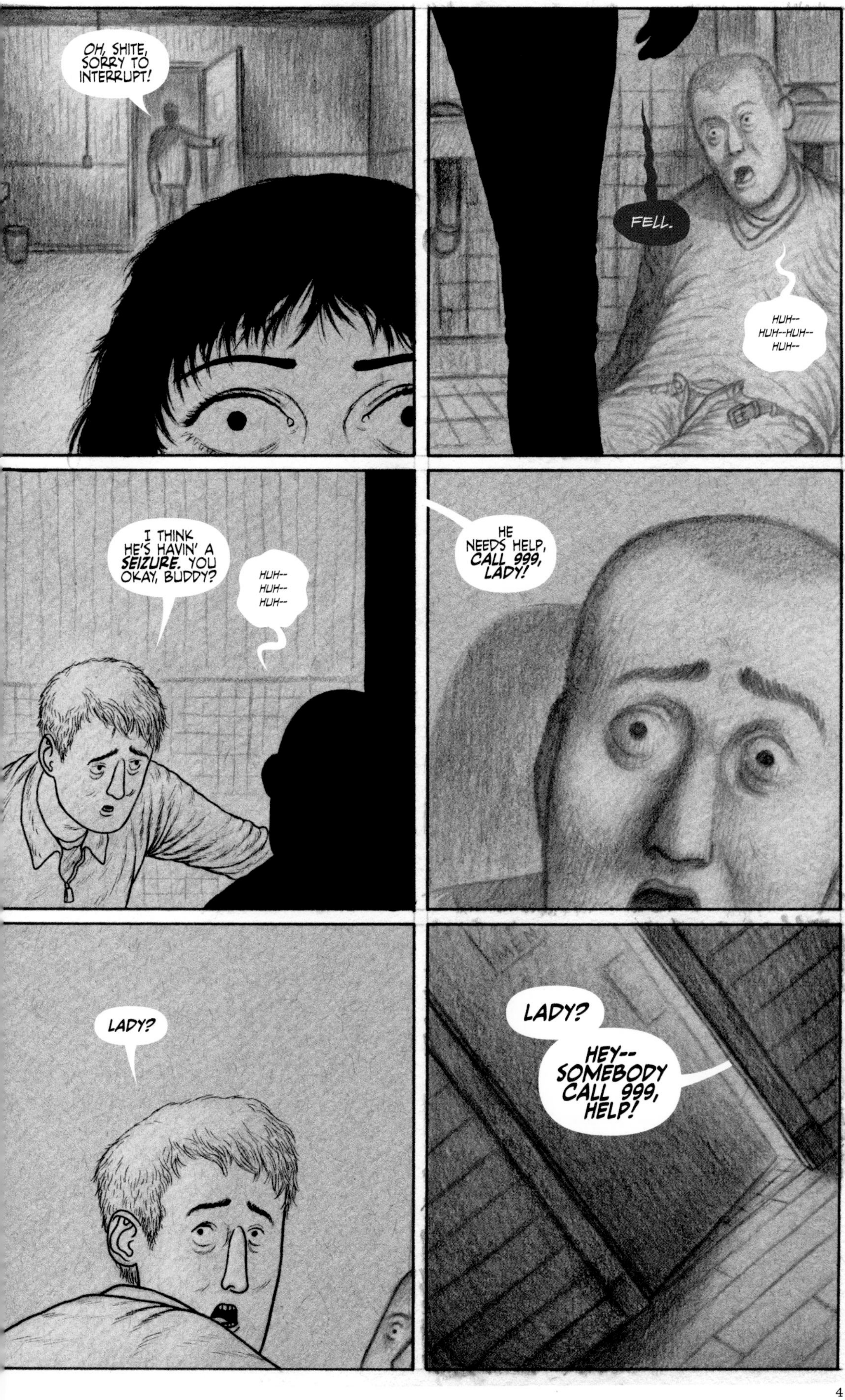
OH, SHITE, SORRY TO INTERRUPT!
FELL.
HUH-- HUH--HUH-- HUH--
I THINK HE'S HAVIN' A SEIZURE. YOU OKAY, BUDDY?
HUH-- HUH-- HUH--
HE NEEDS HELP, CALL 999, LADY!
LADY?
LADY?
HEY-- SOMEBODY CALL 999, HELP!

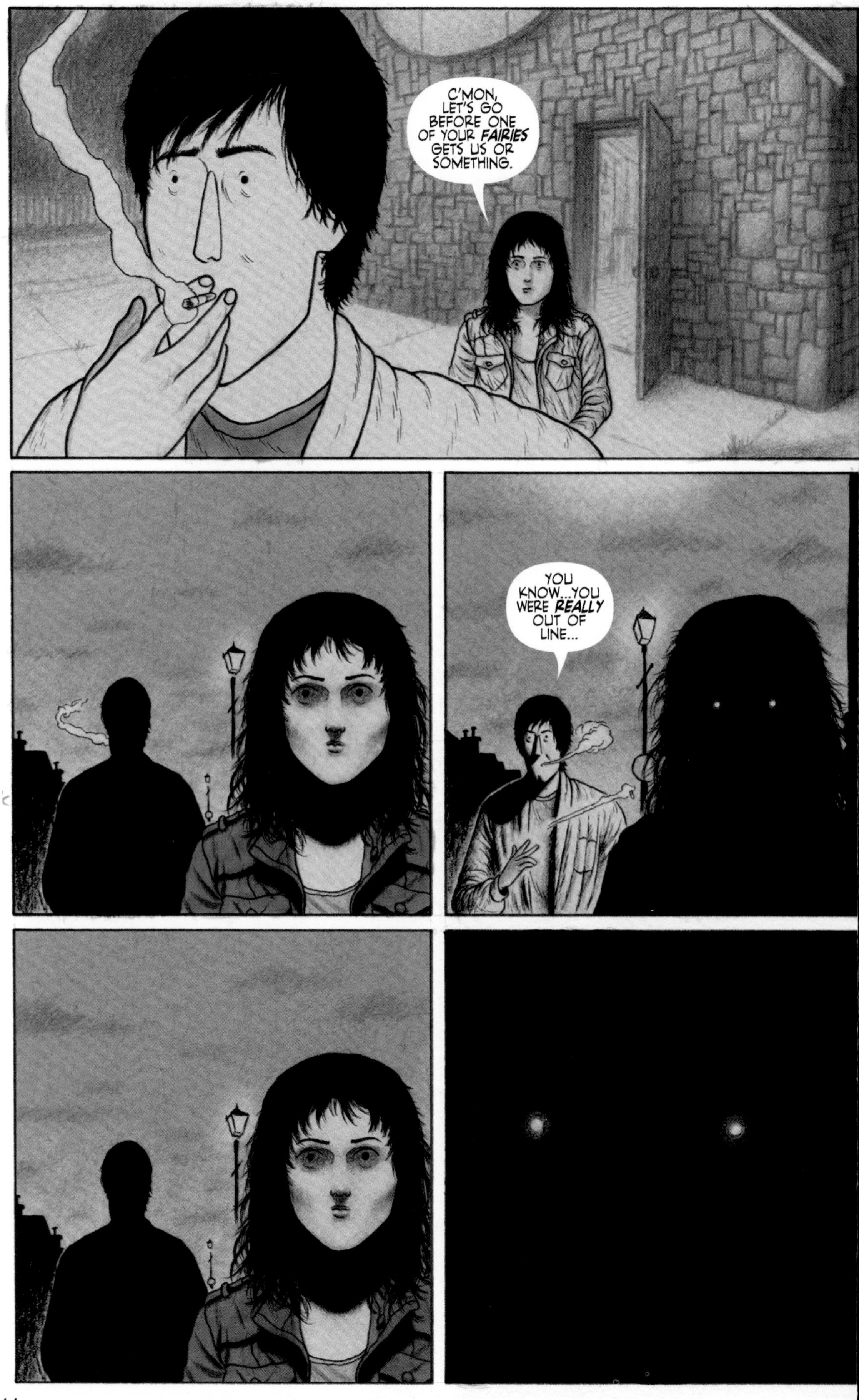
C'MON, LET'S GO BEFORE ONE OF YOUR FAIRIES GETS US OR SOMETHING.
YOU KNOW...YOU WERE REALLY OUT OF LINE...

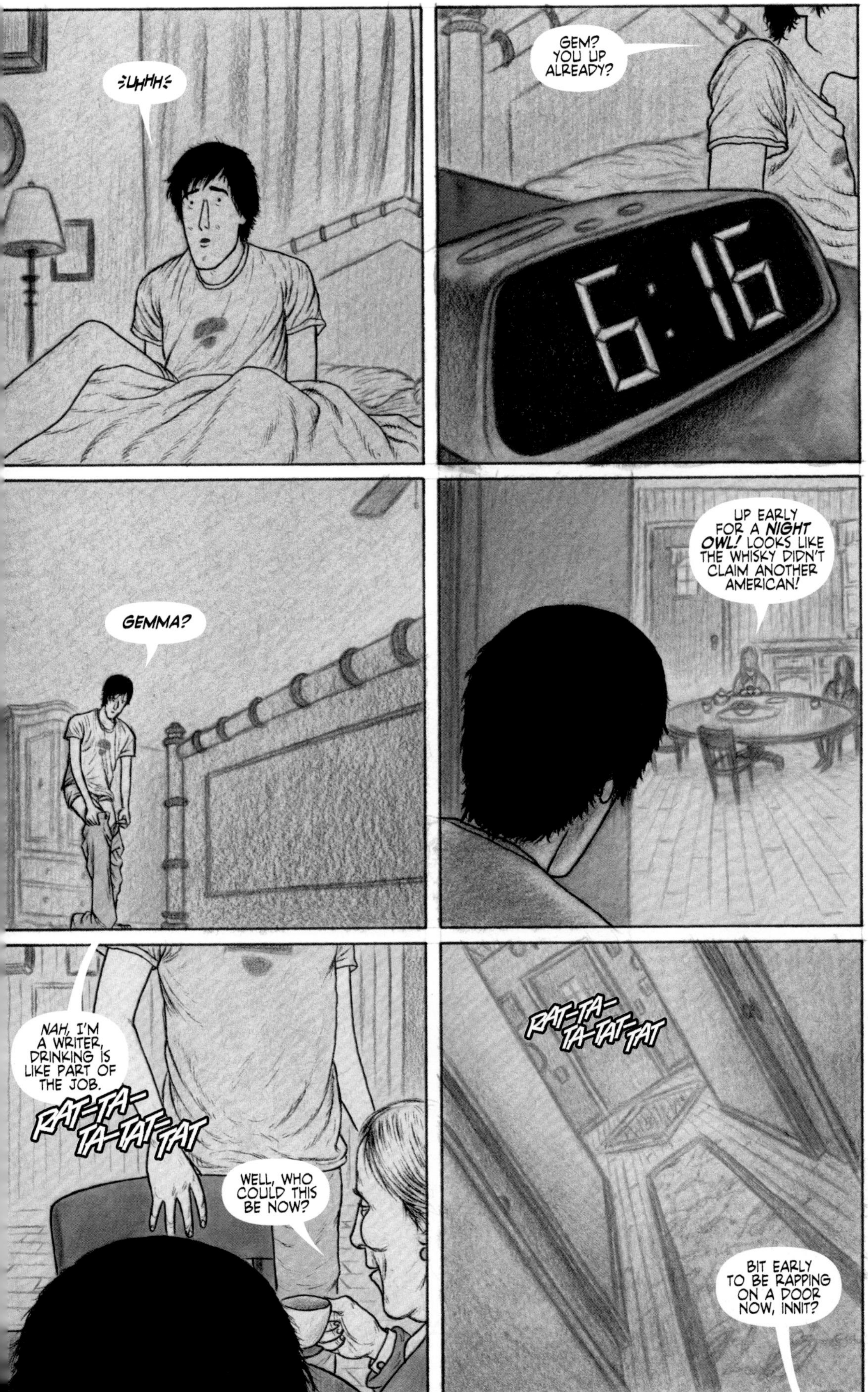
UHHH
GEM? YOU UP ALREADY?
6:16
GEMMA?
UP EARLY FOR A NIGHT OWL! LOOKS LIKE THE WHISKY DIDN'T CLAIM ANOTHER AMERICAN!
NAH, I'M A WRITER, DRINKING IS LIKE PART OF THE JOB.
RAT-TA-TA-TAT-TAT
WELL, WHO COULD THIS BE NOW?
RAT-TA-TA-TAT-TAT
BIT EARLY TO BE RAPPING ON A DOOR NOW, INNIT?

SORRY TO WAKE YOU, MISS. I'M DETECTIVE INSPECTOR MITCHELL AND THIS IS CHIEF INSPECTOR PATERSON.

IT'S OUR DISPLEASURE TO INFORM YOU THAT THERE HAVE BEEN SOME CONCERNING DEVELOPMENTS IN TOWN.

OH MY-- WHAT'S GOING ON?

WE CAN'T DISCLOSE MUCH, BUT WE ARE PLACING AN INFORMAL CURFEW ON THE LOCAL AREA.

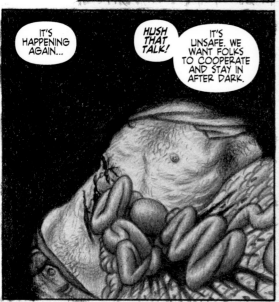

IT'S HAPPENING AGAIN...

HUSH THAT TALK!

IT'S UNSAFE. WE WANT FOLKS TO COOPERATE AND STAY IN AFTER DARK.

IT'S HAPPENING AGAIN THEN... I THOUGHT--

THAT'S ENOUGH OF THAT TALK! WE ARE ON THE CASE, WE ARE JUST ASKING FOR YOUR COOPERATION, AND FOR THE COOPERATION OF YOUR LODGERS.

NATURALLY, BUT, I THOUGHT YOU--

WE APPRECIATE YOUR COOPERATION AND DISCRETION IN THIS MATTER. WE'LL BE NEEDIN' A LIST OF YOUR CURRENT LODGERS.

OF COURSE-- ONE MOMENT.

HERE, PLEASE--

THANK YOU, MUM. WE'LL BE FOLLOWIN' UP SHORTLY.

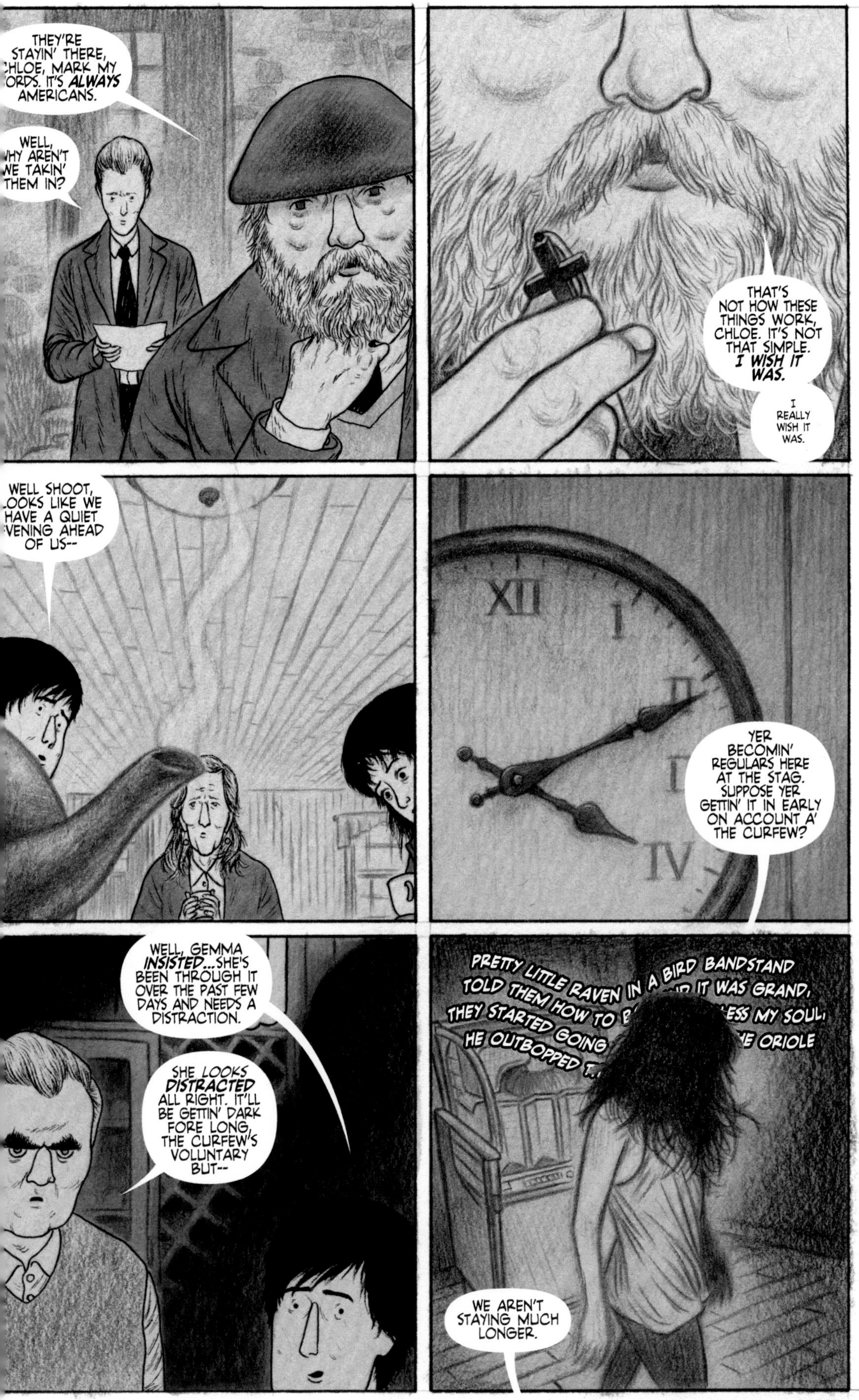
THEY'RE STAYIN' THERE, CHLOE, MARK MY ORDS. IT'S *ALWAYS* AMERICANS.
WELL, HY AREN'T WE TAKIN' THEM IN?
THAT'S NOT HOW THESE THINGS WORK, CHLOE. IT'S NOT THAT SIMPLE. ***I WISH IT WAS.***
I REALLY WISH IT WAS.
WELL SHOOT, OOKS LIKE WE HAVE A QUIET EVENING AHEAD OF US--
YER BECOMIN' REGULARS HERE AT THE STAG. SUPPOSE YER GETTIN' IT IN EARLY ON ACCOUNT A' THE CURFEW?
WELL, GEMMA ***INSISTED***... SHE'S BEEN THROUGH IT OVER THE PAST FEW DAYS AND NEEDS A DISTRACTION.
SHE *LOOKS* ***DISTRACTED*** ALL RIGHT. IT'LL BE GETTIN' DARK FORE LONG. THE CURFEW'S VOLUNTARY BUT--
PRETTY LITTLE RAVEN IN A BIRD BANDSTAND
TOLD THEM HOW TO B
IT WAS GRAND,
THEY STARTED GOING
ESS MY SOUL,
HE OUTBOPPED T
E ORIOLE
WE AREN'T STAYING MUCH LONGER.

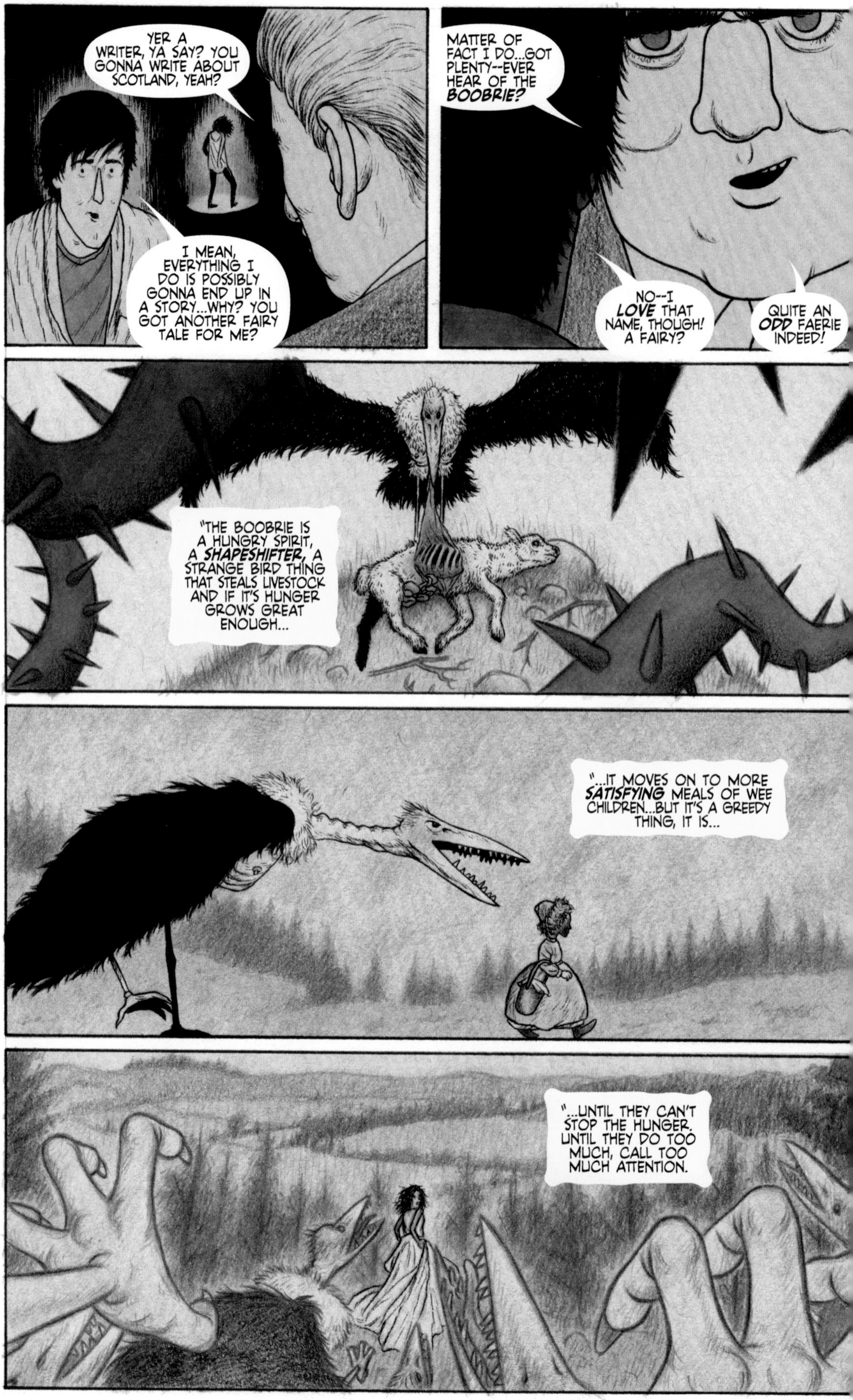

YER A WRITER, YA SAY? YOU GONNA WRITE ABOUT SCOTLAND, YEAH?
I MEAN, EVERYTHING I DO IS POSSIBLY GONNA END UP IN A STORY...WHY? YOU GOT ANOTHER FAIRY TALE FOR ME?
MATTER OF FACT I DO...GOT PLENTY--EVER HEAR OF THE BOOBRIE?
NO--I LOVE THAT NAME, THOUGH! A FAIRY?
QUITE AN ODD FAERIE INDEED!
"THE BOOBRIE IS A HUNGRY SPIRIT, A SHAPESHIFTER, A STRANGE BIRD THING THAT STEALS LIVESTOCK AND IF IT'S HUNGER GROWS GREAT ENOUGH...
"...IT MOVES ON TO MORE SATISFYING MEALS OF WEE CHILDREN...BUT IT'S A GREEDY THING, IT IS...
"...UNTIL THEY CAN'T STOP THE HUNGER. UNTIL THEY DO TOO MUCH, CALL TOO MUCH ATTENTION.

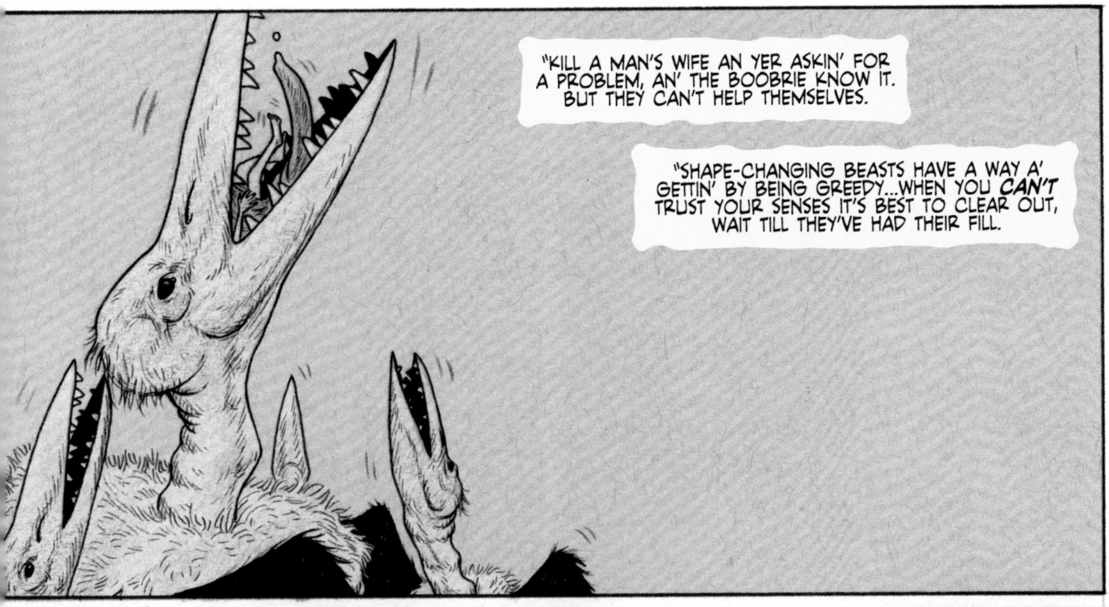
"KILL A MAN'S WIFE AN YER ASKIN' FOR A PROBLEM, AN' THE BOOBRIE KNOW IT. BUT THEY CAN'T HELP THEMSELVES.
"SHAPE-CHANGING BEASTS HAVE A WAY A' GETTIN' BY BEING GREEDY...WHEN YOU *CAN'T* TRUST YOUR SENSES IT'S BEST TO CLEAR OUT, WAIT TILL THEY'VE HAD THEIR FILL.

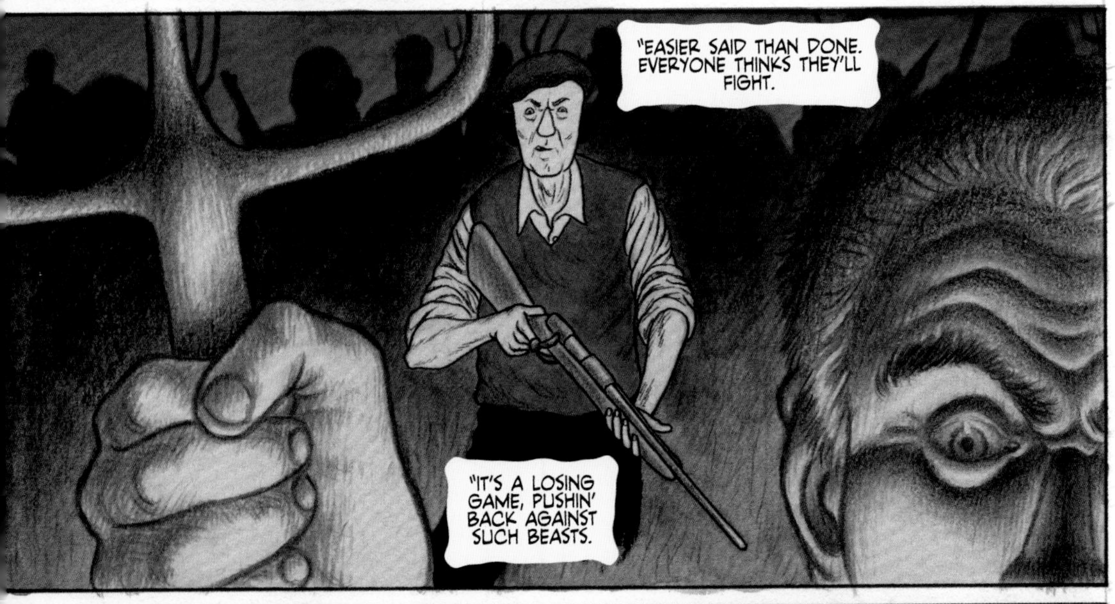
"EASIER SAID THAN DONE. EVERYONE THINKS THEY'LL FIGHT.
"IT'S A LOSING GAME, PUSHIN' BACK AGAINST SUCH BEASTS.

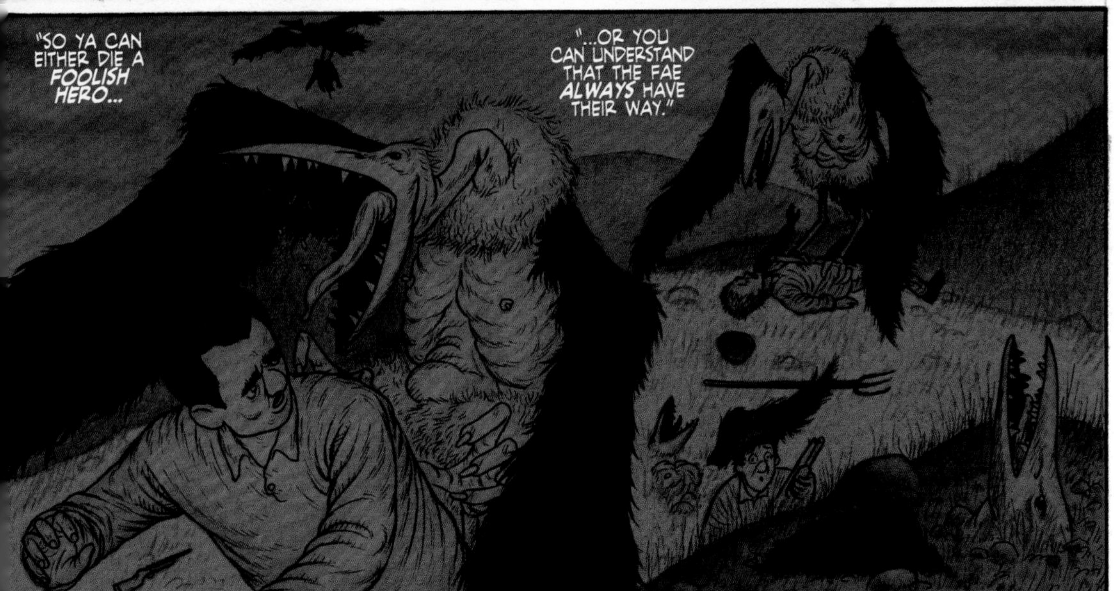
"SO YA CAN EITHER DIE A *FOOLISH HERO*...
"...OR YOU CAN UNDERSTAND THAT THE FAE *ALWAYS* HAVE THEIR WAY."

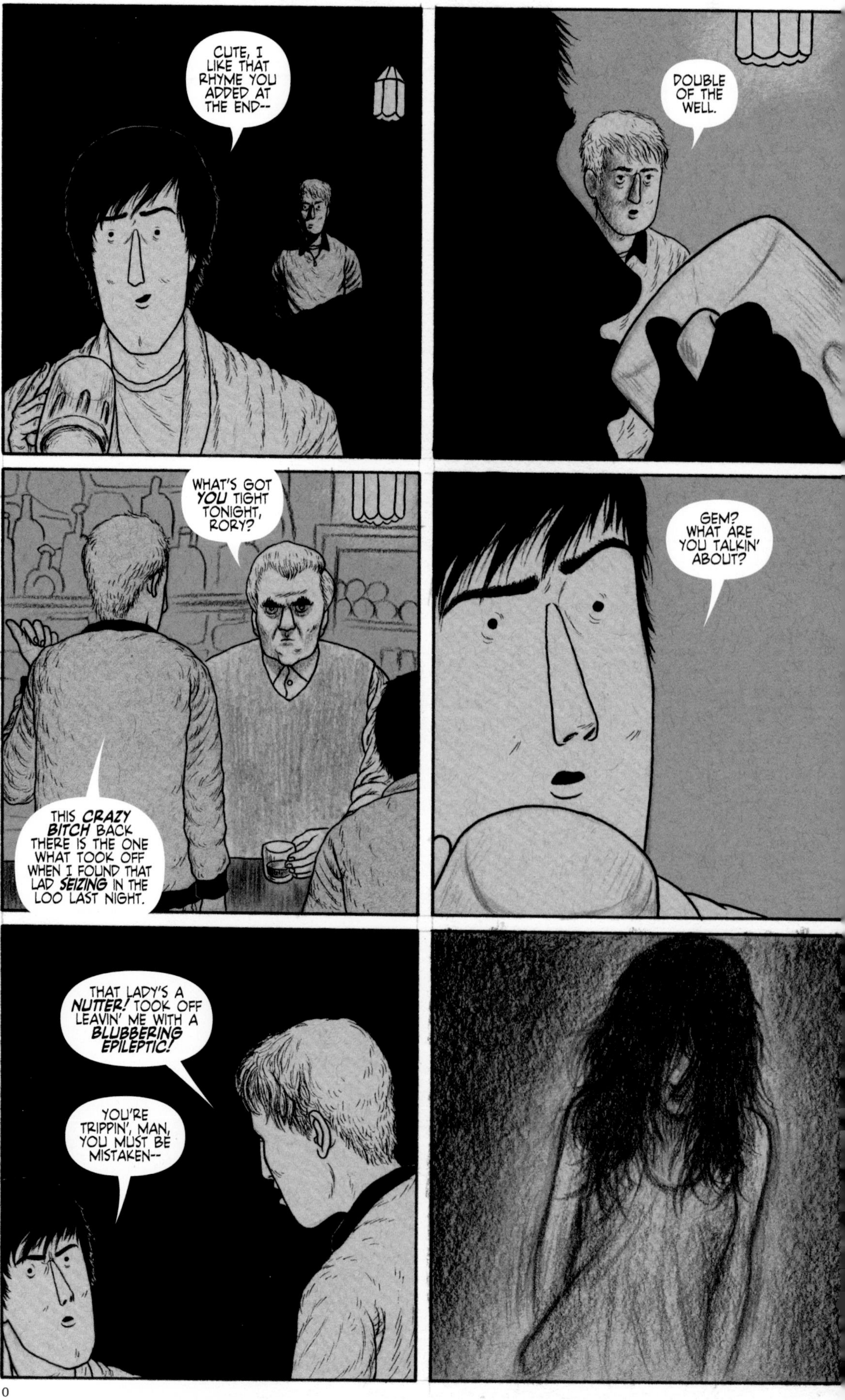
CUTE, I LIKE THAT RHYME YOU ADDED AT THE END--
DOUBLE OF THE WELL.
WHAT'S GOT *YOU* TIGHT TONIGHT, RORY?
THIS ***CRAZY BITCH*** BACK THERE IS THE ONE WHAT TOOK OFF WHEN I FOUND THAT LAD ***SEIZING*** IN THE LOO LAST NIGHT.
GEM? WHAT ARE YOU TALKIN' ABOUT?
THAT LADY'S A ***NUTTER!*** TOOK OFF LEAVIN' ME WITH A ***BLUBBERING EPILEPTIC!***
YOU'RE TRIPPIN', MAN, YOU MUST BE MISTAKEN--

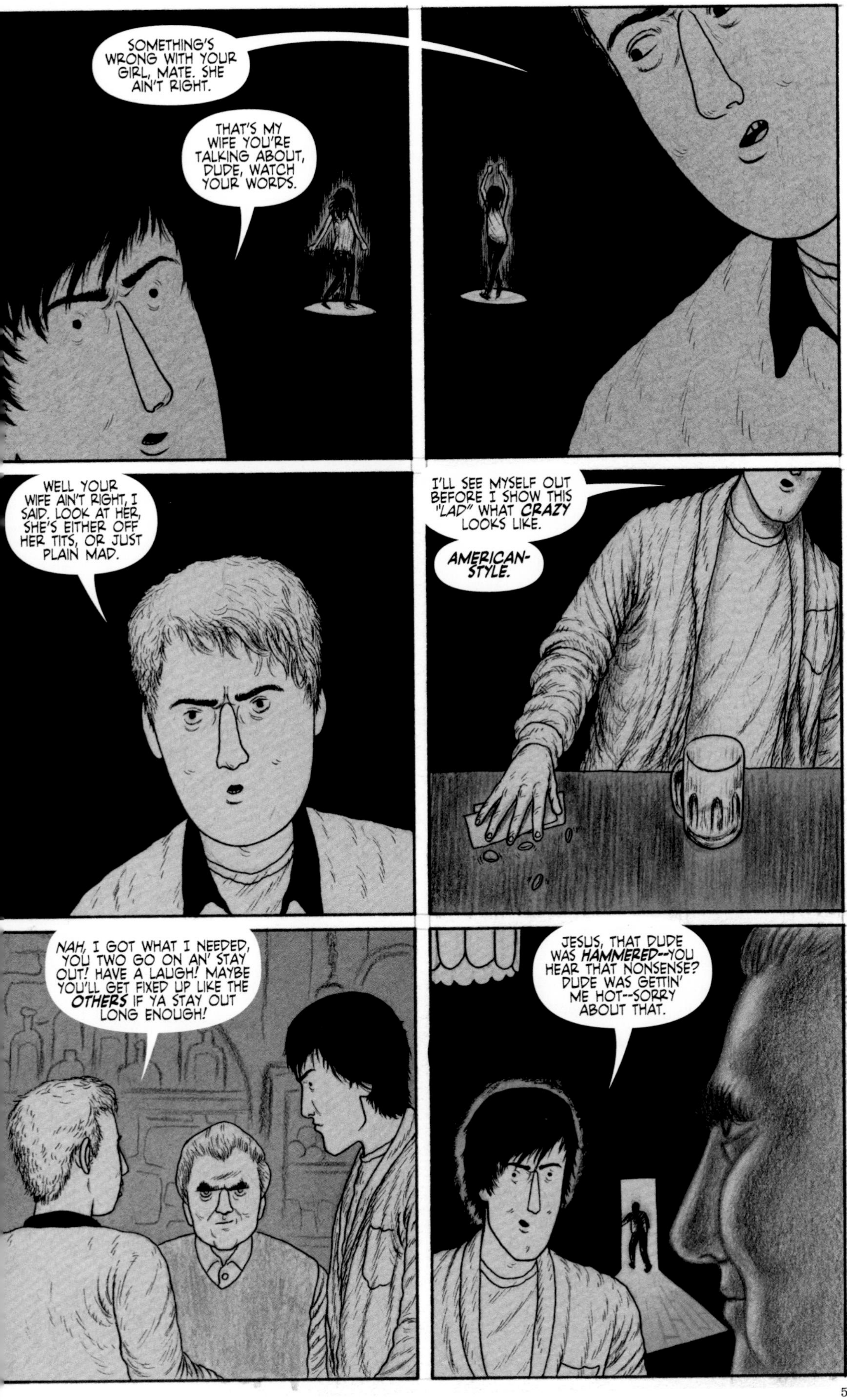
SOMETHING'S WRONG WITH YOUR GIRL, MATE. SHE AIN'T RIGHT.
THAT'S MY WIFE YOU'RE TALKING ABOUT, DUDE, WATCH YOUR WORDS.
WELL YOUR WIFE AIN'T RIGHT, I SAID. LOOK AT HER, SHE'S EITHER OFF HER TITS, OR JUST PLAIN MAD.
I'LL SEE MYSELF OUT BEFORE I SHOW THIS "LAD" WHAT CRAZY LOOKS LIKE.
AMERICAN-STYLE.
NAH, I GOT WHAT I NEEDED, YOU TWO GO ON AN' STAY OUT! HAVE A LAUGH! MAYBE YOU'LL GET FIXED UP LIKE THE OTHERS IF YA STAY OUT LONG ENOUGH!
JESUS, THAT DUDE WAS HAMMERED--YOU HEAR THAT NONSENSE? DUDE WAS GETTIN' ME HOT--SORRY ABOUT THAT.

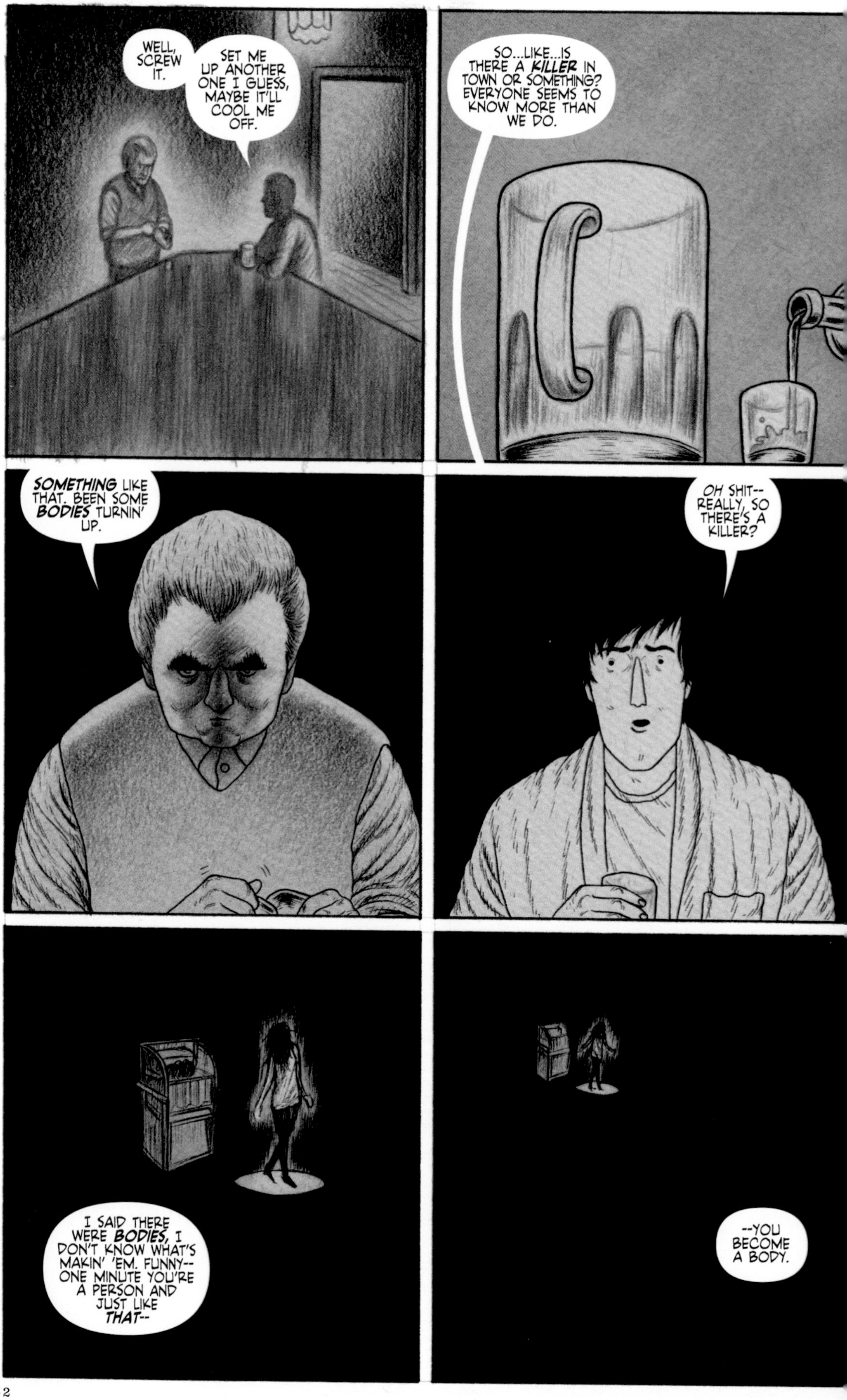
WELL, SCREW IT.
SET ME UP ANOTHER ONE I GUESS, MAYBE IT'LL COOL ME OFF.
SO...LIKE...IS THERE A KILLER IN TOWN OR SOMETHING? EVERYONE SEEMS TO KNOW MORE THAN WE DO.
SOMETHING LIKE THAT. BEEN SOME BODIES TURNIN' UP.
OH SHIT-- REALLY, SO THERE'S A KILLER?
I SAID THERE WERE BODIES, I DON'T KNOW WHAT'S MAKIN' 'EM. FUNNY-- ONE MINUTE YOU'RE A PERSON AND JUST LIKE THAT--
--YOU BECOME A BODY.

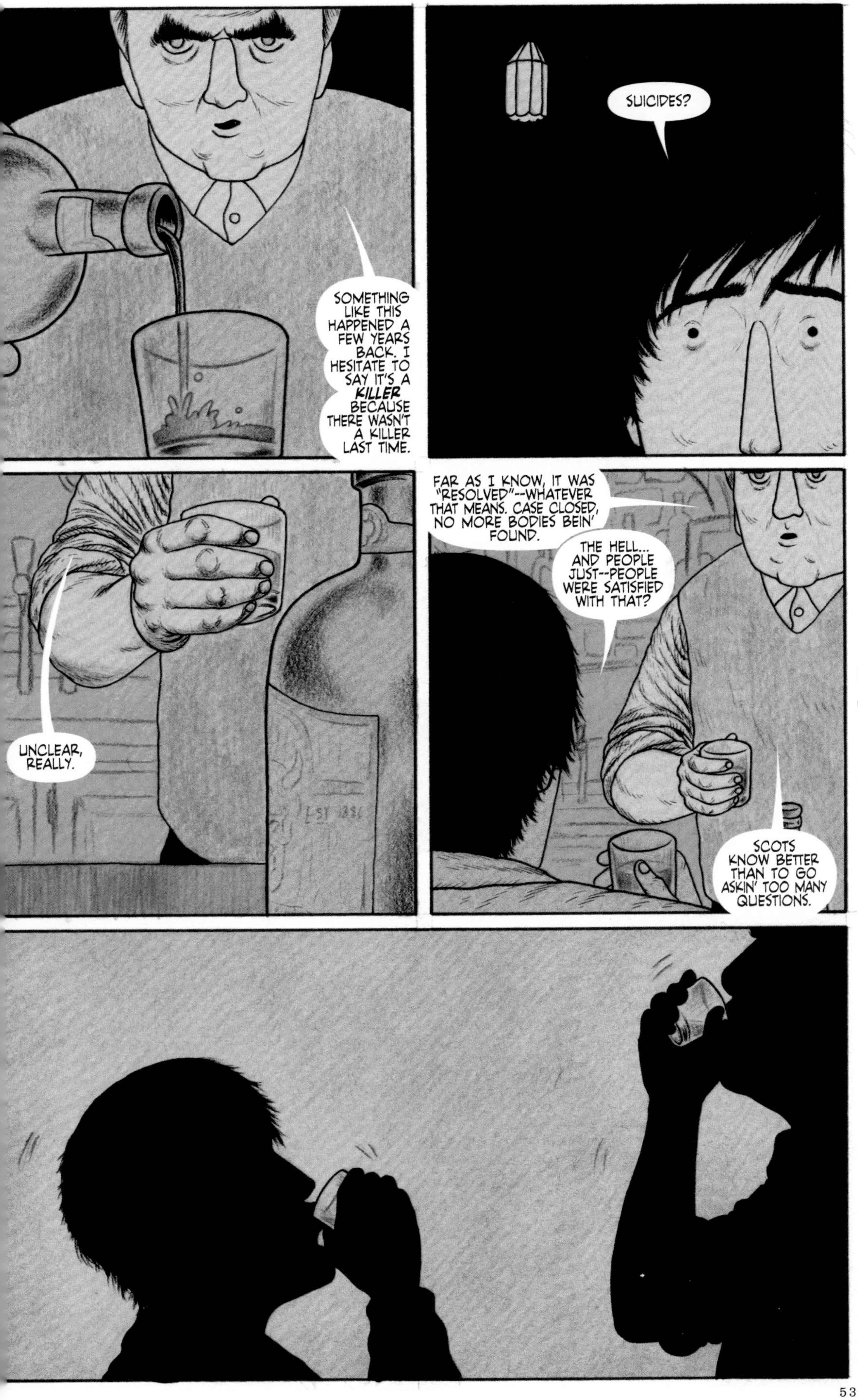
SOMETHING LIKE THIS HAPPENED A FEW YEARS BACK. I HESITATE TO SAY IT'S A KILLER BECAUSE THERE WASN'T A KILLER LAST TIME.
SUICIDES?
UNCLEAR, REALLY.
FAR AS I KNOW, IT WAS "RESOLVED"--WHATEVER THAT MEANS. CASE CLOSED, NO MORE BODIES BEIN' FOUND.
THE HELL... AND PEOPLE JUST--PEOPLE WERE SATISFIED WITH THAT?
SCOTS KNOW BETTER THAN TO GO ASKIN' TOO MANY QUESTIONS.

JUST BE CAREFUL, *LAY LOW*--AND STAY OFF THE STREETS AT NIGHT. IF YER GONNA GO OUT, MAYBE DON'T GO *ALONE*.

DAMN, THIS IS *NOT* THE TRIP WE WERE HOPING FOR. YA KNOW...UP ON STORR GEMMA HAD A...WELL WE LOST--

SHE'S GONE, MATE. DIDN'T SEE HER SLIP OFF, MIGHT WANNA CHECK, IT'S STARTIN' TO GET DARK.

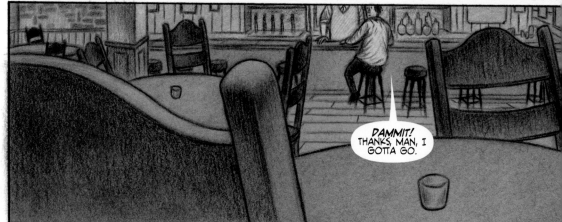

DAMMIT! THANKS, MAN, I GOTTA GO.

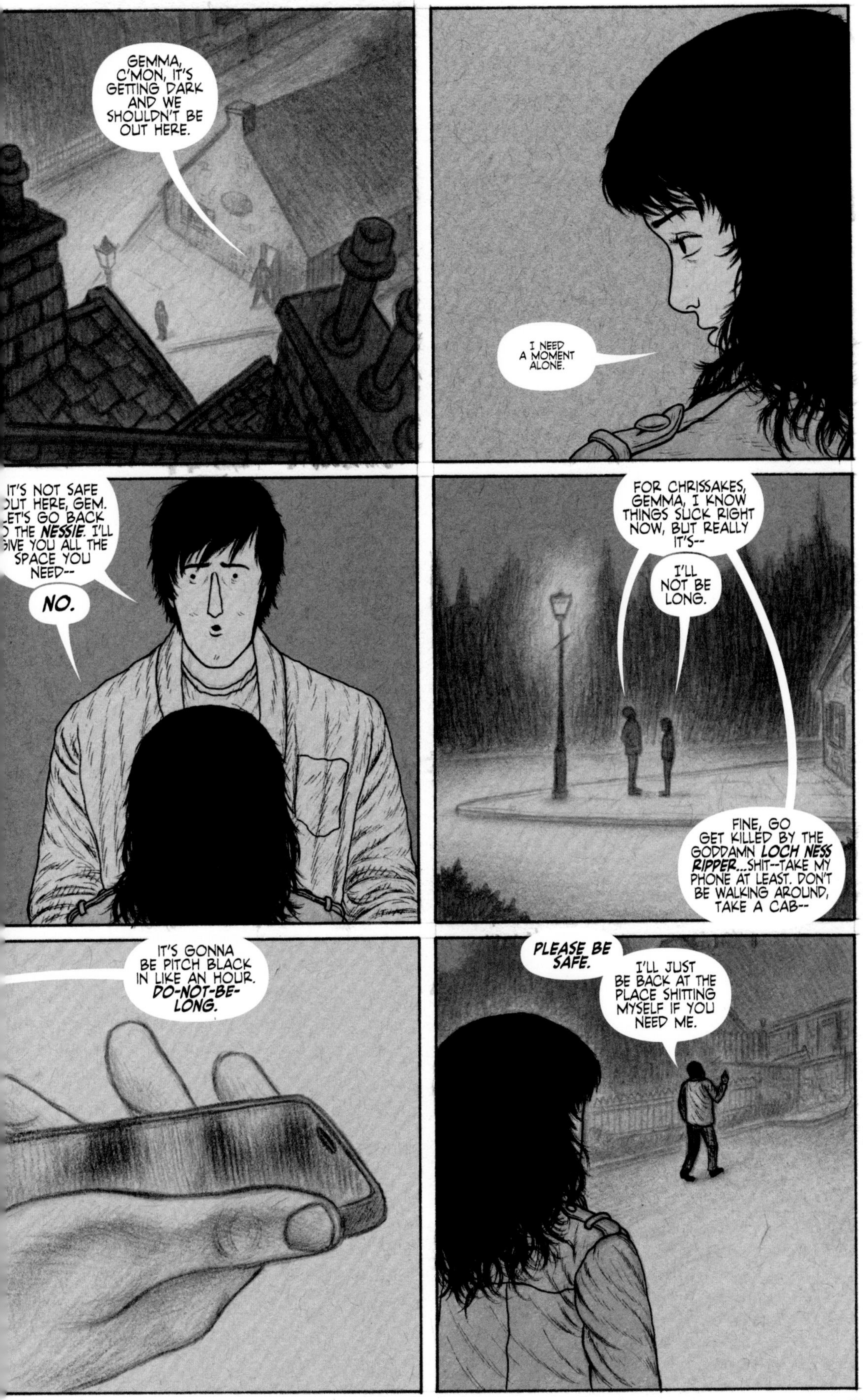
GEMMA, C'MON, IT'S GETTING DARK AND WE SHOULDN'T BE OUT HERE.
I NEED A MOMENT ALONE.
IT'S NOT SAFE OUT HERE, GEM. LET'S GO BACK TO THE *NESSIE*. I'LL GIVE YOU ALL THE SPACE YOU NEED--
NO.
FOR CHRISSAKES, GEMMA, I KNOW THINGS SUCK RIGHT NOW, BUT REALLY IT'S--
I'LL NOT BE LONG.
FINE, GO GET KILLED BY THE GODDAMN *LOCH NESS RIPPER*...SHIT--TAKE MY PHONE AT LEAST. DON'T BE WALKING AROUND, TAKE A CAB--
IT'S GONNA BE PITCH BLACK IN LIKE AN HOUR. *DO-NOT-BE-LONG.*
PLEASE BE SAFE.
I'LL JUST BE BACK AT THE PLACE SHITTING MYSELF IF YOU NEED ME.

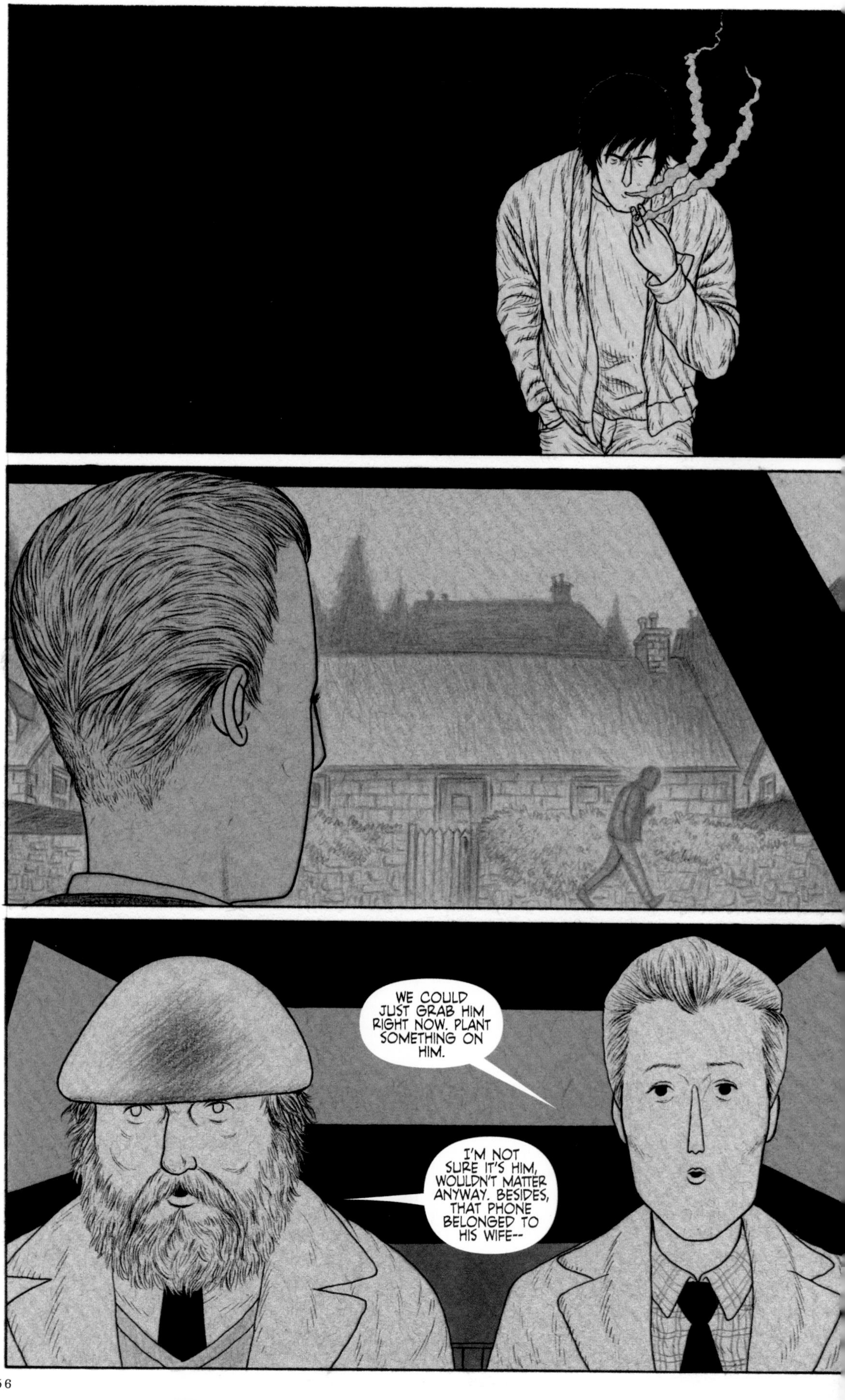

WE COULD JUST GRAB HIM RIGHT NOW. PLANT SOMETHING ON HIM.
I'M NOT SURE IT'S HIM, WOULDN'T MATTER ANYWAY. BESIDES, THAT PHONE BELONGED TO HIS WIFE--

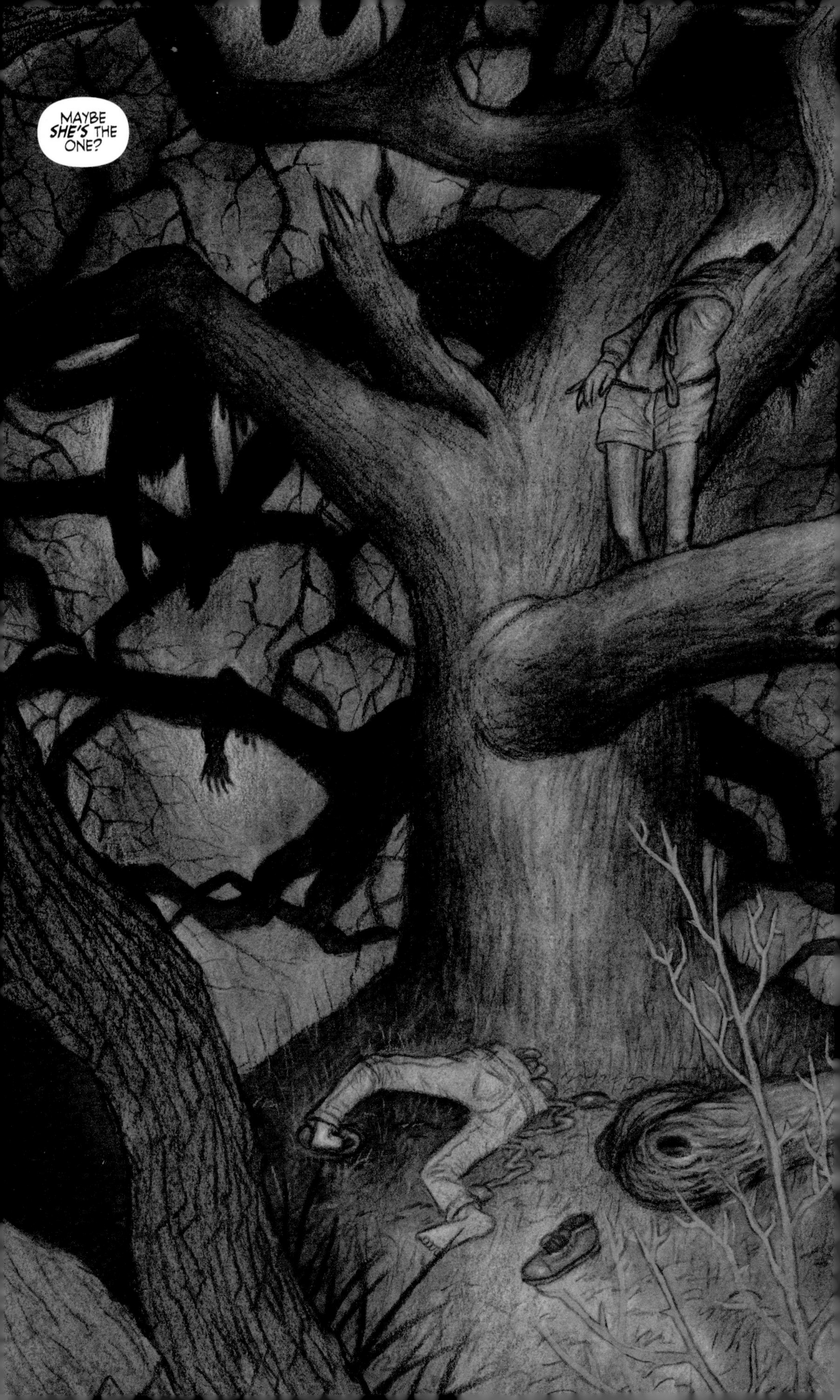
MAYBE SHE'S THE ONE?

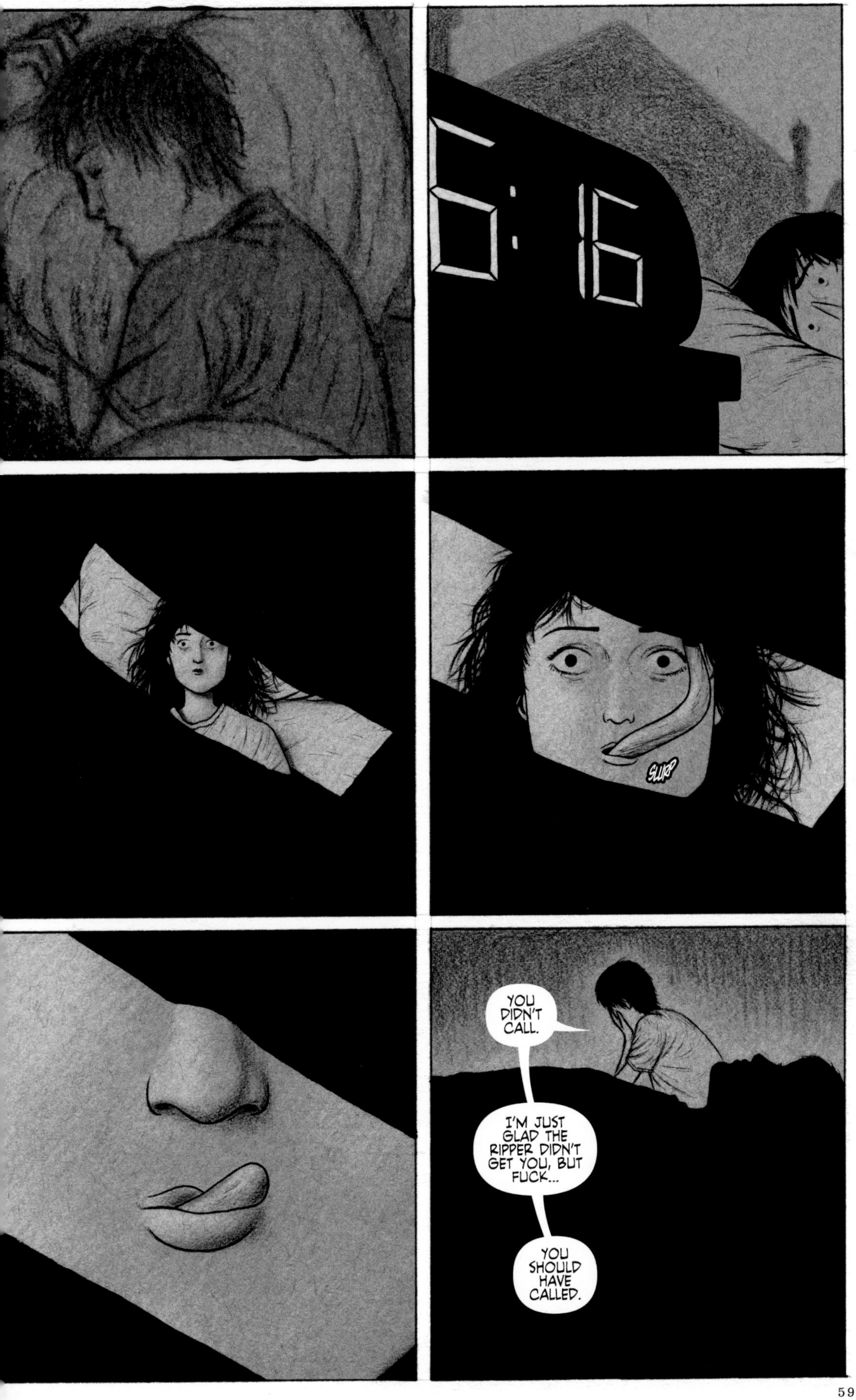
5:16
SLURP
YOU DIDN'T CALL.
I'M JUST GLAD THE RIPPER DIDN'T GET YOU, BUT FUCK...
YOU SHOULD HAVE CALLED.

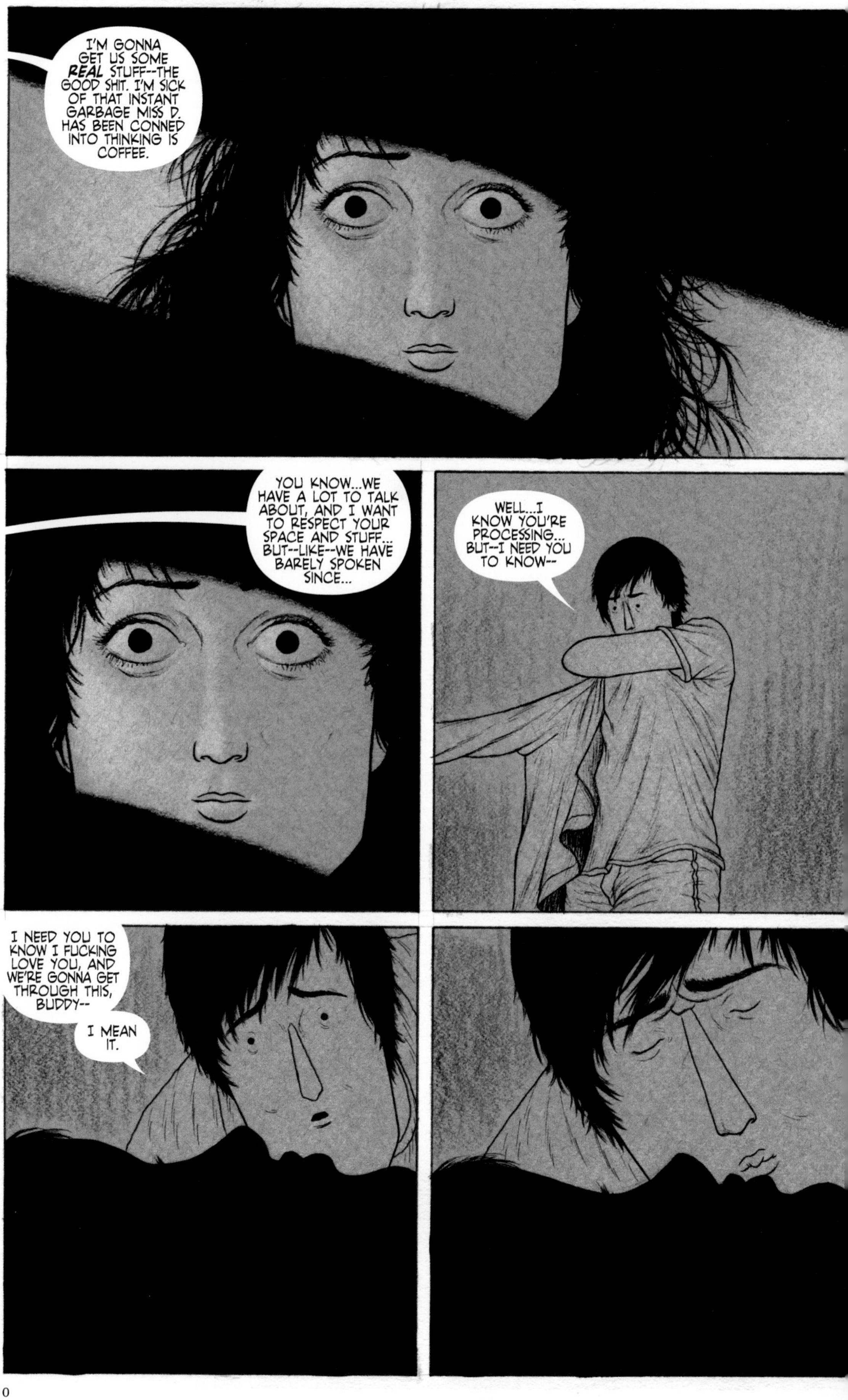
I'M GONNA GET US SOME REAL STUFF--THE GOOD SHIT. I'M SICK OF THAT INSTANT GARBAGE MISS D. HAS BEEN CONNED INTO THINKING IS COFFEE.
YOU KNOW...WE HAVE A LOT TO TALK ABOUT, AND I WANT TO RESPECT YOUR SPACE AND STUFF... BUT--LIKE--WE HAVE BARELY SPOKEN SINCE...
WELL...I KNOW YOU'RE PROCESSING... BUT--I NEED YOU TO KNOW--
I NEED YOU TO KNOW I FUCKING LOVE YOU, AND WE'RE GONNA GET THROUGH THIS, BUDDY--
I MEAN IT.

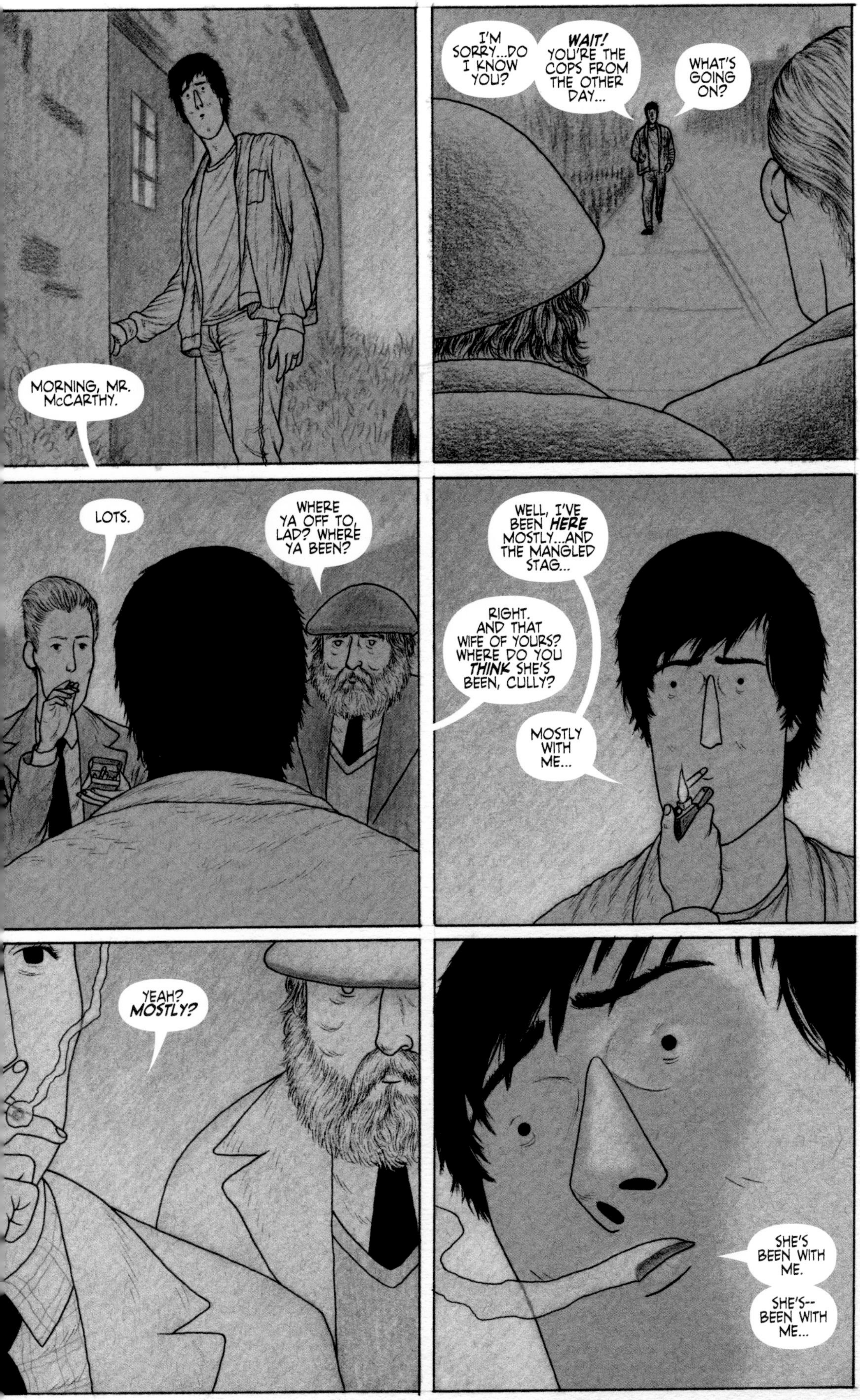
MORNING, MR. McCARTHY.
I'M SORRY...DO I KNOW YOU?
WAIT! YOU'RE THE COPS FROM THE OTHER DAY...
WHAT'S GOING ON?
LOTS.
WHERE YA OFF TO, LAD? WHERE YA BEEN?
WELL, I'VE BEEN HERE MOSTLY...AND THE MANGLED STAG...
RIGHT. AND THAT WIFE OF YOURS? WHERE DO YOU THINK SHE'S BEEN, CULLY?
MOSTLY WITH ME...
YEAH? MOSTLY?
SHE'S BEEN WITH ME.
SHE'S-- BEEN WITH ME...

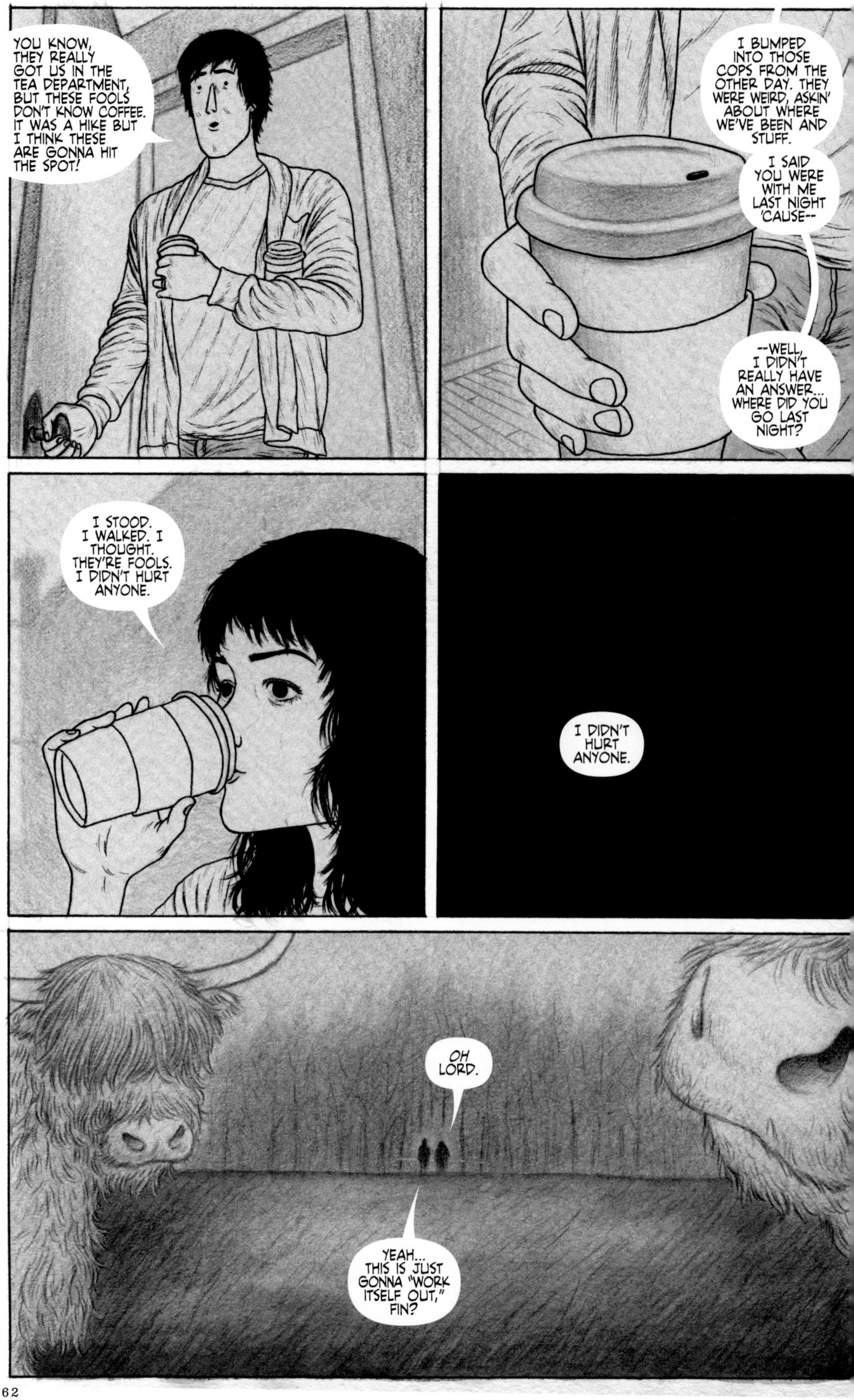
YOU KNOW, THEY REALLY GOT US IN THE TEA DEPARTMENT, BUT THESE FOOLS DON'T KNOW COFFEE. IT WAS A HIKE BUT I THINK THESE ARE GONNA HIT THE SPOT!
I BUMPED INTO THOSE COPS FROM THE OTHER DAY. THEY WERE WEIRD, ASKIN' ABOUT WHERE WE'VE BEEN AND STUFF.
I SAID YOU WERE WITH ME LAST NIGHT 'CAUSE--
--WELL, I DIDN'T REALLY HAVE AN ANSWER... WHERE DID YOU GO LAST NIGHT?
I STOOD. I WALKED. I THOUGHT. THEY'RE FOOLS. I DIDN'T HURT ANYONE.
I DIDN'T HURT ANYONE.
OH LORD.
YEAH... THIS IS JUST GONNA "WORK ITSELF OUT," FIN?

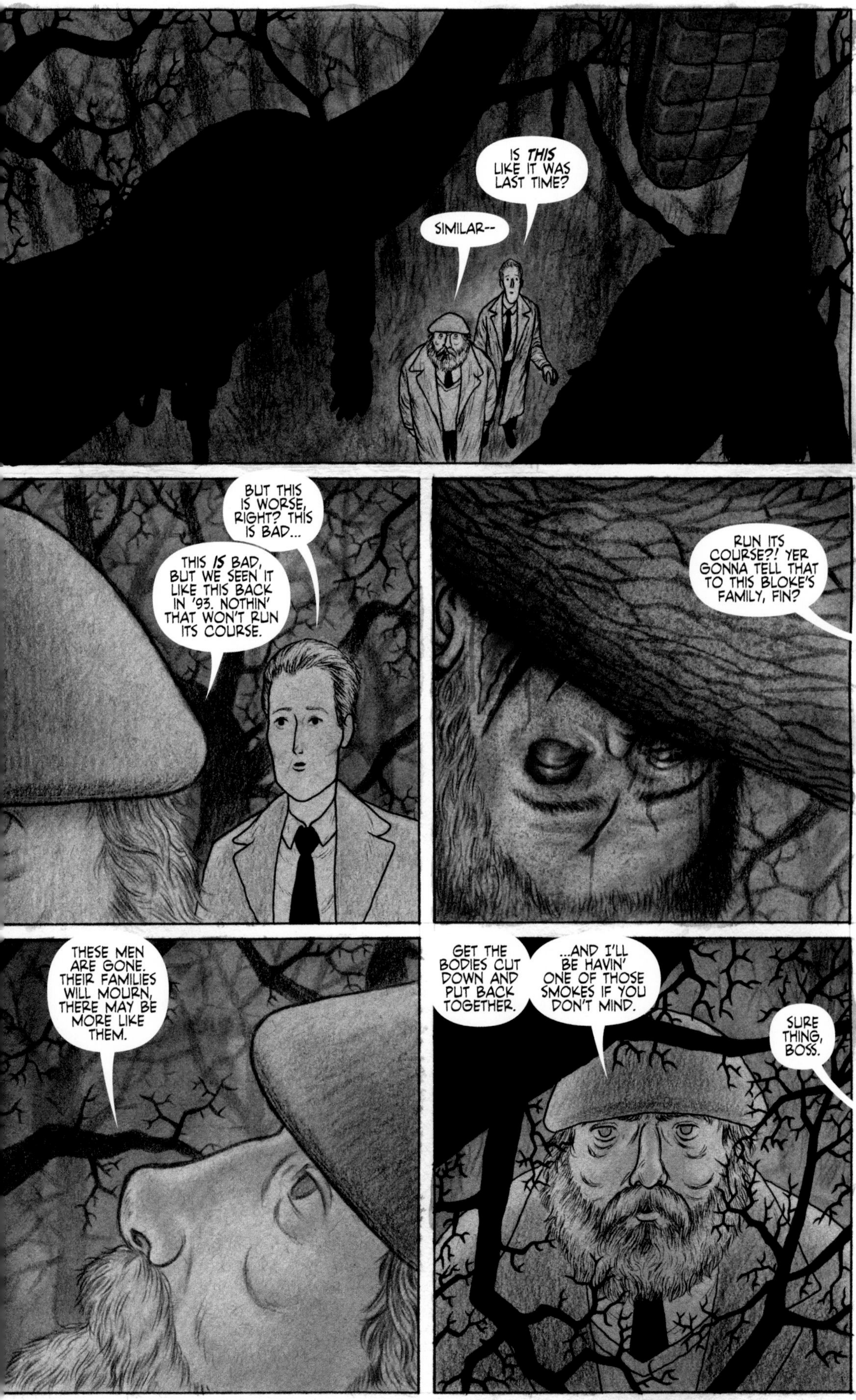

IS THIS LIKE IT WAS LAST TIME?
SIMILAR--
BUT THIS IS WORSE, RIGHT? THIS IS BAD...
THIS IS BAD, BUT WE SEEN IT LIKE THIS BACK IN '93. NOTHIN' THAT WON'T RUN ITS COURSE.
RUN ITS COURSE?! YER GONNA TELL THAT TO THIS BLOKE'S FAMILY, FIN?
THESE MEN ARE GONE. THEIR FAMILIES WILL MOURN, THERE MAY BE MORE LIKE THEM.
GET THE BODIES CUT DOWN AND PUT BACK TOGETHER.
...AND I'LL BE HAVIN' ONE OF THOSE SMOKES IF YOU DON'T MIND.
SURE THING, BOSS.

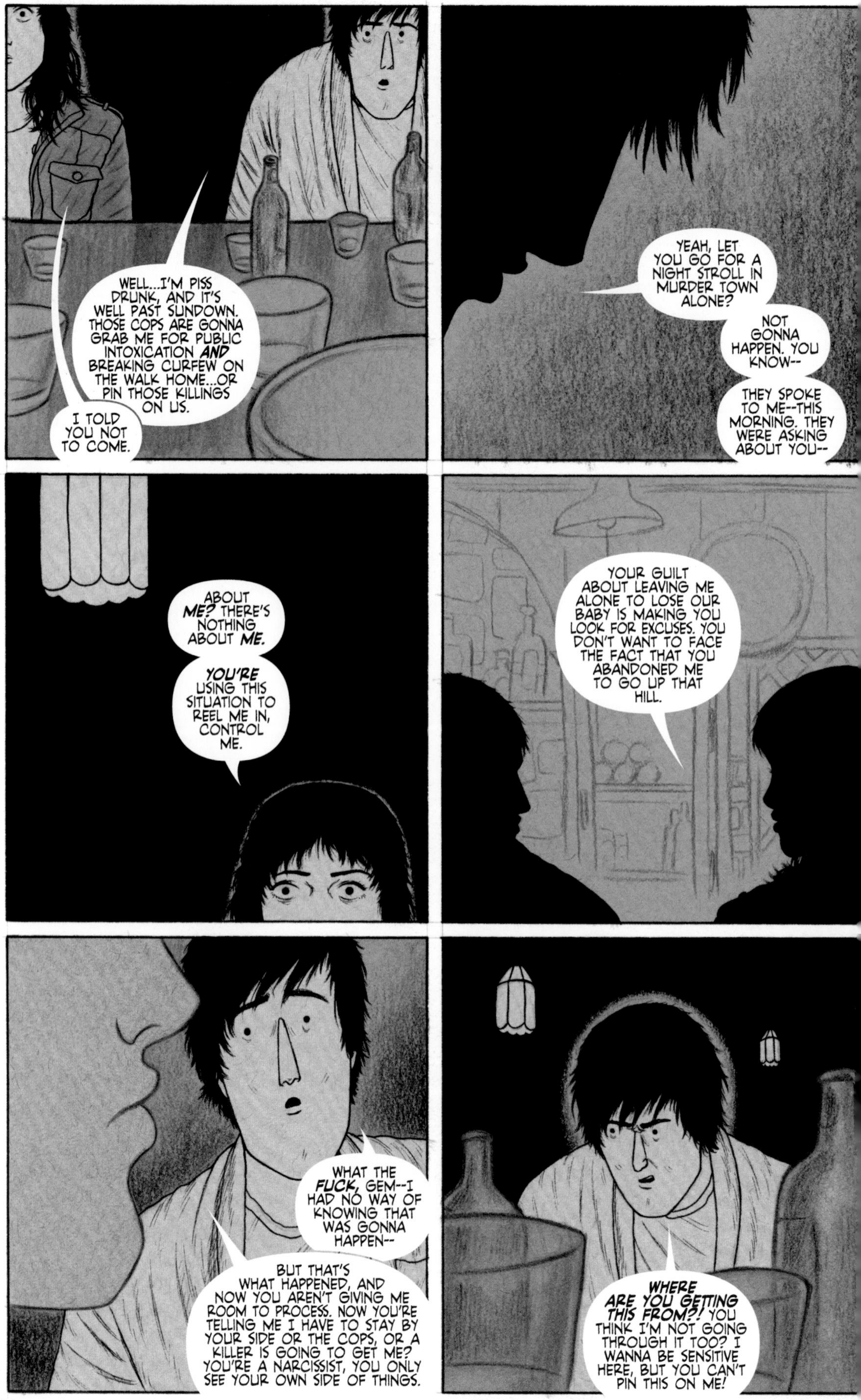
I TOLD YOU NOT TO COME.
WELL...I'M PISS DRUNK, AND IT'S WELL PAST SUNDOWN. THOSE COPS ARE GONNA GRAB ME FOR PUBLIC INTOXICATION AND BREAKING CURFEW ON THE WALK HOME...OR PIN THOSE KILLINGS ON US.
YEAH, LET YOU GO FOR A NIGHT STROLL IN MURDER TOWN ALONE?
NOT GONNA HAPPEN. YOU KNOW--
THEY SPOKE TO ME--THIS MORNING. THEY WERE ASKING ABOUT YOU--
ABOUT ME? THERE'S NOTHING ABOUT ME.
YOU'RE USING THIS SITUATION TO REEL ME IN, CONTROL ME.
YOUR GUILT ABOUT LEAVING ME ALONE TO LOSE OUR BABY IS MAKING YOU LOOK FOR EXCUSES. YOU DON'T WANT TO FACE THE FACT THAT YOU ABANDONED ME TO GO UP THAT HILL.
WHAT THE FUCK, GEM--I HAD NO WAY OF KNOWING THAT WAS GONNA HAPPEN--
BUT THAT'S WHAT HAPPENED, AND NOW YOU AREN'T GIVING ME ROOM TO PROCESS. NOW YOU'RE TELLING ME I HAVE TO STAY BY YOUR SIDE OR THE COPS, OR A KILLER IS GOING TO GET ME? YOU'RE A NARCISSIST, YOU ONLY SEE YOUR OWN SIDE OF THINGS.
WHERE ARE YOU GETTING THIS FROM?! YOU THINK I'M NOT GOING THROUGH IT TOO? I WANNA BE SENSITIVE HERE, BUT YOU CAN'T PIN THIS ON ME!

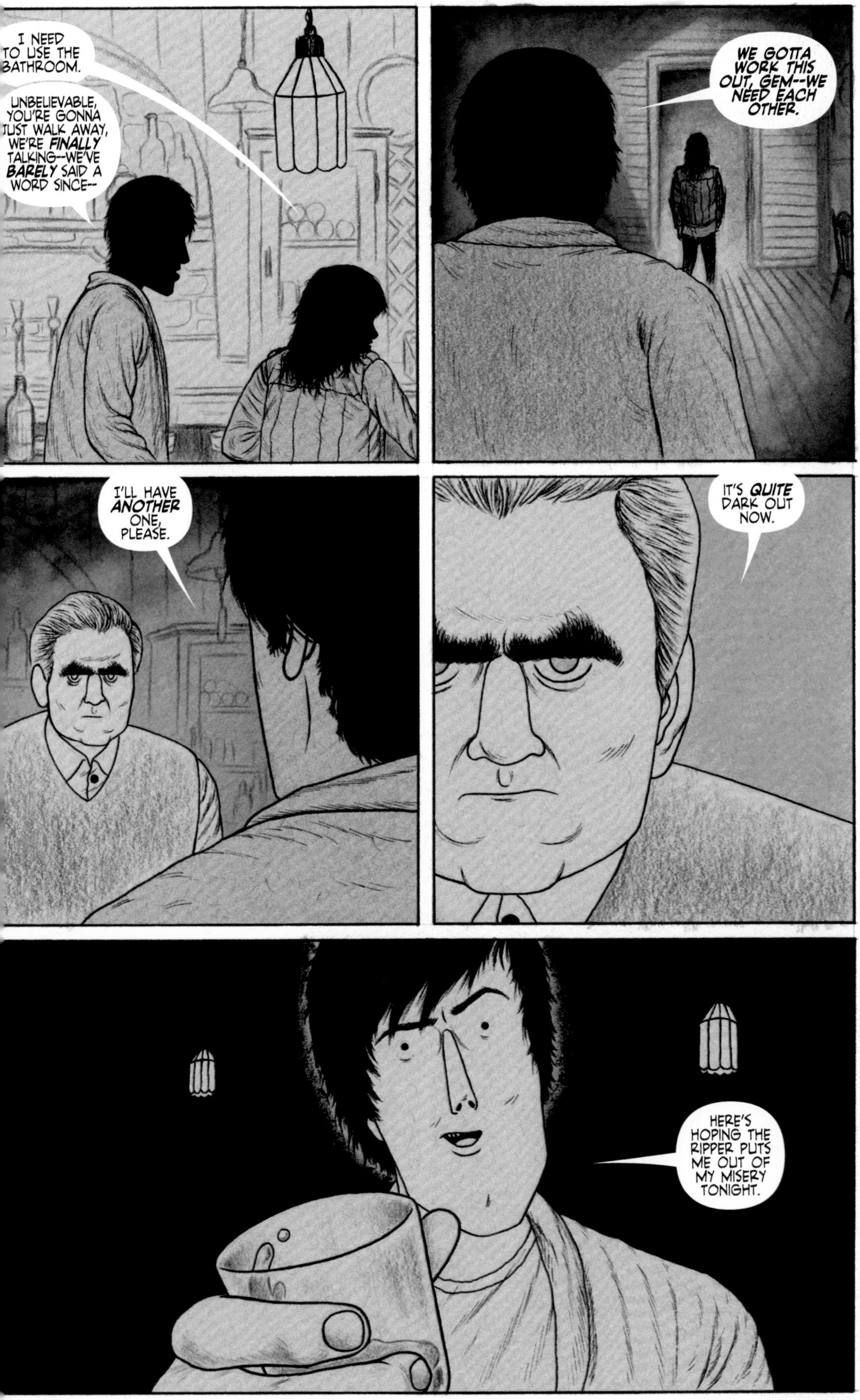
I NEED TO USE THE BATHROOM.
UNBELIEVABLE, YOU'RE GONNA JUST WALK AWAY, WE'RE FINALLY TALKING--WE'VE BARELY SAID A WORD SINCE--
WE GOTTA WORK THIS OUT, GEM--WE NEED EACH OTHER.
I'LL HAVE ANOTHER ONE, PLEASE.
IT'S QUITE DARK OUT NOW.
HERE'S HOPING THE RIPPER PUTS ME OUT OF MY MISERY TONIGHT.

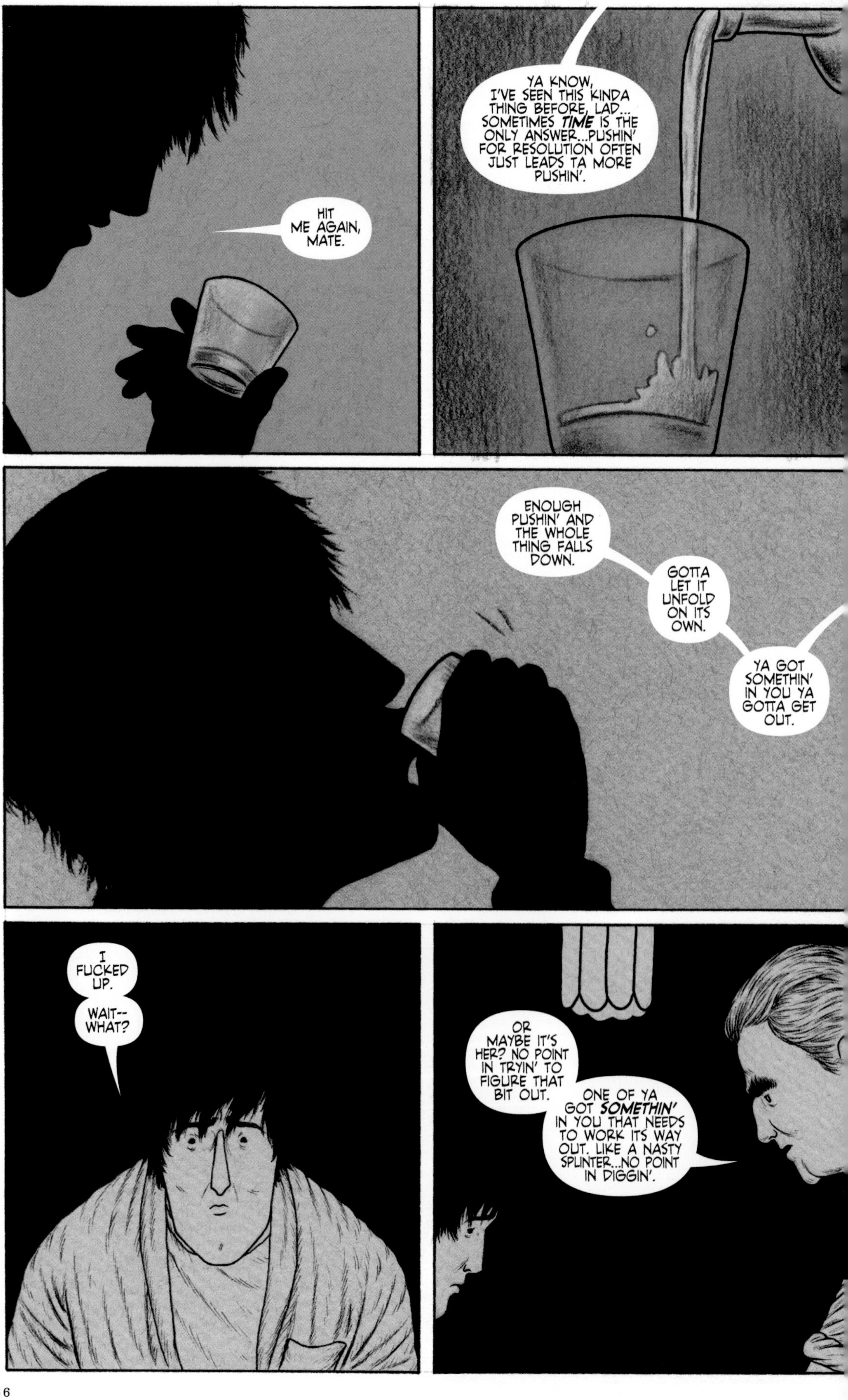
HIT ME AGAIN, MATE.
YA KNOW, I'VE SEEN THIS KINDA THING BEFORE, LAD... SOMETIMES *TIME* IS THE ONLY ANSWER...PUSHIN' FOR RESOLUTION OFTEN JUST LEADS TA MORE PUSHIN'.
ENOUGH PUSHIN' AND THE WHOLE THING FALLS DOWN.
GOTTA LET IT UNFOLD ON ITS OWN.
YA GOT SOMETHIN' IN YOU YA GOTTA GET OUT.
I FUCKED UP.
WAIT-- WHAT?
OR MAYBE IT'S HER? NO POINT IN TRYIN' TO FIGURE THAT BIT OUT.
ONE OF YA GOT *SOMETHIN'* IN YOU THAT NEEDS TO WORK ITS WAY OUT. LIKE A NASTY SPLINTER...NO POINT IN DIGGIN'.

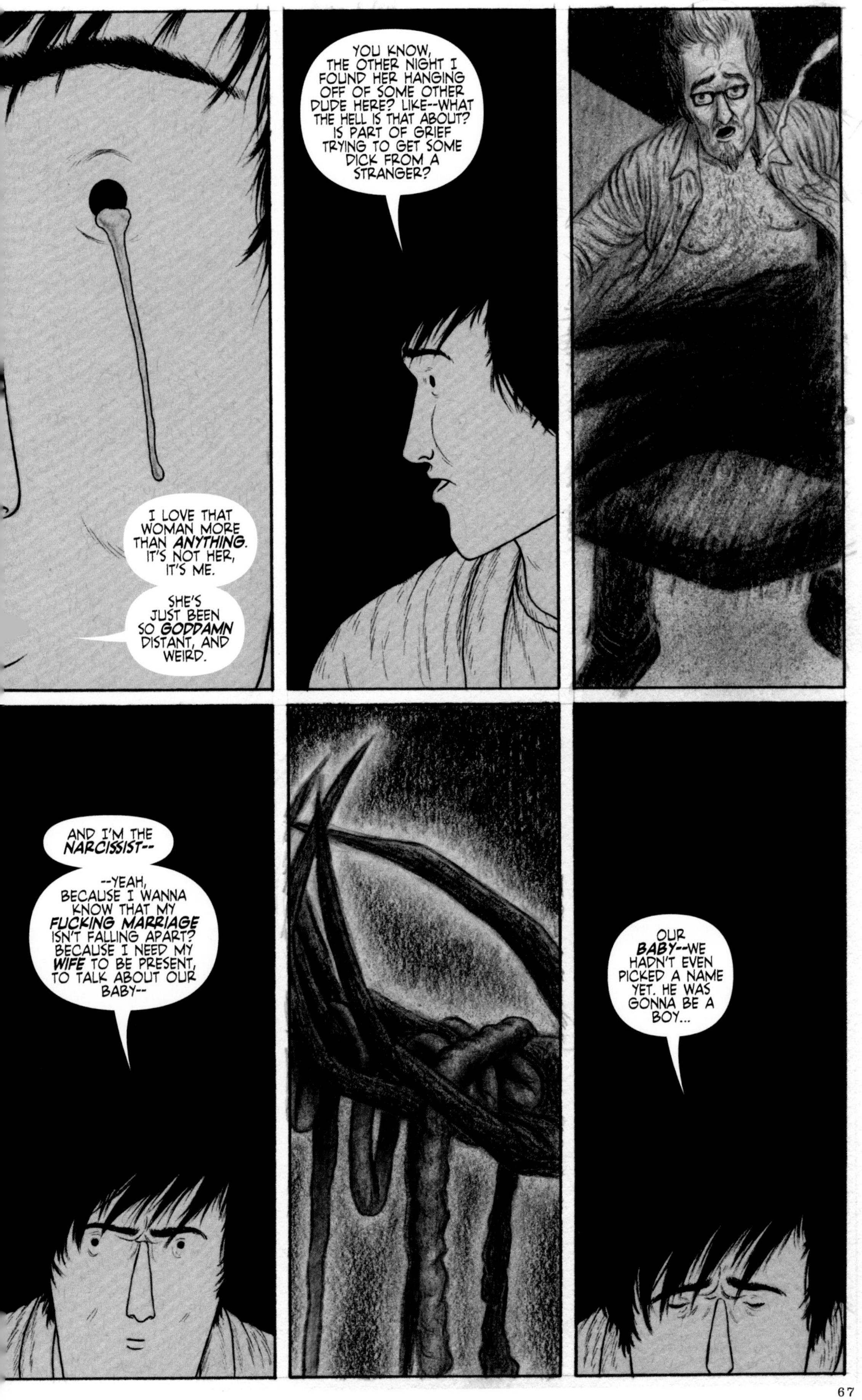
I LOVE THAT WOMAN MORE THAN ANYTHING. IT'S NOT HER, IT'S ME.
SHE'S JUST BEEN SO GODDAMN DISTANT, AND WEIRD.
YOU KNOW, THE OTHER NIGHT I FOUND HER HANGING OFF OF SOME OTHER DUDE HERE? LIKE--WHAT THE HELL IS THAT ABOUT? IS PART OF GRIEF TRYING TO GET SOME DICK FROM A STRANGER?
AND I'M THE NARCISSIST--
--YEAH, BECAUSE I WANNA KNOW THAT MY FUCKING MARRIAGE ISN'T FALLING APART? BECAUSE I NEED MY WIFE TO BE PRESENT, TO TALK ABOUT OUR BABY--
OUR BABY--WE HADN'T EVEN PICKED A NAME YET. HE WAS GONNA BE A BOY...

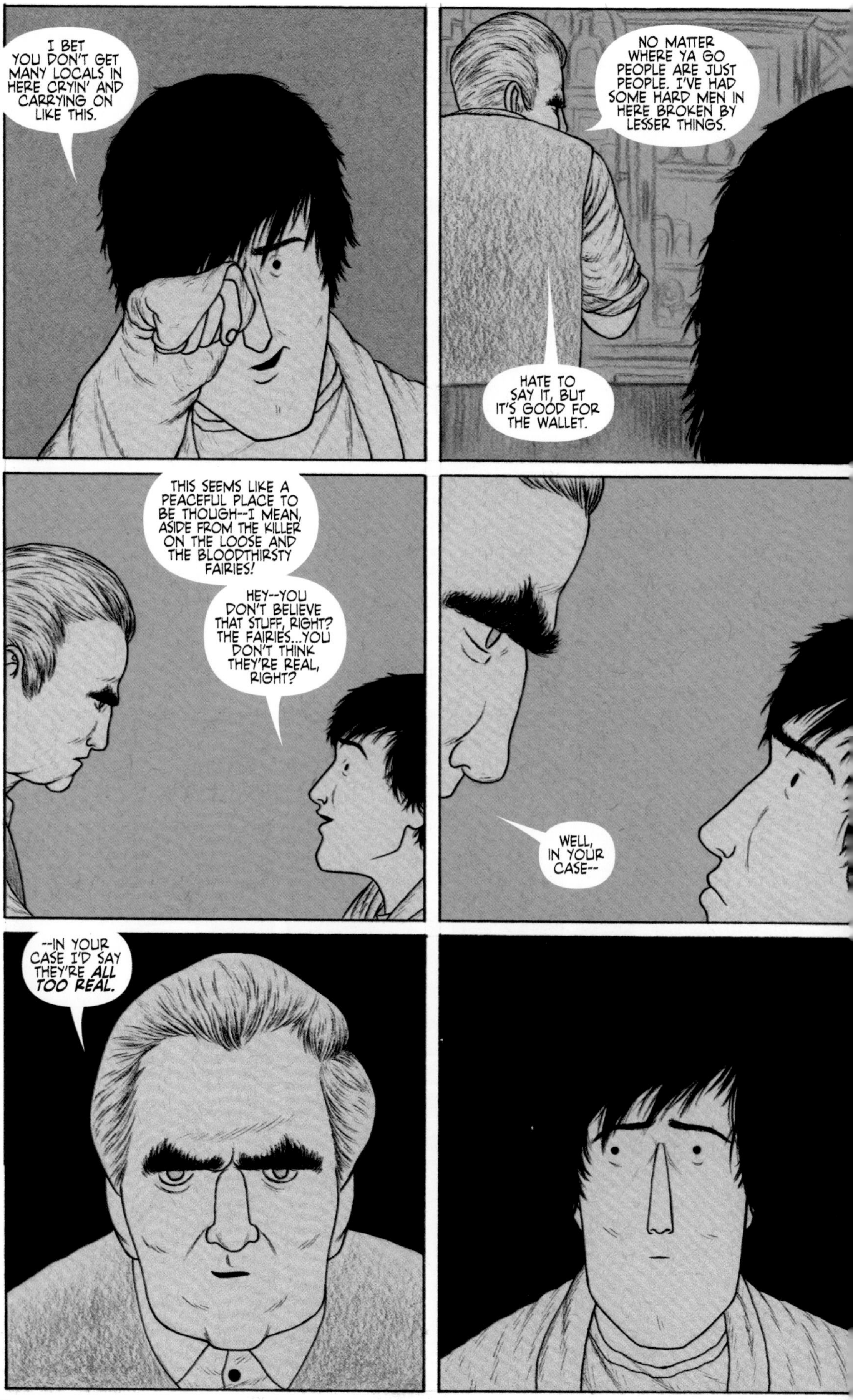
I BET YOU DON'T GET MANY LOCALS IN HERE CRYIN' AND CARRYING ON LIKE THIS.
NO MATTER WHERE YA GO PEOPLE ARE JUST PEOPLE. I'VE HAD SOME HARD MEN IN HERE BROKEN BY LESSER THINGS.
HATE TO SAY IT, BUT IT'S GOOD FOR THE WALLET.
THIS SEEMS LIKE A PEACEFUL PLACE TO BE THOUGH--I MEAN, ASIDE FROM THE KILLER ON THE LOOSE AND THE BLOODTHIRSTY FAIRIES!
HEY--YOU DON'T BELIEVE THAT STUFF, RIGHT? THE FAIRIES...YOU DON'T THINK THEY'RE REAL, RIGHT?
WELL, IN YOUR CASE--
--IN YOUR CASE I'D SAY THEY'RE ALL TOO REAL.

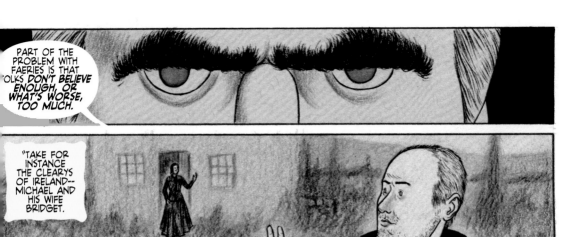

PART OF THE PROBLEM WITH FAERIES IS THAT FOLKS *DON'T BELIEVE ENOUGH*, OR WHAT'S WORSE, *TOO MUCH.*

"TAKE FOR INSTANCE THE CLEARYS OF IRELAND-- MICHAEL AND HIS WIFE BRIDGET.

"HIS WORK IN *CLONMEL* LEFT HER TO FIND HER WAY WITHOUT HER HUSBAND FOR SOME TIME BACK IN *BALLYVADLEA.*

"BRIDGET THRIVED BECOMIN' A SUCCESSFUL DRESSMAKER. WHILE MICHAEL WAS AWAY SHE EXPERIENCED A TASTE OF INDEPENDENCE--A SELF-MADE WOMAN.

"WHEN MICHAEL RETURNED HE FOUND A MUCH *DIFFERENT* WOMAN THAN THE ONE HE LEFT BEHIND ALL THOSE MONTHS AGO.

"MAYBE THERE WAS SOMETHING DIFFERENT ABOUT *HIM* TOO.

"HE CAME TO SUSPECT SOMETHING *DARK* HAD HAPPENED WHILE HE WAS AWAY.

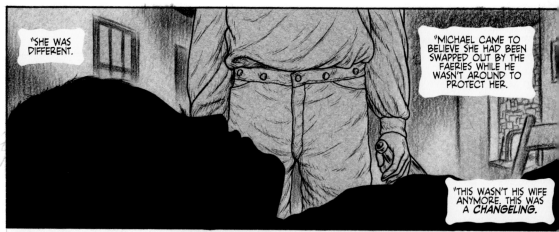

"SHE WAS DIFFERENT.

"MICHAEL CAME TO BELIEVE SHE HAD BEEN SWAPPED OUT BY THE FAERIES WHILE HE WASN'T AROUND TO PROTECT HER.

"THIS WASN'T HIS WIFE ANYMORE. THIS WAS A *CHANGELING.*

"FORE LONG SHE UP AN' VANISHED, NOT SO MUCH AS A WORD EVEN TO HER DEAREST FRIENDS.

CLEARY'S DRESS SHOPPE & SEAMSTRESS

CLOSED

"SHE WAS MISSING AND ALL OLD MICHAEL HAD TA SAY WAS THAT THE *FAERIES* HAD STOLEN OFF WITH HER IN THE NIGHT.

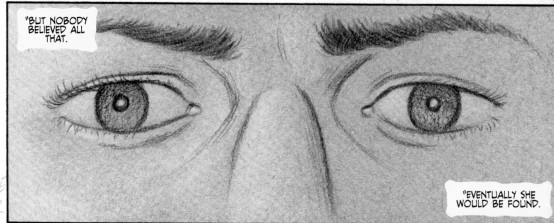

"BUT NOBODY BELIEVED ALL THAT.

"EVENTUALLY SHE WOULD BE FOUND.

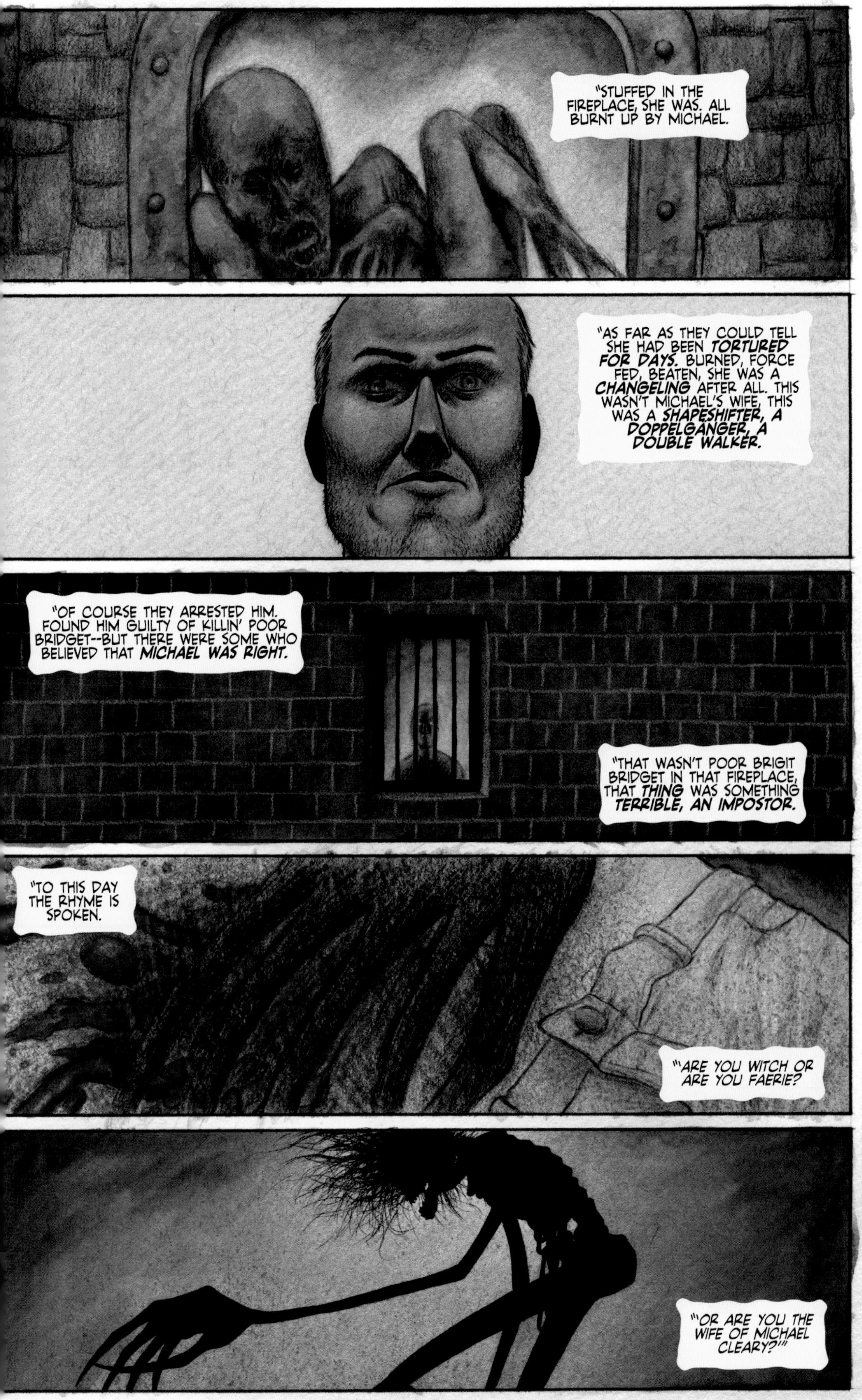
"STUFFED IN THE FIREPLACE, SHE WAS. ALL BURNT UP BY MICHAEL.
"AS FAR AS THEY COULD TELL SHE HAD BEEN TORTURED FOR DAYS. BURNED, FORCE FED, BEATEN, SHE WAS A CHANGELING AFTER ALL. THIS WASN'T MICHAEL'S WIFE, THIS WAS A SHAPESHIFTER, A DOPPELGÄNGER, A DOUBLE WALKER.
"OF COURSE THEY ARRESTED HIM. FOUND HIM GUILTY OF KILLIN' POOR BRIDGET--BUT THERE WERE SOME WHO BELIEVED THAT MICHAEL WAS RIGHT.
"THAT WASN'T POOR BRIGIT BRIDGET IN THAT FIREPLACE, THAT THING WAS SOMETHING TERRIBLE, AN IMPOSTOR.
"TO THIS DAY THE RHYME IS SPOKEN.
"'ARE YOU WITCH OR ARE YOU FAERIE?
"OR ARE YOU THE WIFE OF MICHAEL CLEARY?'"

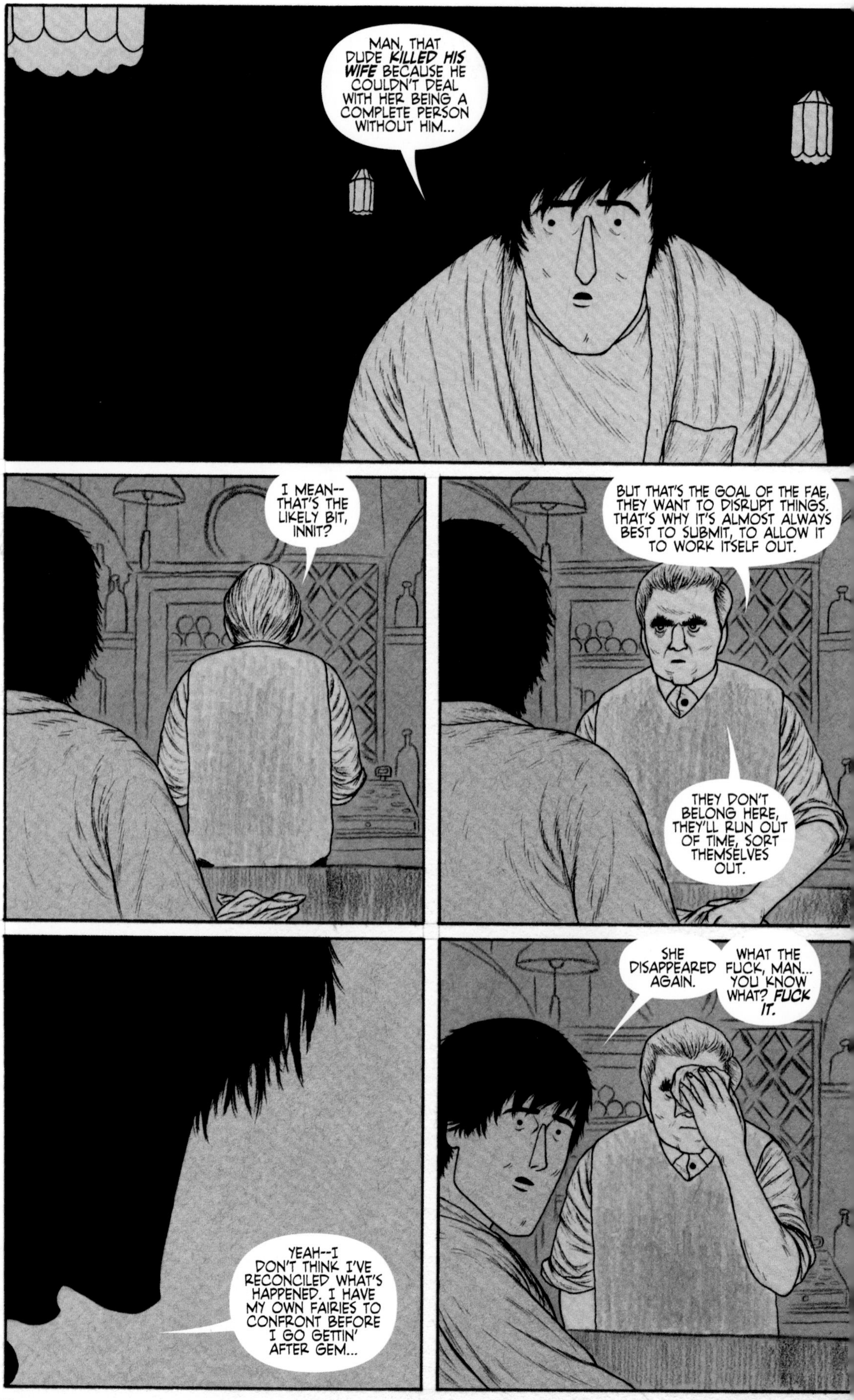
MAN, THAT DUDE **KILLED HIS WIFE** BECAUSE HE COULDN'T DEAL WITH HER BEING A COMPLETE PERSON WITHOUT HIM...
I MEAN-- THAT'S THE LIKELY BIT, INNIT?
BUT THAT'S THE GOAL OF THE FAE, THEY WANT TO DISRUPT THINGS. THAT'S WHY IT'S ALMOST ALWAYS BEST TO SUBMIT, TO ALLOW IT TO WORK ITSELF OUT.
THEY DON'T BELONG HERE, THEY'LL RUN OUT OF TIME, SORT THEMSELVES OUT.
YEAH--I DON'T THINK I'VE RECONCILED WHAT'S HAPPENED. I HAVE MY OWN FAIRIES TO CONFRONT BEFORE I GO GETTIN' AFTER GEM...
SHE DISAPPEARED AGAIN.
WHAT THE FUCK, MAN... YOU KNOW WHAT? **FUCK IT.**

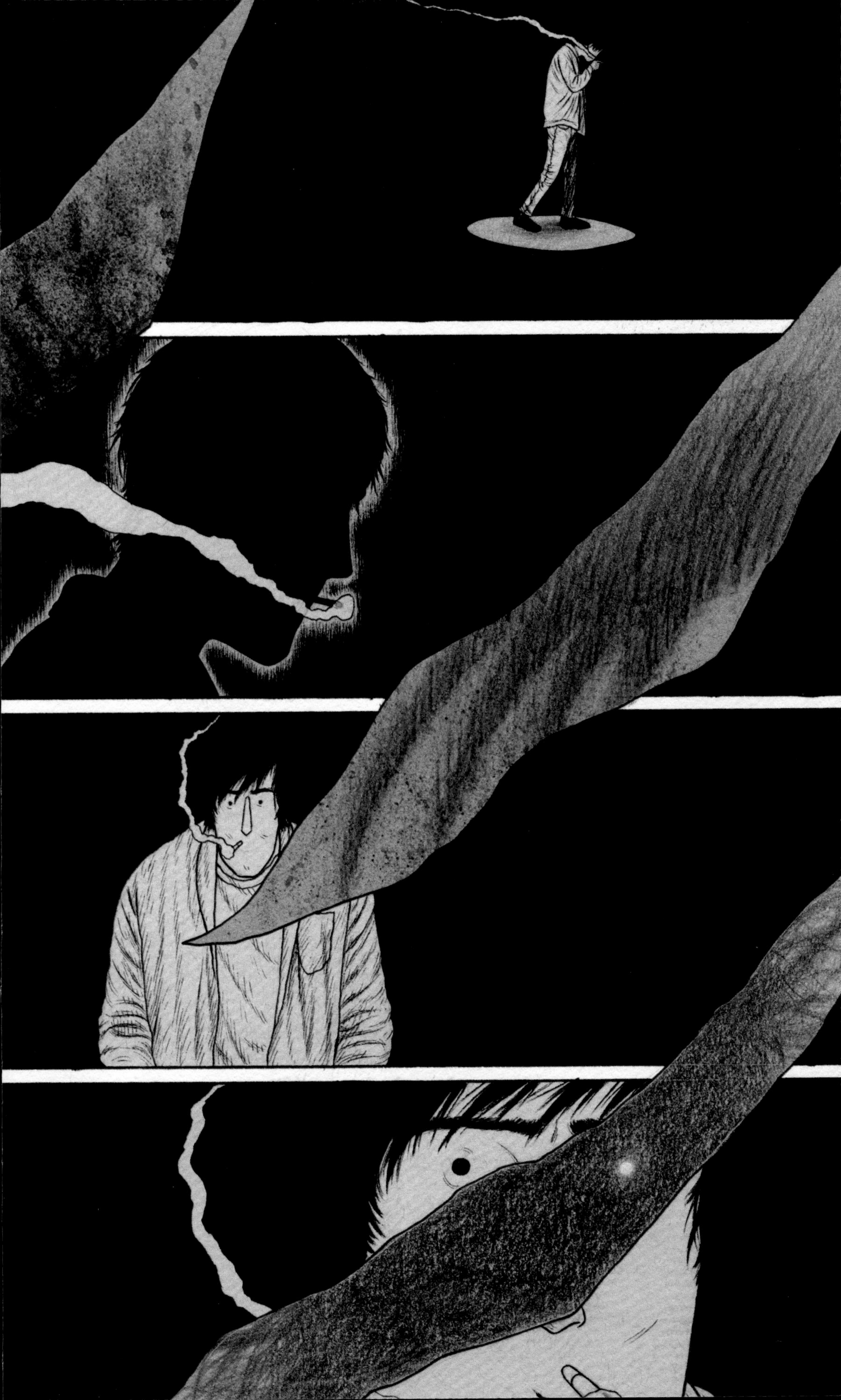

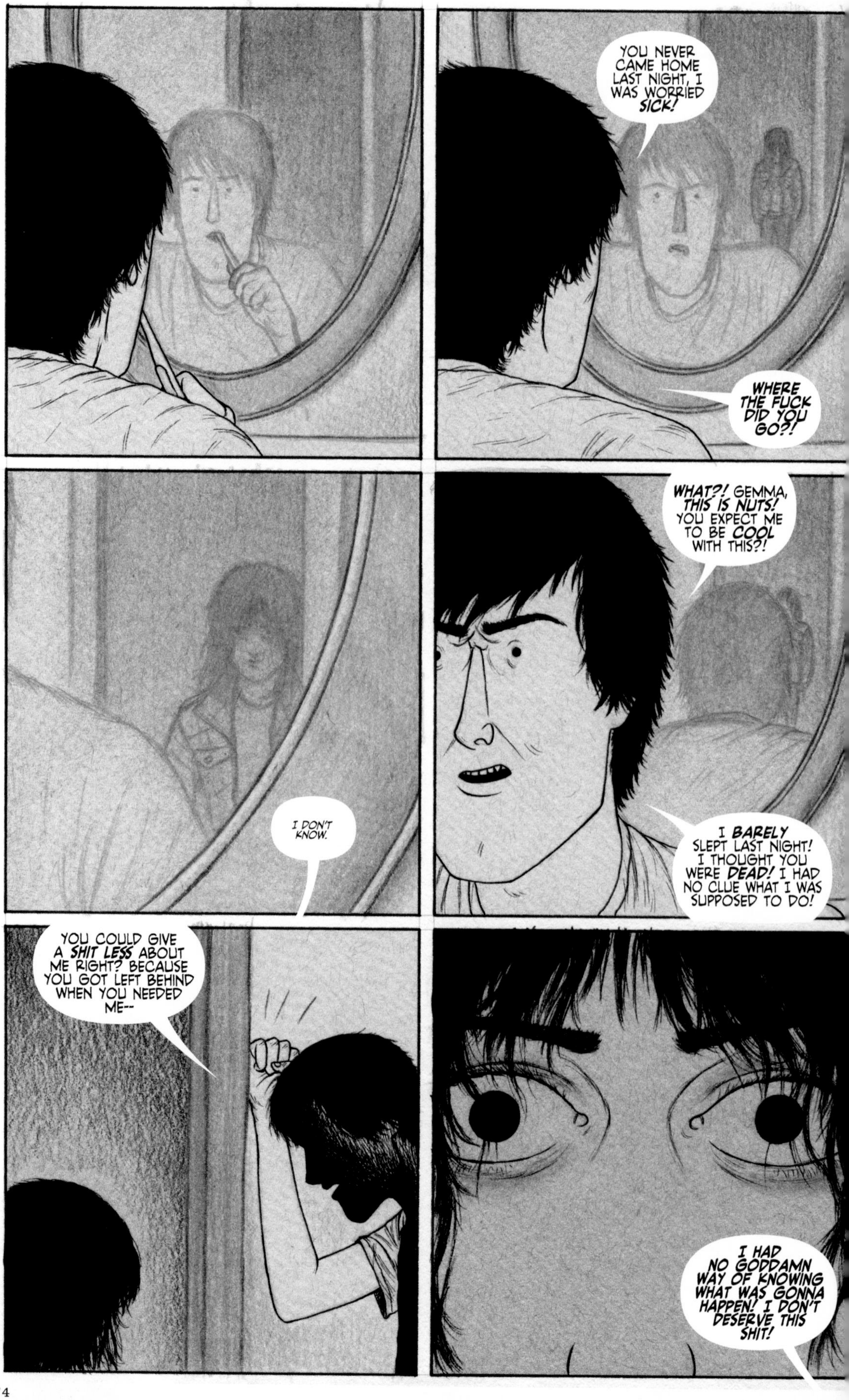
YOU NEVER CAME HOME LAST NIGHT, I WAS WORRIED SICK!
WHERE THE FUCK DID YOU GO?!
I DON'T KNOW.
WHAT?! GEMMA, THIS IS NUTS! YOU EXPECT ME TO BE COOL WITH THIS?!
I BARELY SLEPT LAST NIGHT! I THOUGHT YOU WERE DEAD! I HAD NO CLUE WHAT I WAS SUPPOSED TO DO!
YOU COULD GIVE A SHIT LESS ABOUT ME RIGHT? BECAUSE YOU GOT LEFT BEHIND WHEN YOU NEEDED ME--
I HAD NO GODDAMN WAY OF KNOWING WHAT WAS GONNA HAPPEN! I DON'T DESERVE THIS SHIT!

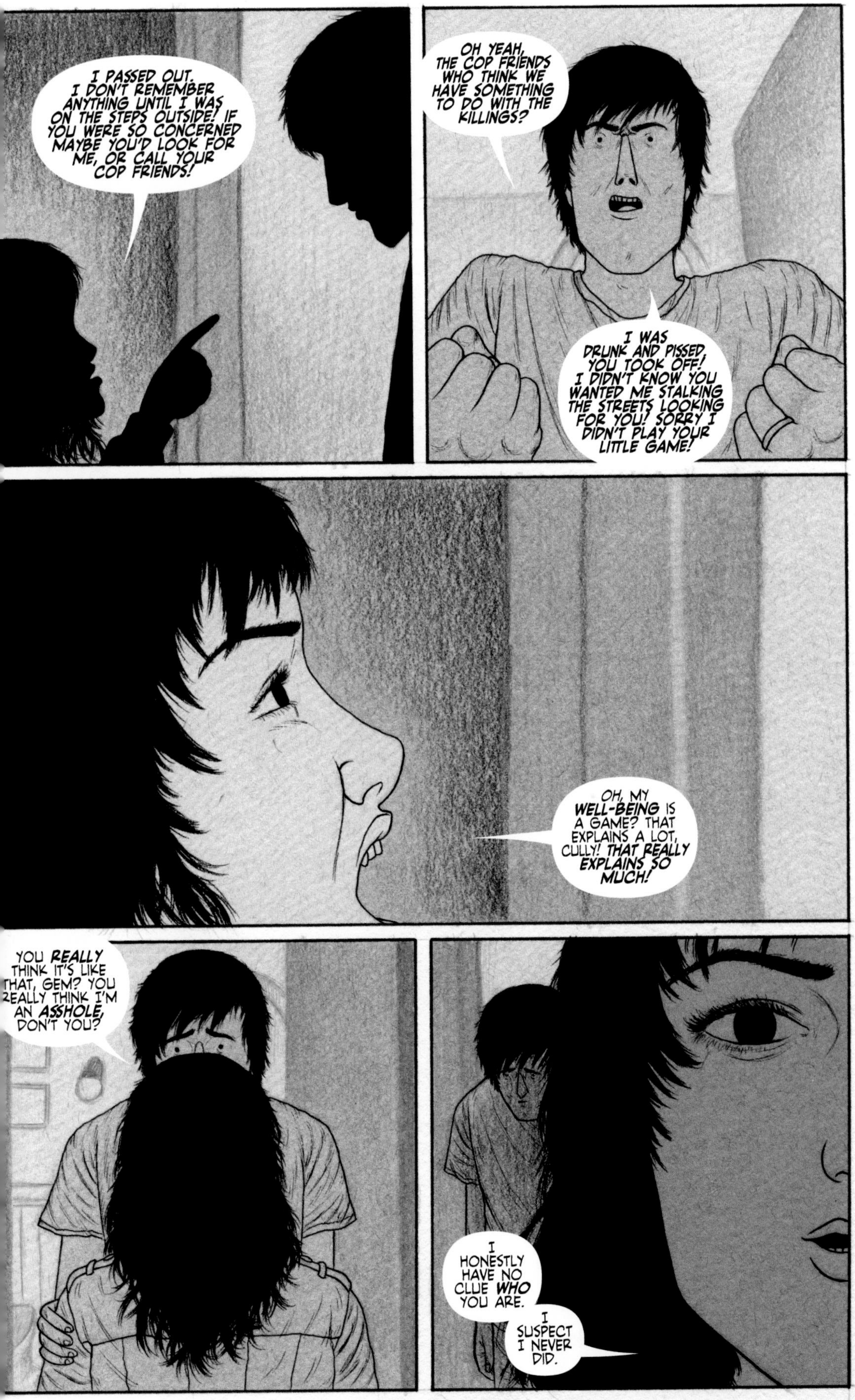
I PASSED OUT. I DON'T REMEMBER ANYTHING UNTIL I WAS ON THE STEPS OUTSIDE! IF YOU WERE SO CONCERNED MAYBE YOU'D LOOK FOR ME, OR CALL YOUR COP FRIENDS!
OH YEAH, THE COP FRIENDS WHO THINK WE HAVE SOMETHING TO DO WITH THE KILLINGS?
I WAS DRUNK AND PISSED, YOU TOOK OFF! I DIDN'T KNOW YOU WANTED ME STALKING THE STREETS LOOKING FOR YOU! SORRY I DIDN'T PLAY YOUR LITTLE GAME!
OH, MY WELL-BEING IS A GAME? THAT EXPLAINS A LOT, CULLY! THAT REALLY EXPLAINS SO MUCH!
YOU REALLY THINK IT'S LIKE THAT, GEM? YOU REALLY THINK I'M AN ASSHOLE, DON'T YOU?
I HONESTLY HAVE NO CLUE WHO YOU ARE.
I SUSPECT I NEVER DID.

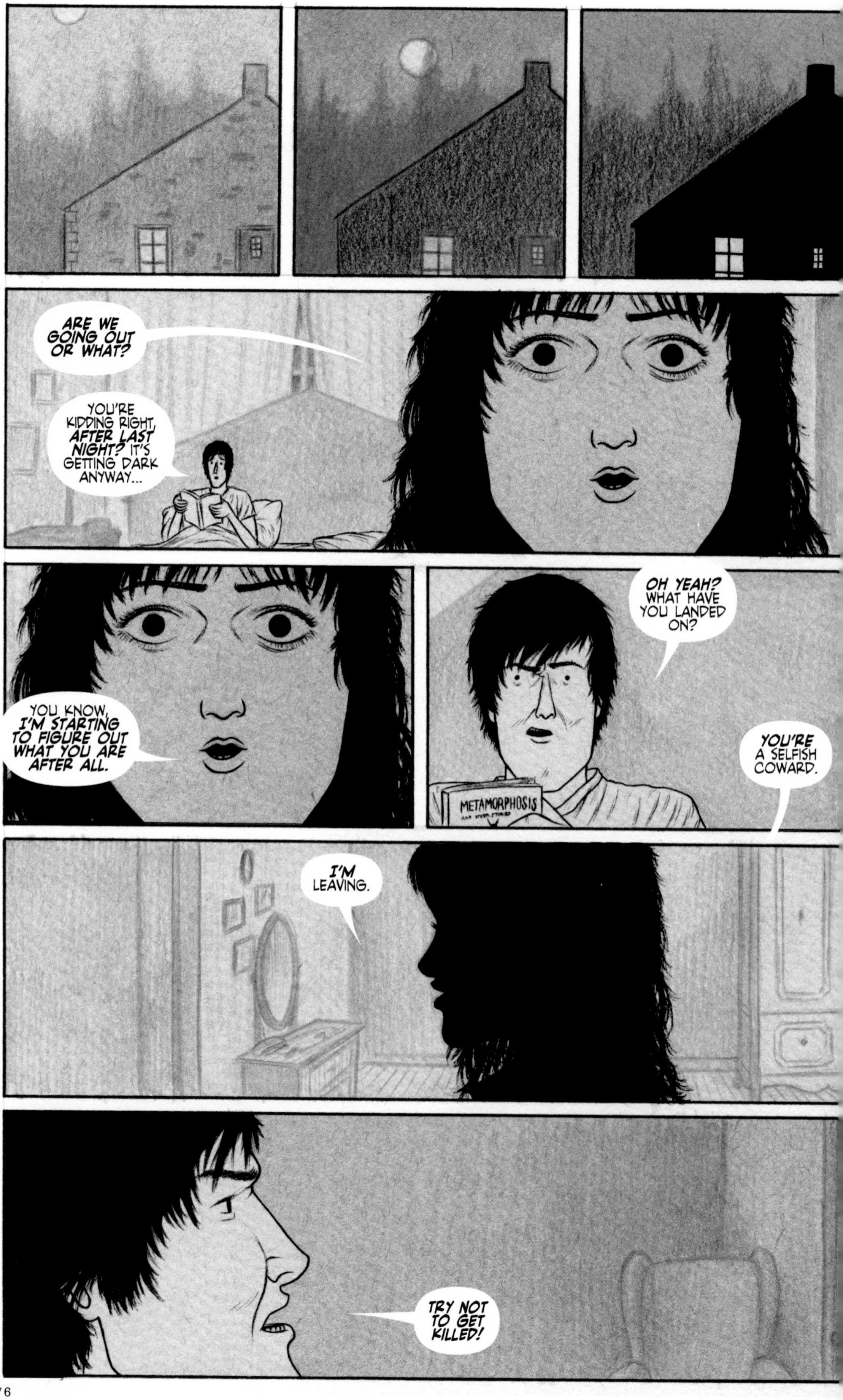

ARE WE GOING OUT OR WHAT?
YOU'RE KIDDING RIGHT, AFTER LAST NIGHT? IT'S GETTING DARK ANYWAY...
YOU KNOW, I'M STARTING TO FIGURE OUT WHAT YOU ARE AFTER ALL.
OH YEAH? WHAT HAVE YOU LANDED ON?
METAMORPHOSIS
YOU'RE A SELFISH COWARD.
I'M LEAVING.
TRY NOT TO GET KILLED!

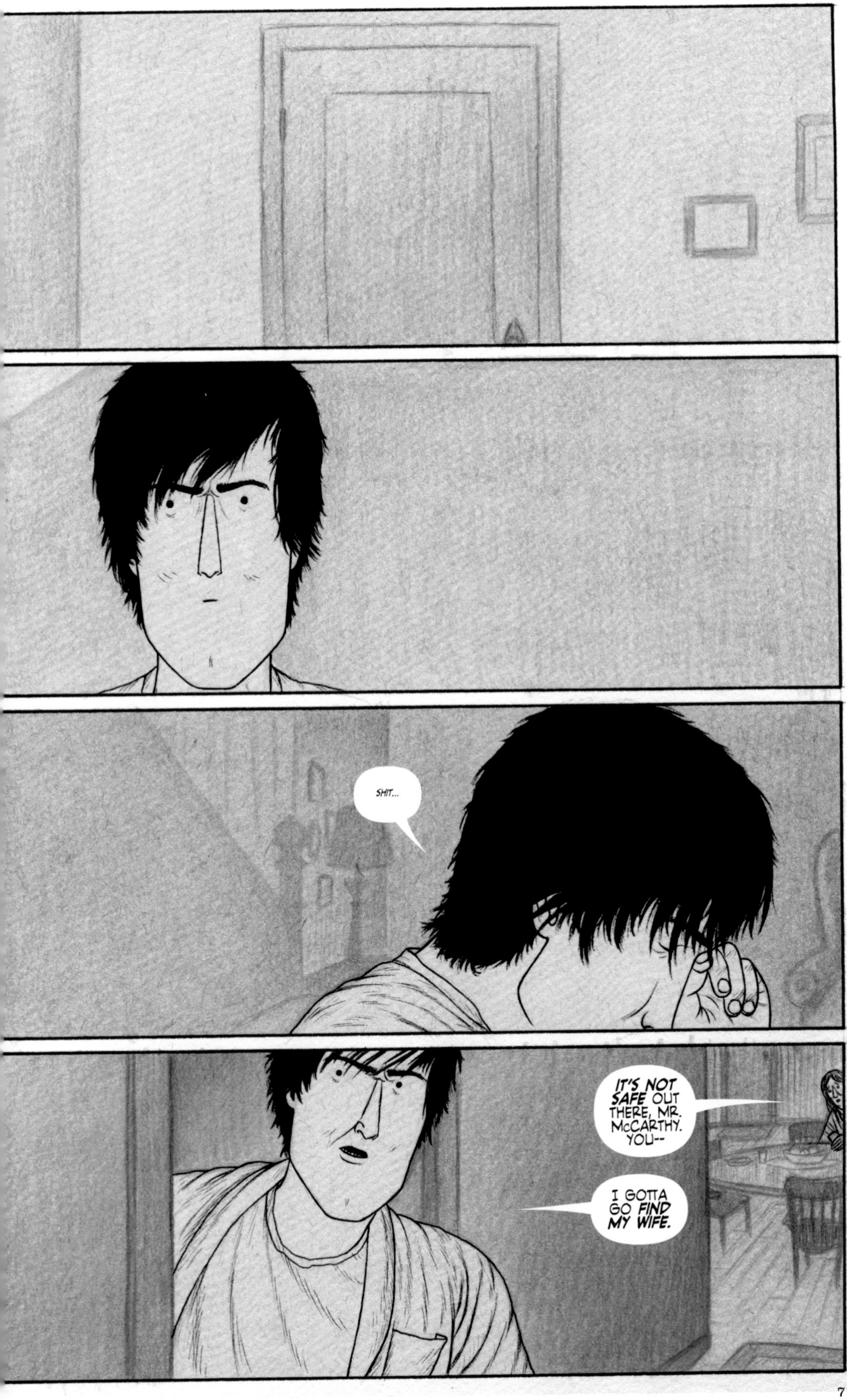
SHIT...
IT'S NOT SAFE OUT THERE, MR. McCARTHY. YOU--
I GOTTA GO FIND MY WIFE.

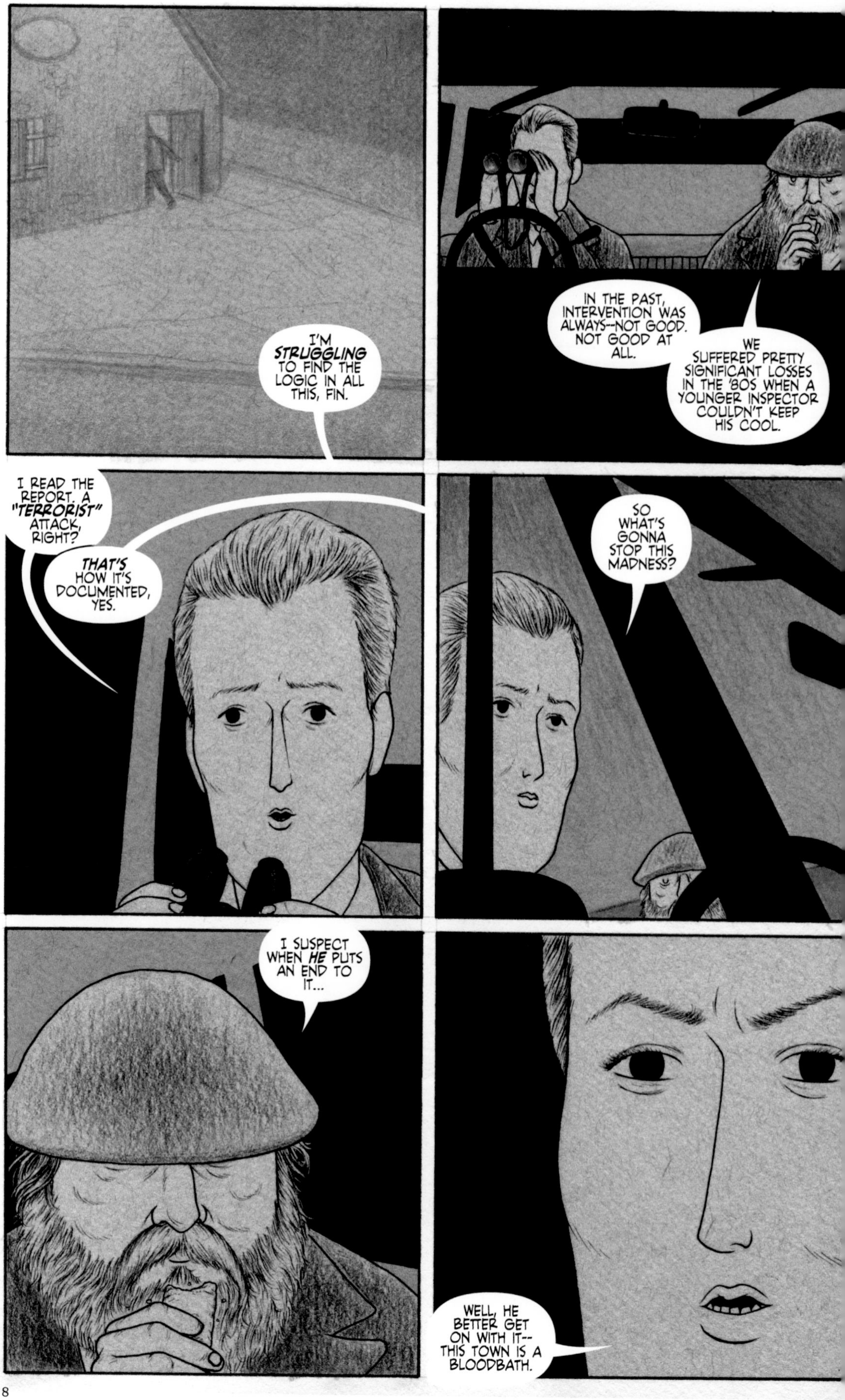
I'M STRUGGLING TO FIND THE LOGIC IN ALL THIS, FIN.
IN THE PAST, INTERVENTION WAS ALWAYS--NOT GOOD. NOT GOOD AT ALL.
WE SUFFERED PRETTY SIGNIFICANT LOSSES IN THE '80S WHEN A YOUNGER INSPECTOR COULDN'T KEEP HIS COOL.
I READ THE REPORT. A "TERRORIST" ATTACK, RIGHT?
THAT'S HOW IT'S DOCUMENTED, YES.
SO WHAT'S GONNA STOP THIS MADNESS?
I SUSPECT WHEN HE PUTS AN END TO IT...
WELL, HE BETTER GET ON WITH IT-- THIS TOWN IS A BLOODBATH.

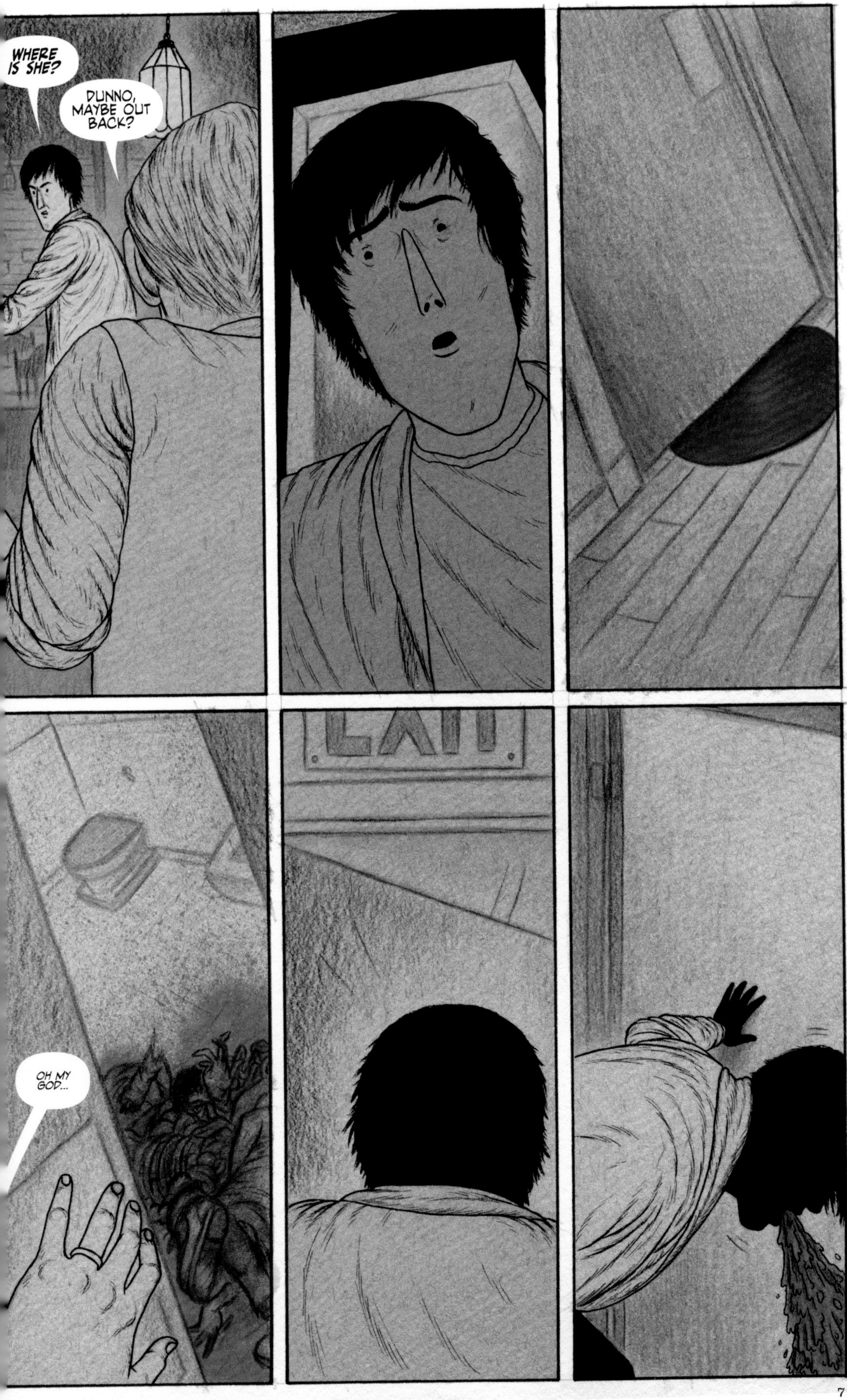
WHERE IS SHE?
DUNNO, MAYBE OUT BACK?
OH MY GOD...

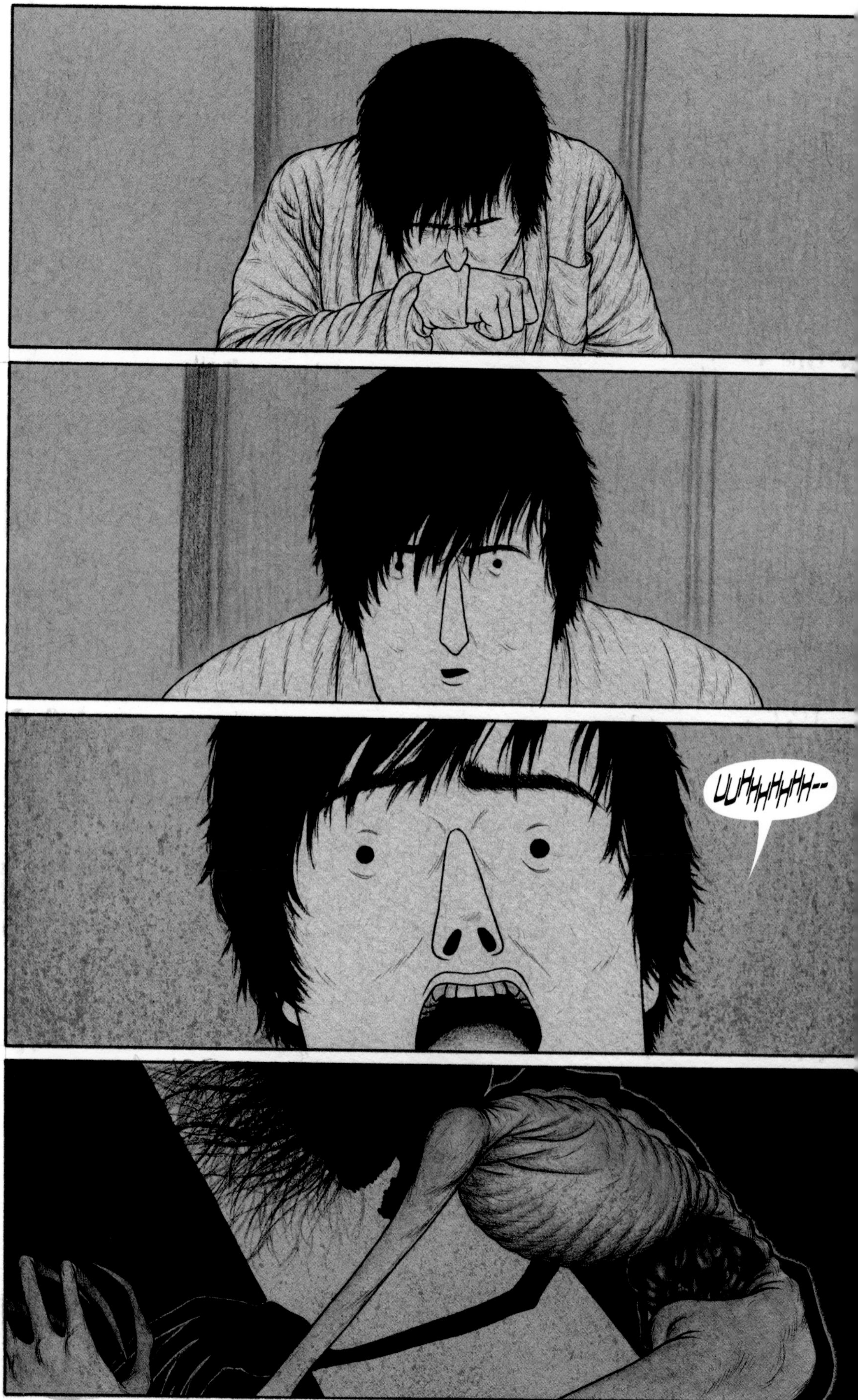
UUHHHHHH--

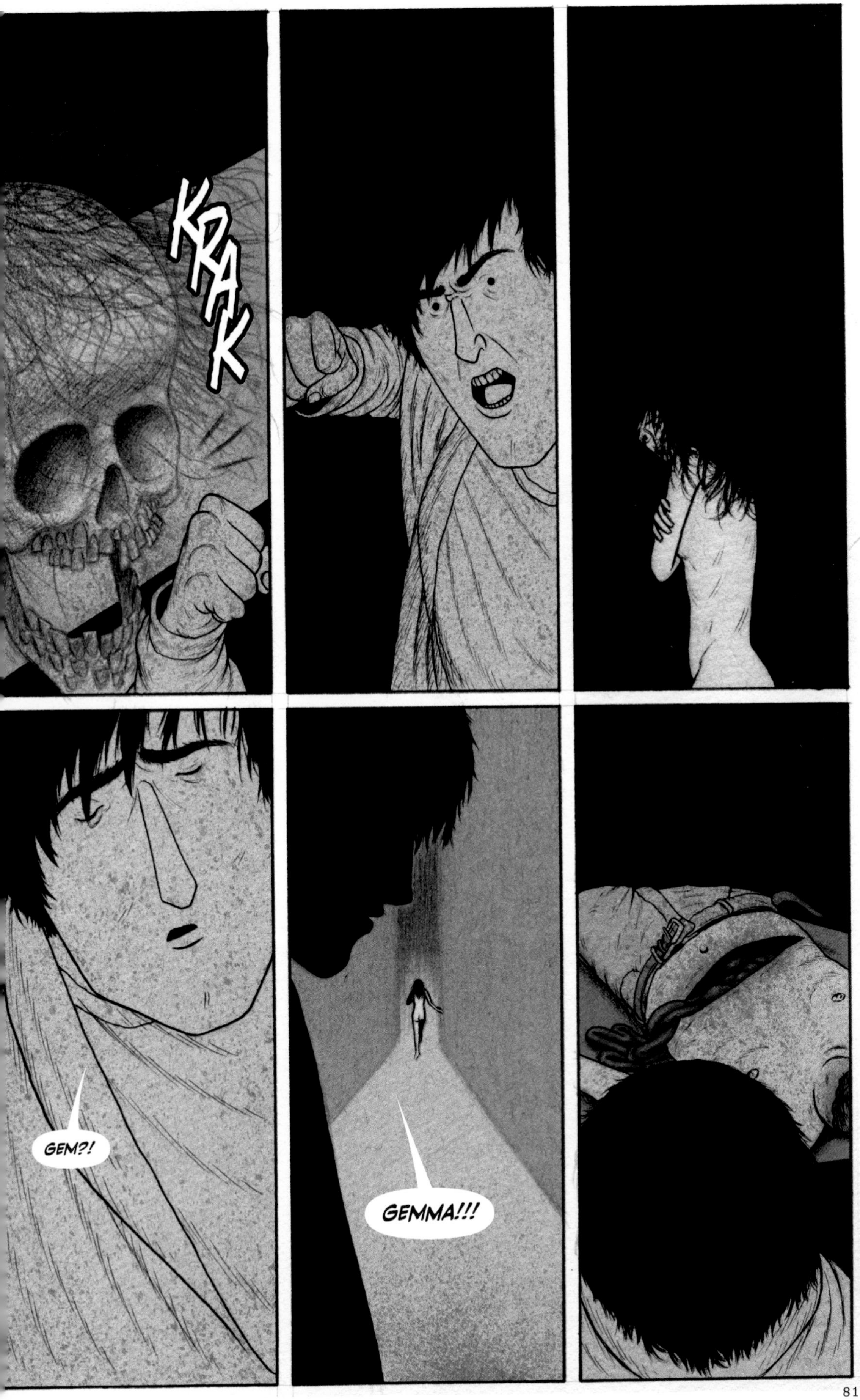
KRAK
GEM?!
GEMMA!!!

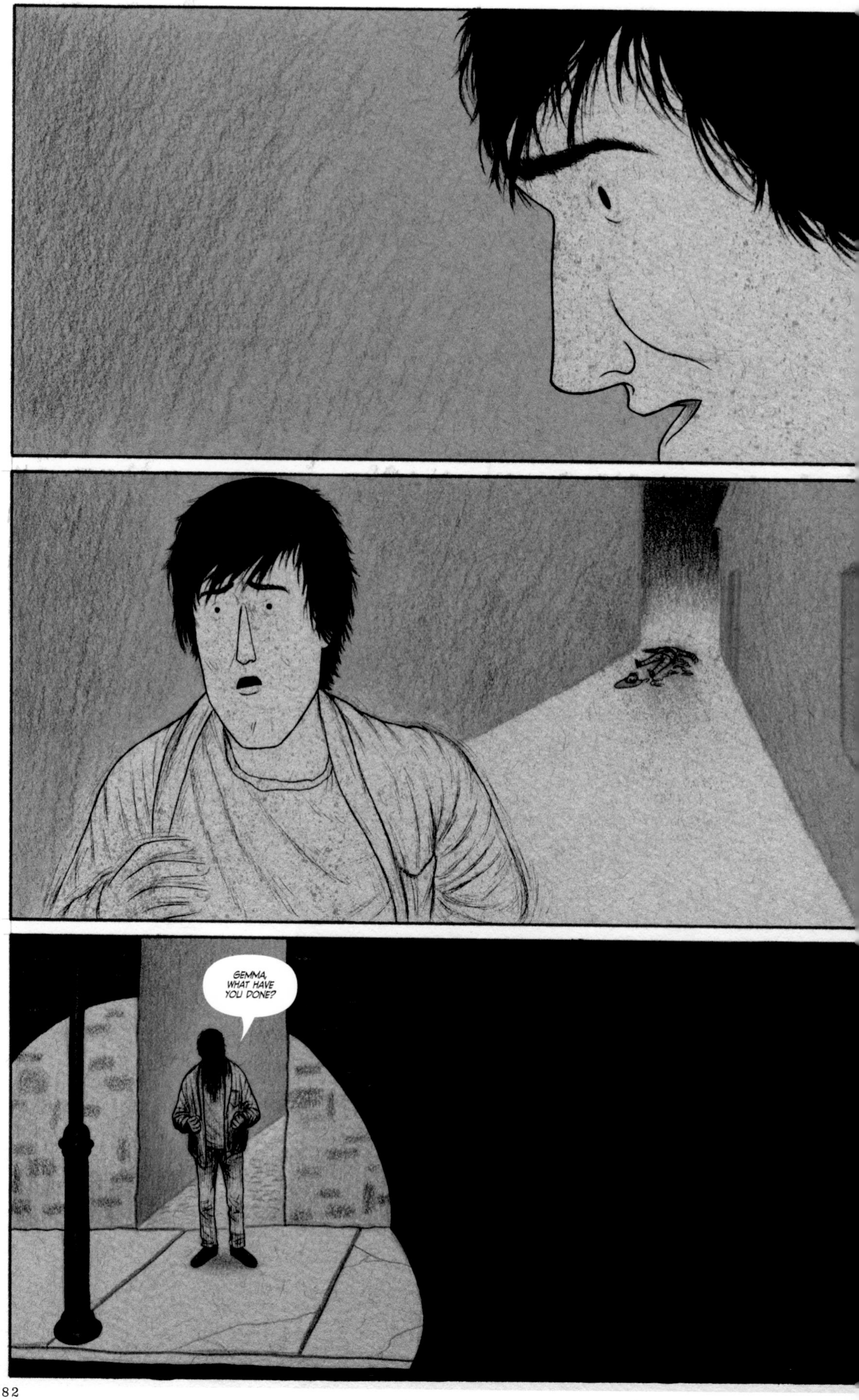
GEMMA, WHAT HAVE YOU DONE?

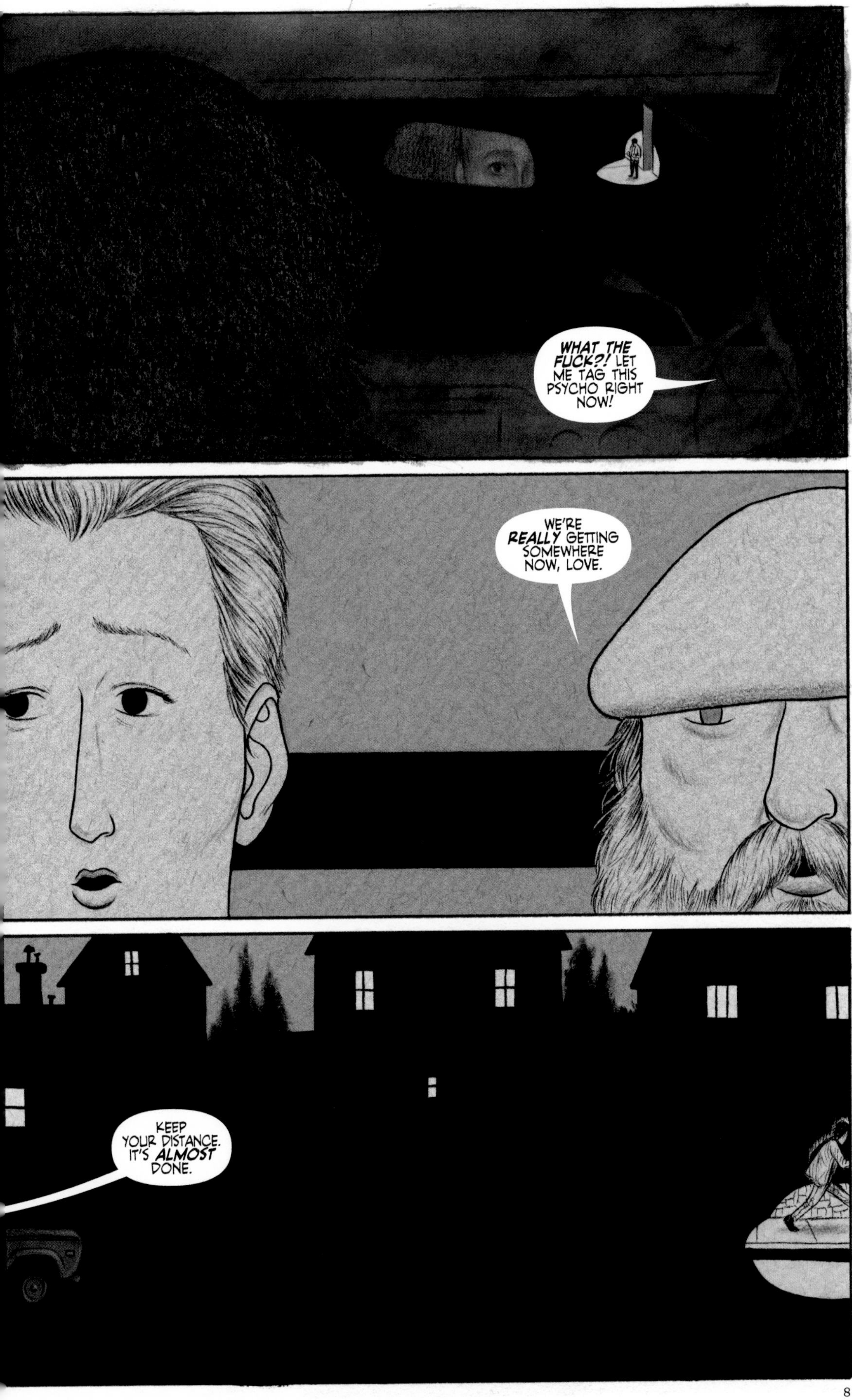
WHAT THE FUCK?! LET ME TAG THIS PSYCHO RIGHT NOW!
WE'RE REALLY GETTING SOMEWHERE NOW, LOVE.
KEEP YOUR DISTANCE. IT'S ALMOST DONE.

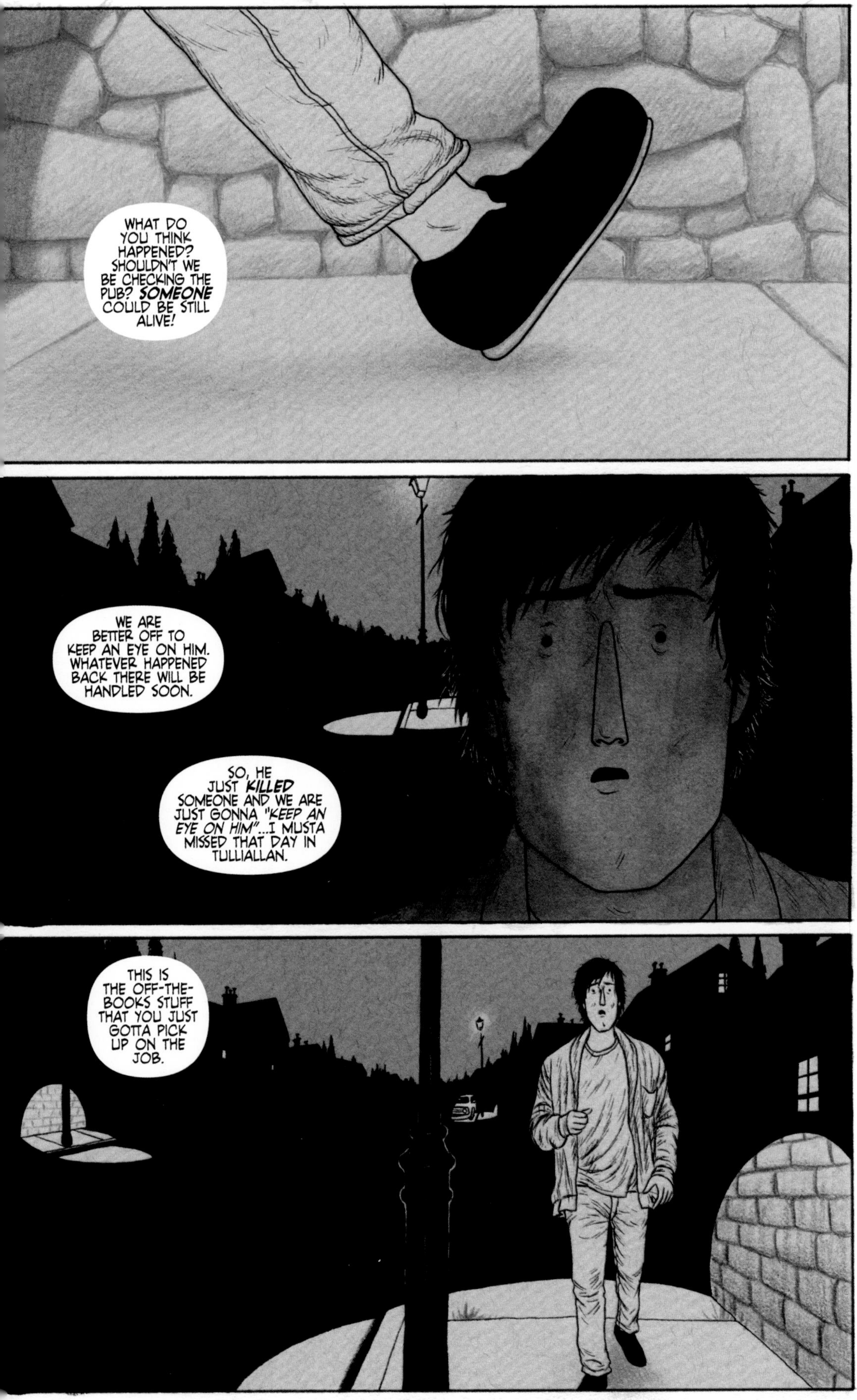
WHAT DO YOU THINK HAPPENED? SHOULDN'T WE BE CHECKING THE PUB? **SOMEONE** COULD BE STILL ALIVE!
WE ARE BETTER OFF TO KEEP AN EYE ON HIM. WHATEVER HAPPENED BACK THERE WILL BE HANDLED SOON.
SO, HE JUST **KILLED** SOMEONE AND WE ARE JUST GONNA *"KEEP AN EYE ON HIM"*...I MUSTA MISSED THAT DAY IN TULLIALLAN.
THIS IS THE OFF-THE-BOOKS STUFF THAT YOU JUST GOTTA PICK UP ON THE JOB.

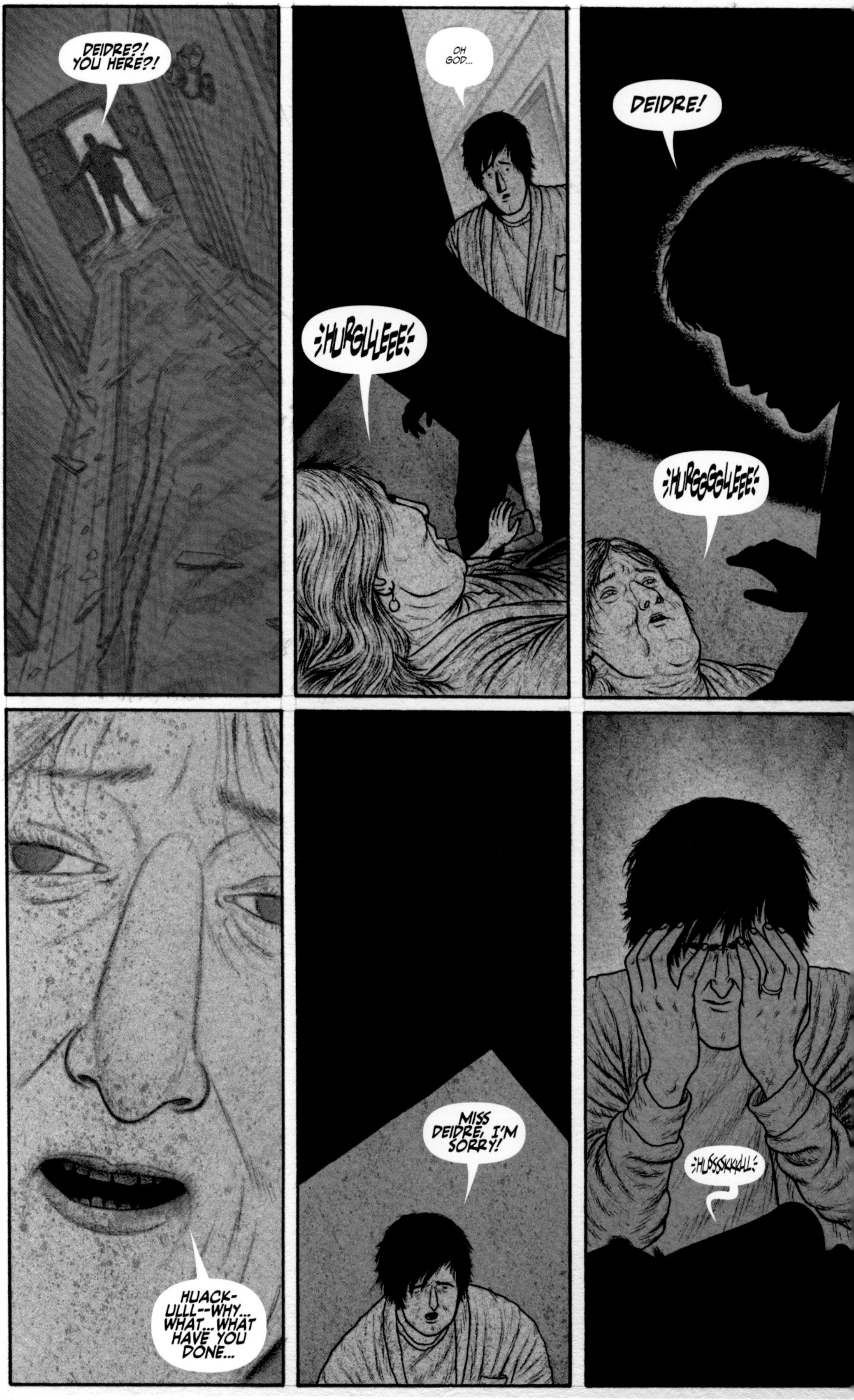
DEIDRE?! YOU HERE?!
OH GOD...
HURGLLLEEE
DEIDRE!
HURGGGLLEEE
HUACK-ULLL--WHY... WHAT... WHAT HAVE YOU DONE...
MISS DEIDRE, I'M SORRY!
HUSSSKKKLL

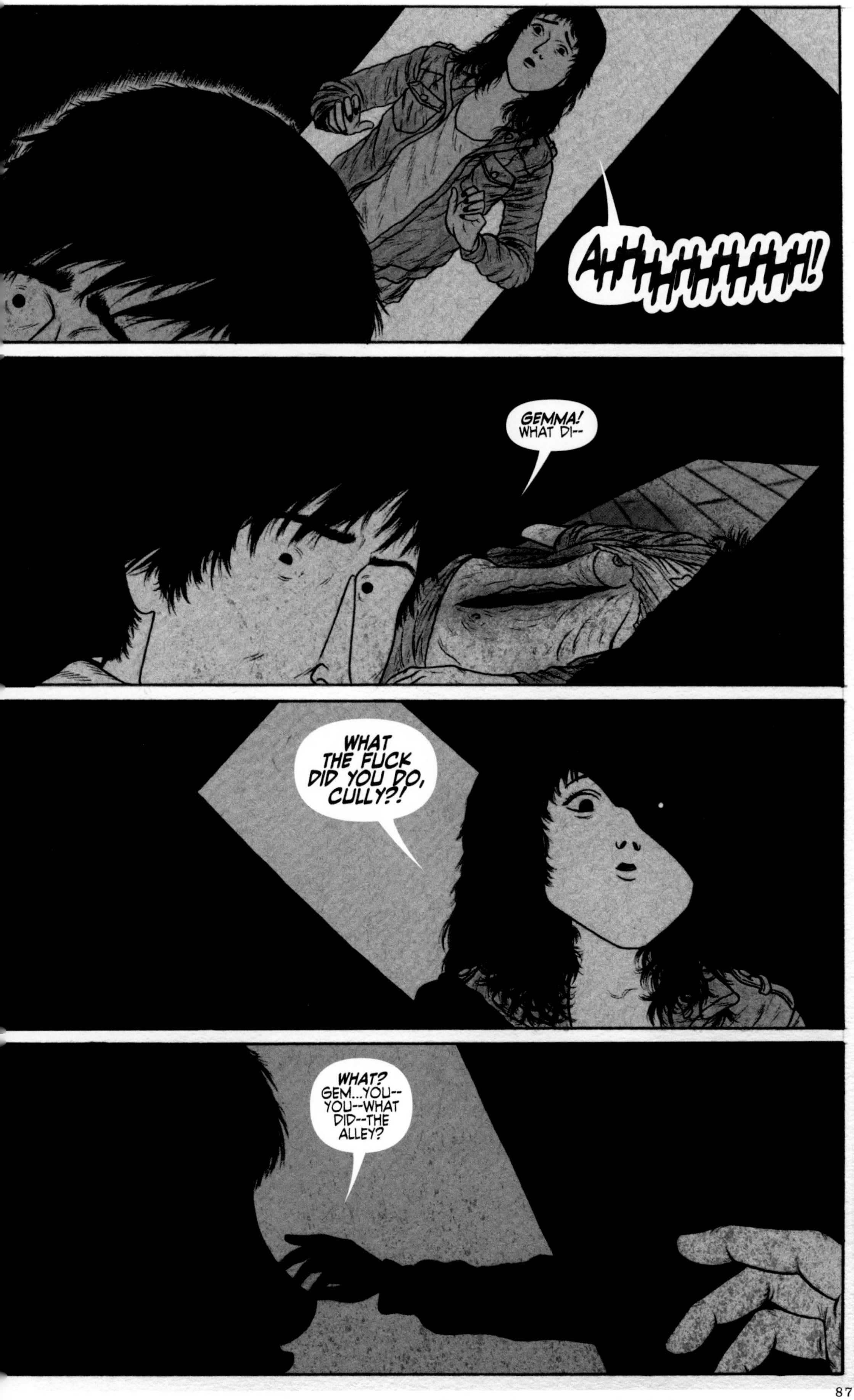
AHHHHHHHHHH!
GEMMA! WHAT DI--
WHAT THE FUCK DID YOU DO, CULLY?!
WHAT? GEM...YOU-- YOU--WHAT DID--THE ALLEY?

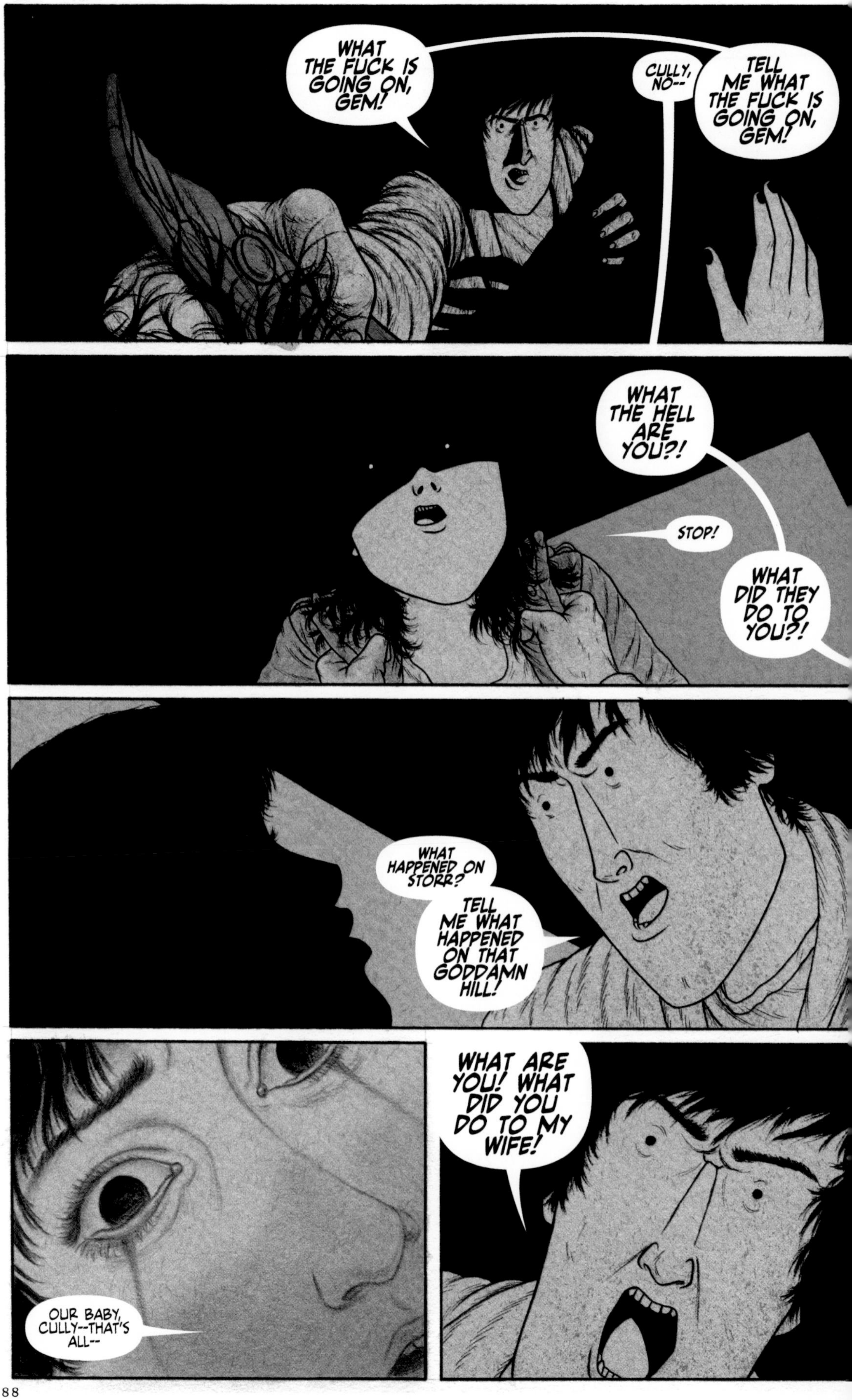
WHAT THE FUCK IS GOING ON, GEM!
CULLY, NO--
TELL ME WHAT THE FUCK IS GOING ON, GEM!
WHAT THE HELL ARE YOU?!
STOP!
WHAT DID THEY DO TO YOU?!
WHAT HAPPENED ON STORR?
TELL ME WHAT HAPPENED ON THAT GODDAMN HILL!
OUR BABY, CULLY--THAT'S ALL--
WHAT ARE YOU! WHAT DID YOU DO TO MY WIFE!

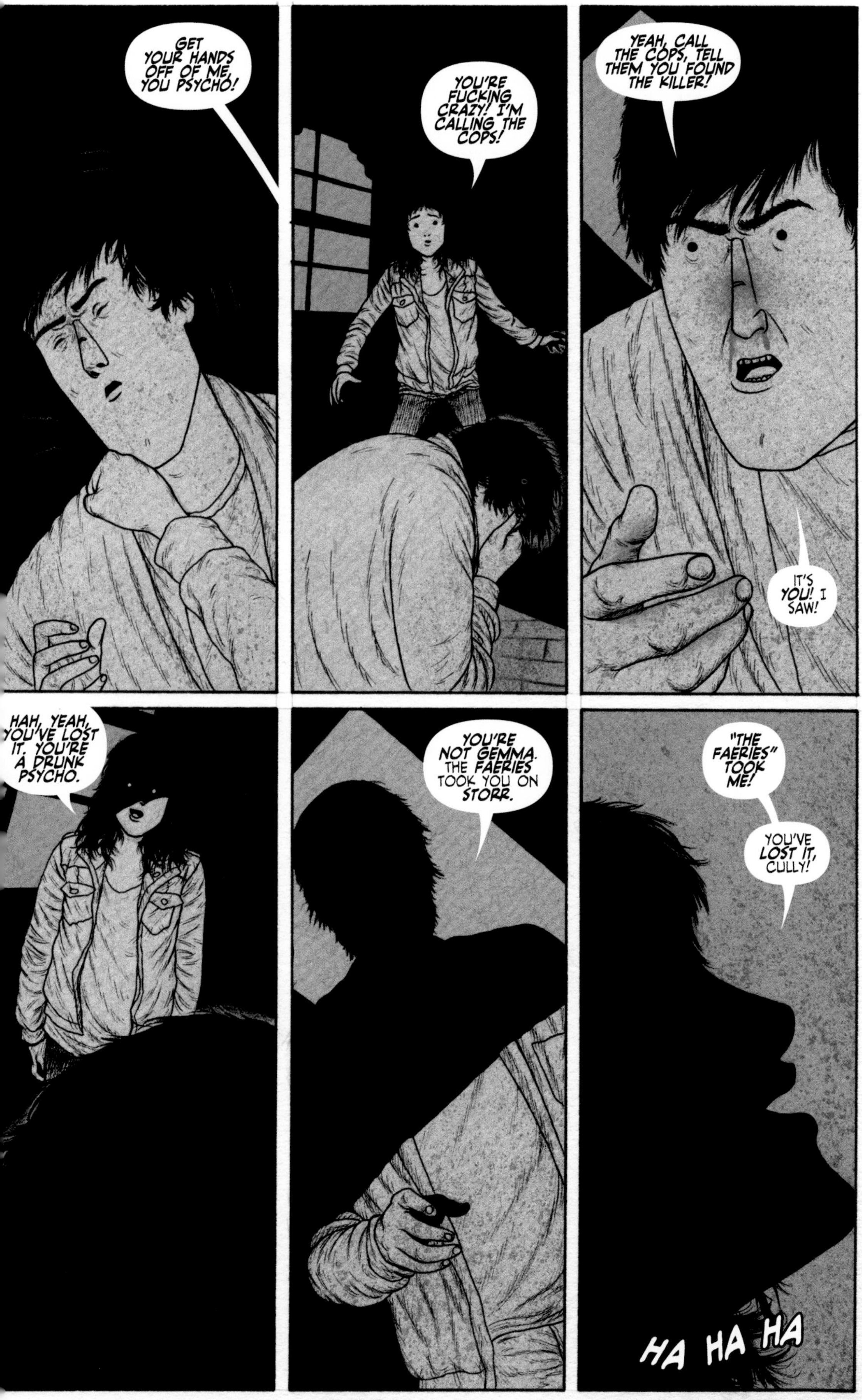
GET YOUR HANDS OFF OF ME, YOU PSYCHO!
YOU'RE FUCKING CRAZY! I'M CALLING THE COPS!
YEAH, CALL THE COPS, TELL THEM YOU FOUND THE KILLER!
IT'S YOU! I SAW!
HAH, YEAH, YOU'VE LOST IT. YOU'RE A DRUNK PSYCHO.
YOU'RE NOT GEMMA. THE FAERIES TOOK YOU ON STORR.
"THE FAERIES" TOOK ME!
YOU'VE LOST IT, CULLY!
HA HA HA

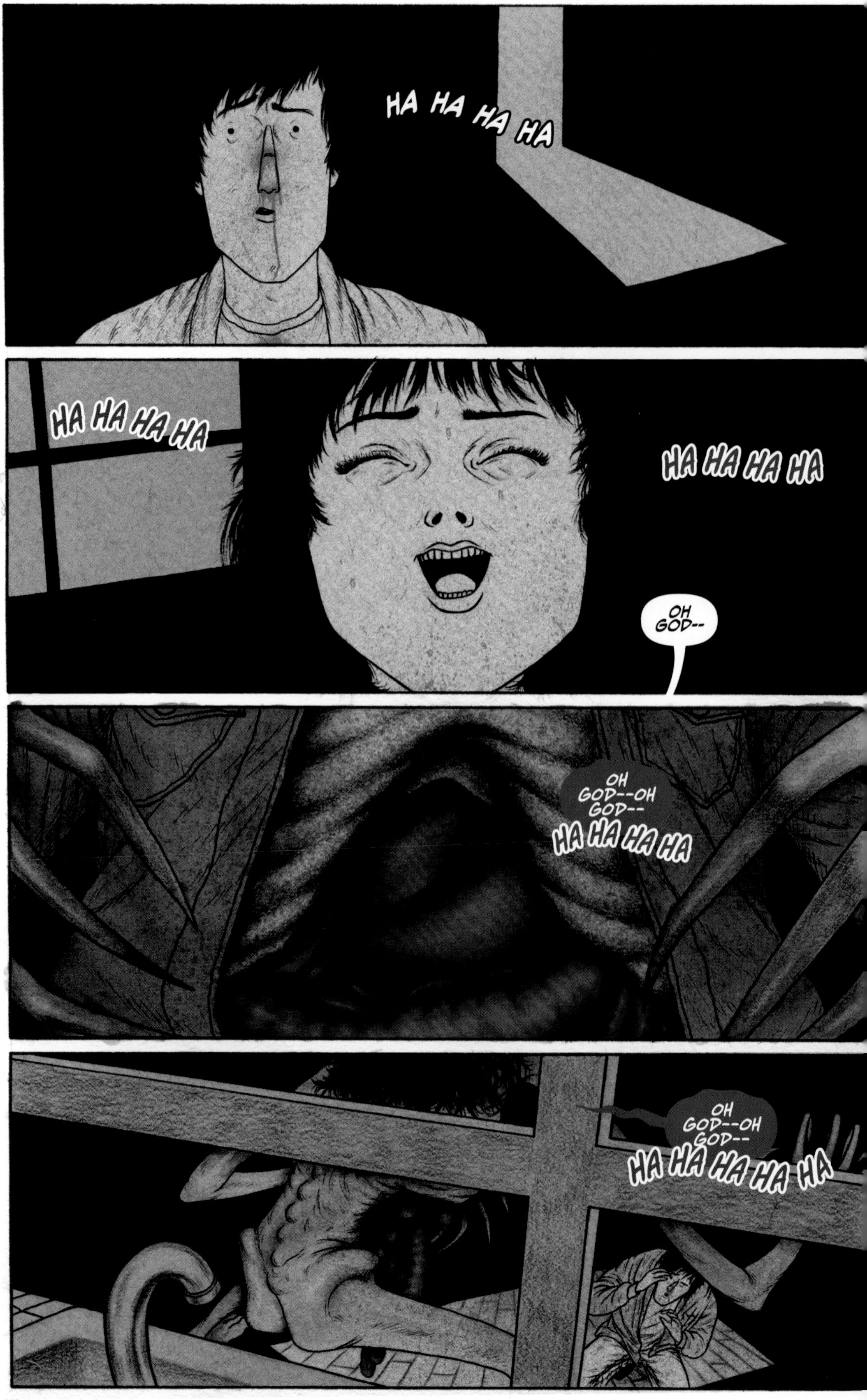
HA HA HA HA
HA HA HA HA
HA HA HA HA
OH GOD--
OH GOD--OH GOD--
HA HA HA HA
OH GOD--OH GOD--
HA HA HA HA HA HA

AHHHHH!
UNGH... NO!
NO?
NO.
NO!
NO, NO, NO, NO GOD!
HA HA HA HA HA

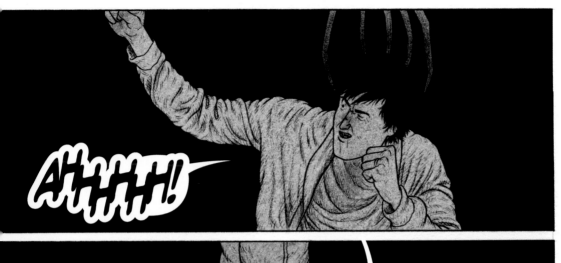

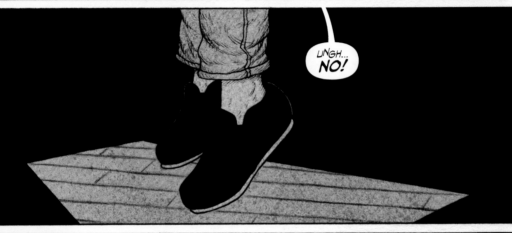

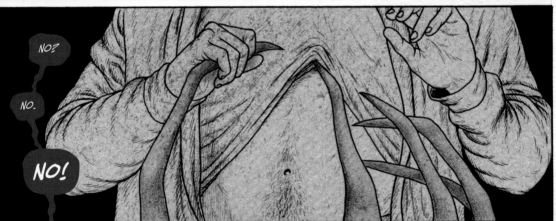

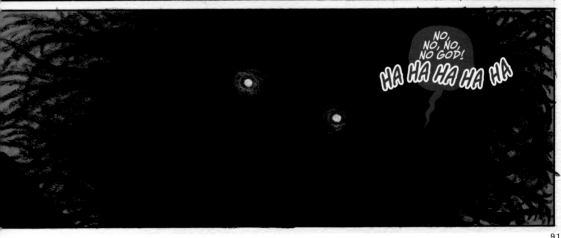

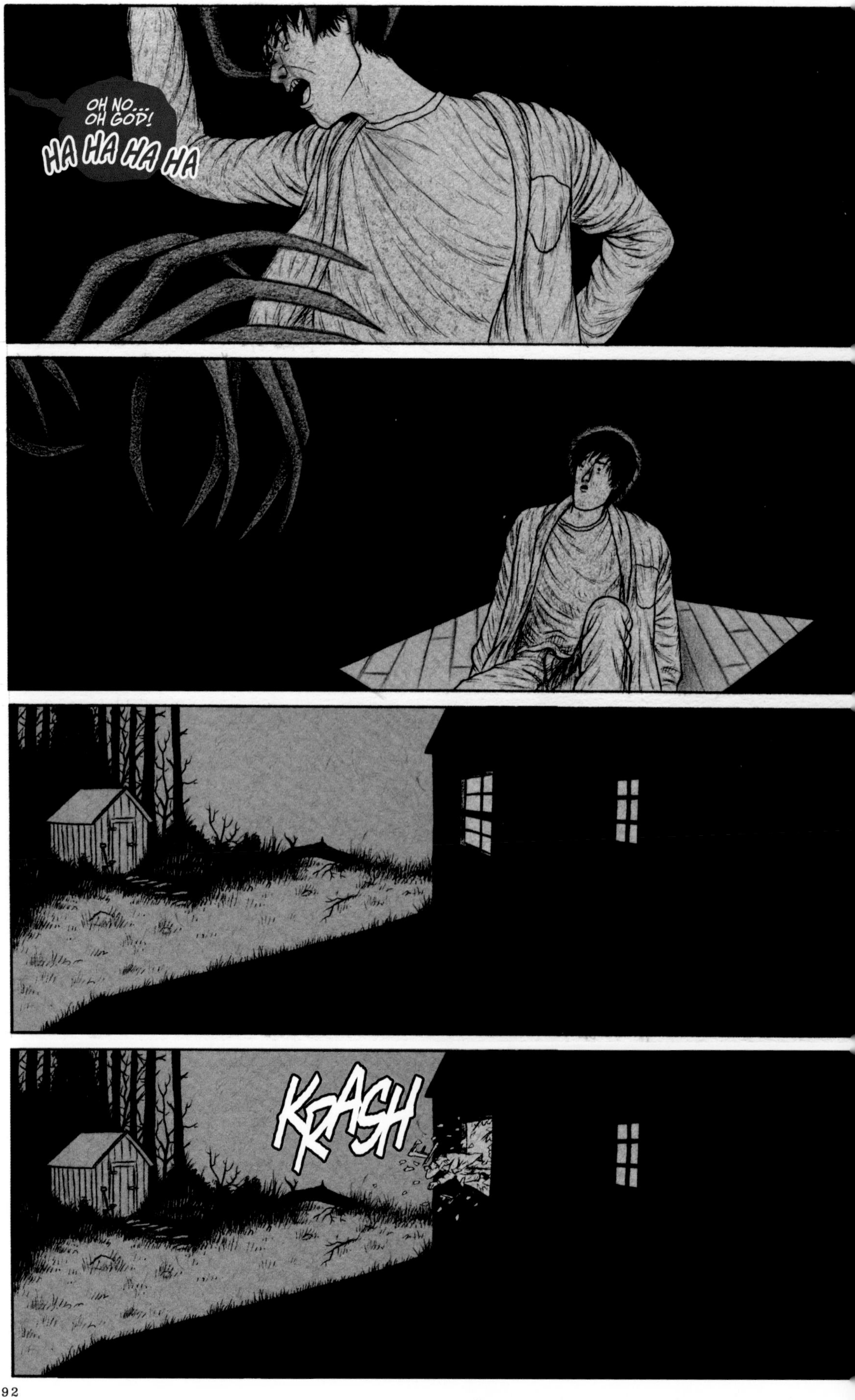
OH NO... OH GOD!
HA HA HA HA
KRASH

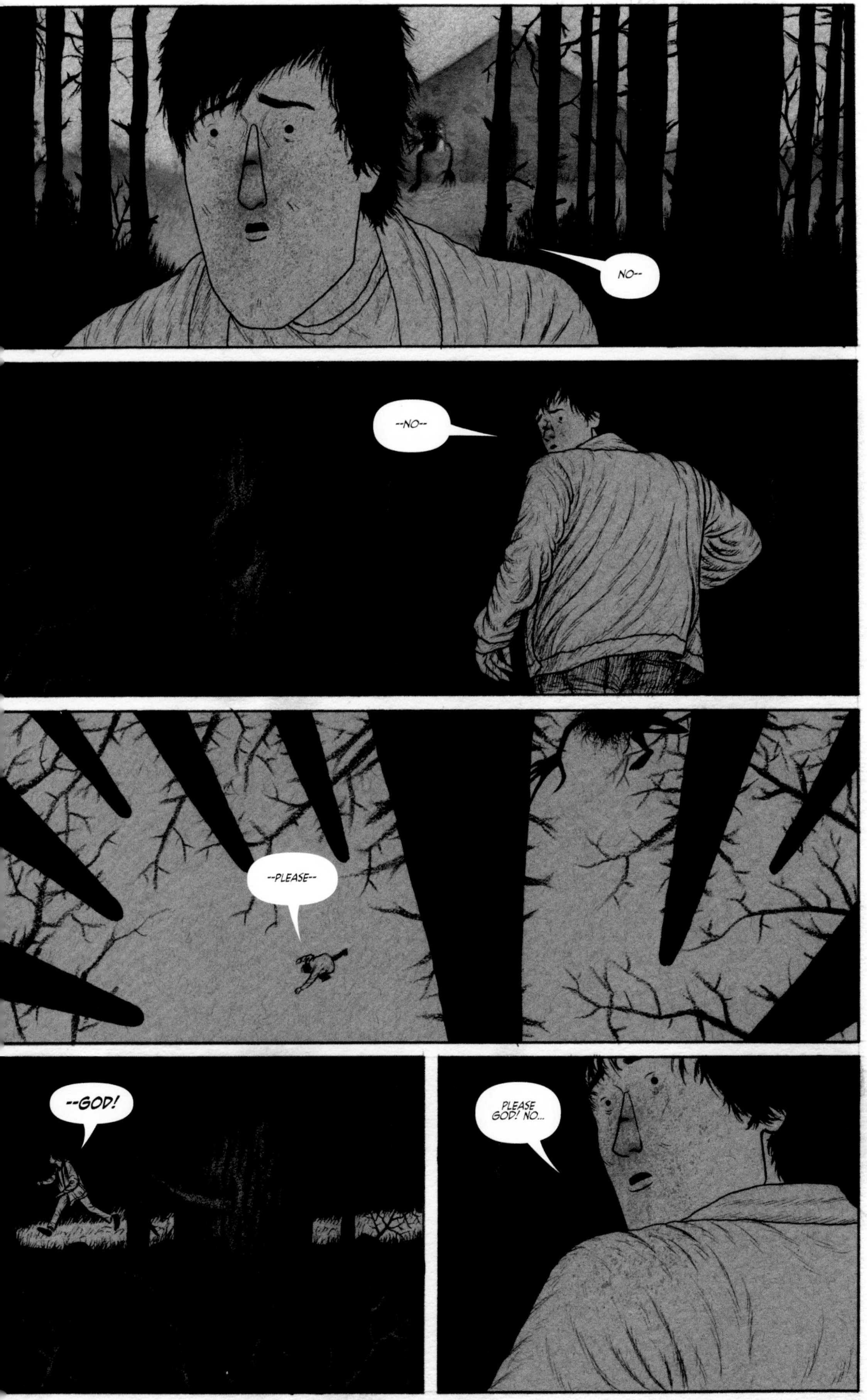
NO--
--NO--
--PLEASE--
--GOD!
PLEASE GOD! NO...

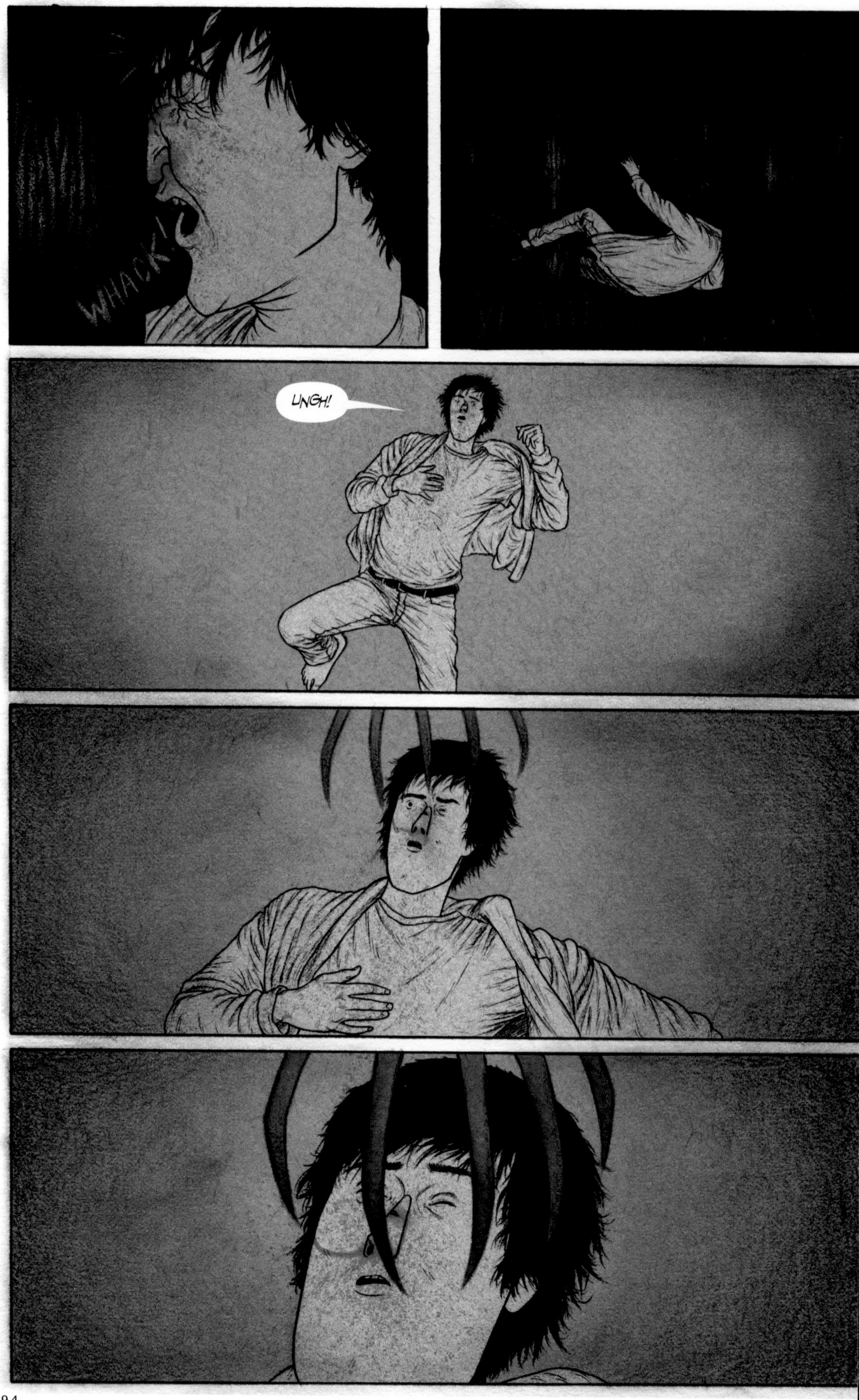
WHACK!
UNGH!

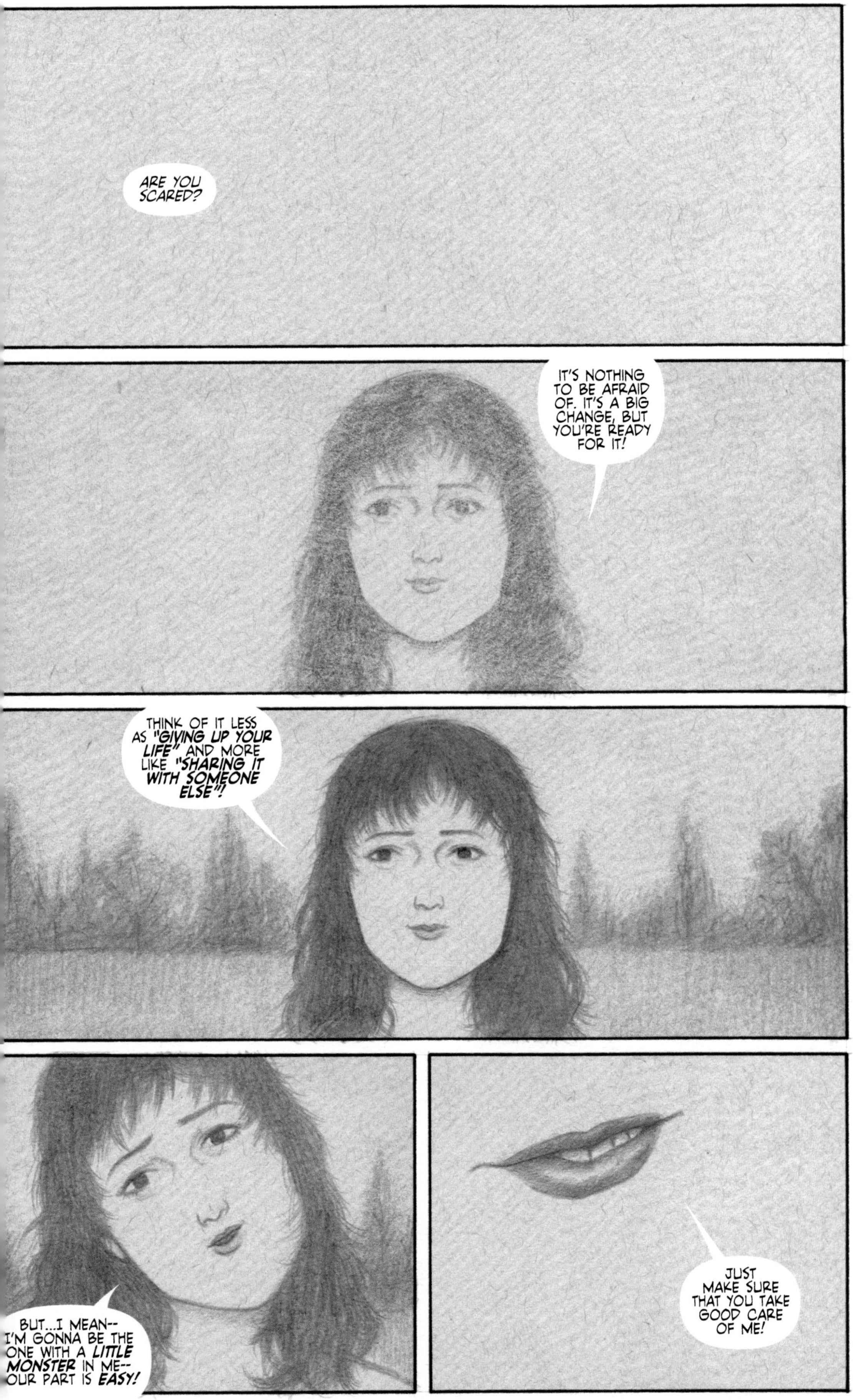
ARE YOU SCARED?
IT'S NOTHING TO BE AFRAID OF. IT'S A BIG CHANGE, BUT YOU'RE READY FOR IT!
THINK OF IT LESS AS *"GIVING UP YOUR LIFE"* AND MORE LIKE *"SHARING IT WITH SOMEONE ELSE"*!
BUT...I MEAN-- I'M GONNA BE THE ONE WITH A *LITTLE MONSTER* IN ME-- OUR PART IS *EASY!*
JUST MAKE SURE THAT YOU TAKE GOOD CARE OF ME!

I GUESS I *AM* AFRAID. *I'M HAPPY,* I SWEAR THAT, IT'S JUST LIKE...*A LOT* RIGHT NOW.

FOR THE NEXT 9 MONTHS I'M GONNA BE SCARED. *HELL,* AFTER THAT I GUESS I'LL BE SCARED, TOO!

LIKE, WHAT IF *SOMETHING* HAPPENS?

OH, SOMETHING WILL HAPPEN, SOMETHING HAS HAPPENED.

LIKE, RIGHT NOW. YOU THINK THE BABY IS *DEAD,* REMEMBER?

YOU HAD A *MISCARRIAGE* ON STORR...

I'M *STILL* PREGNANT. THINGS *CHANGED,* BUT I'M STILL GOING TO BE A MOTHER.

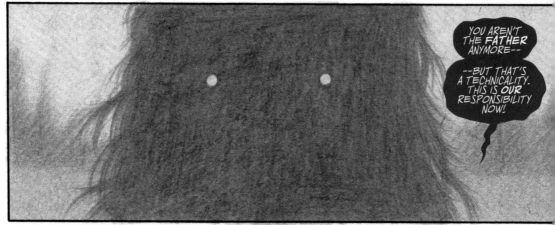

YOU AREN'T THE *FATHER* ANYMORE--

--BUT THAT'S A TECHNICALITY. THIS IS *OUR* RESPONSIBILITY NOW!

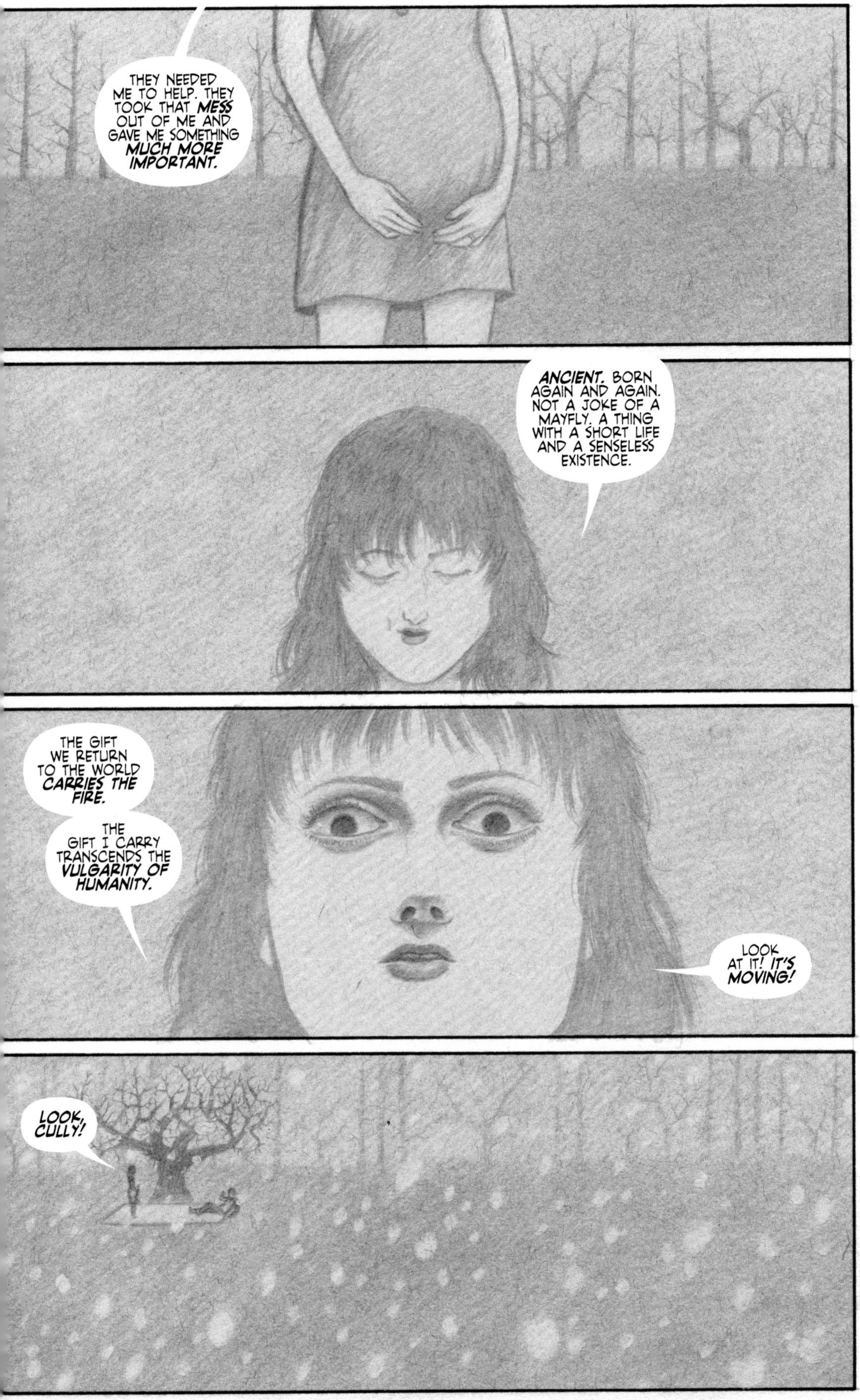
THEY NEEDED ME TO HELP. THEY TOOK THAT MESS OUT OF ME AND GAVE ME SOMETHING MUCH MORE IMPORTANT.
ANCIENT. BORN AGAIN AND AGAIN. NOT A JOKE OF A MAYFLY. A THING WITH A SHORT LIFE AND A SENSELESS EXISTENCE.
THE GIFT WE RETURN TO THE WORLD CARRIES THE FIRE.
THE GIFT I CARRY TRANSCENDS THE VULGARITY OF HUMANITY.
LOOK AT IT! IT'S MOVING!
LOOK, CULLY!

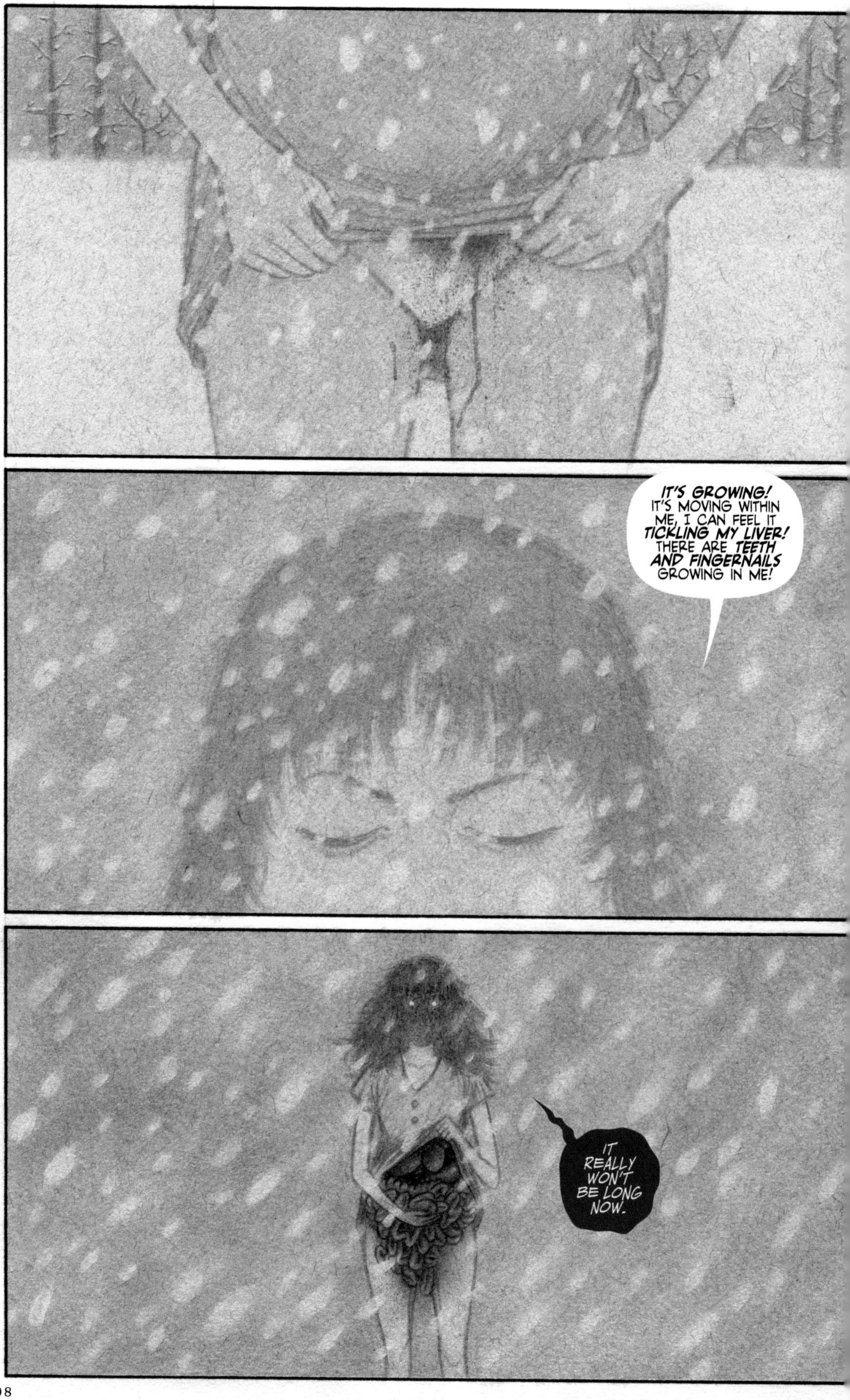
IT'S GROWING! IT'S MOVING WITHIN ME, I CAN FEEL IT TICKLING MY LIVER! THERE ARE TEETH AND FINGERNAILS GROWING IN ME!
IT REALLY WON'T BE LONG NOW.

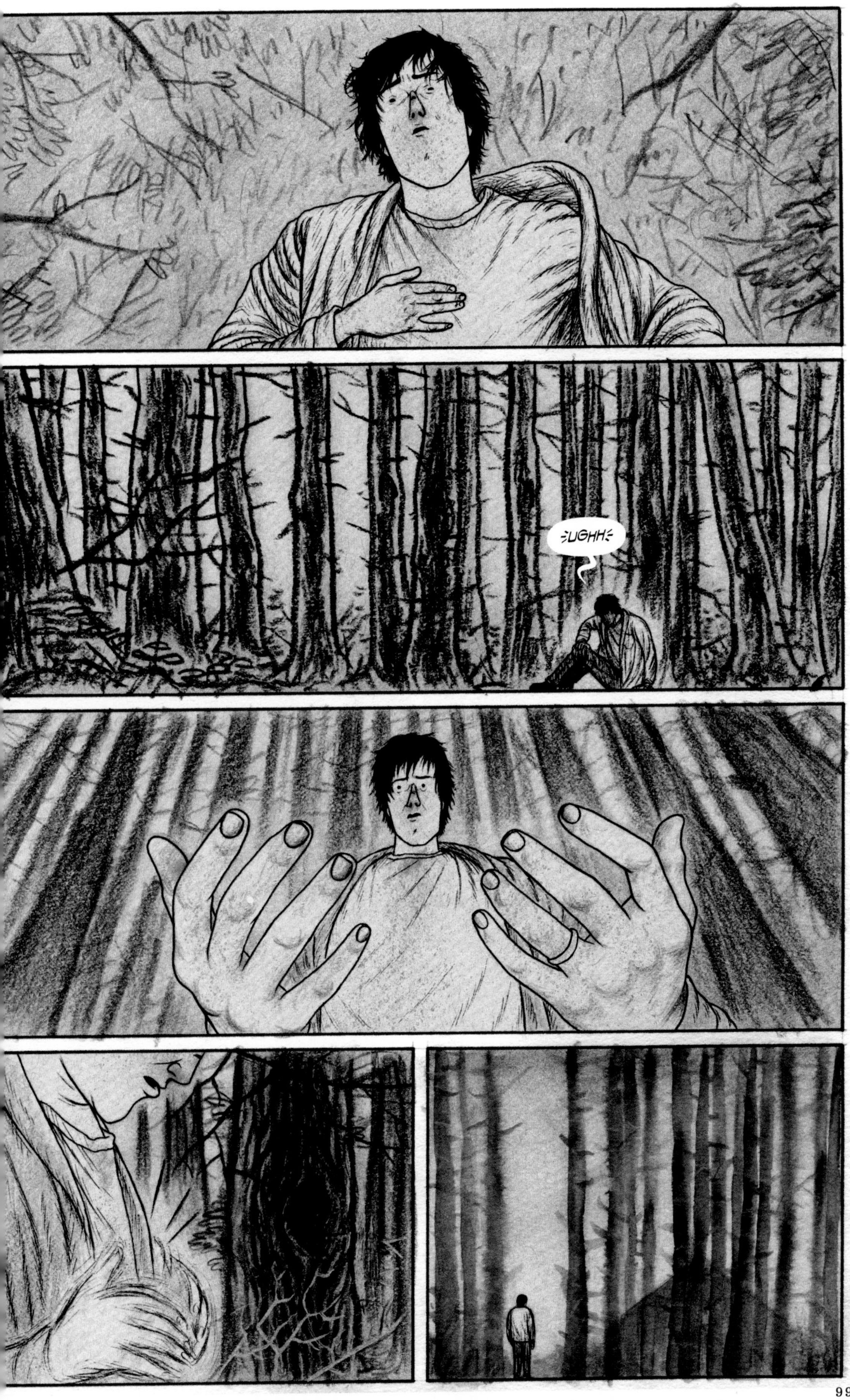
UGHH

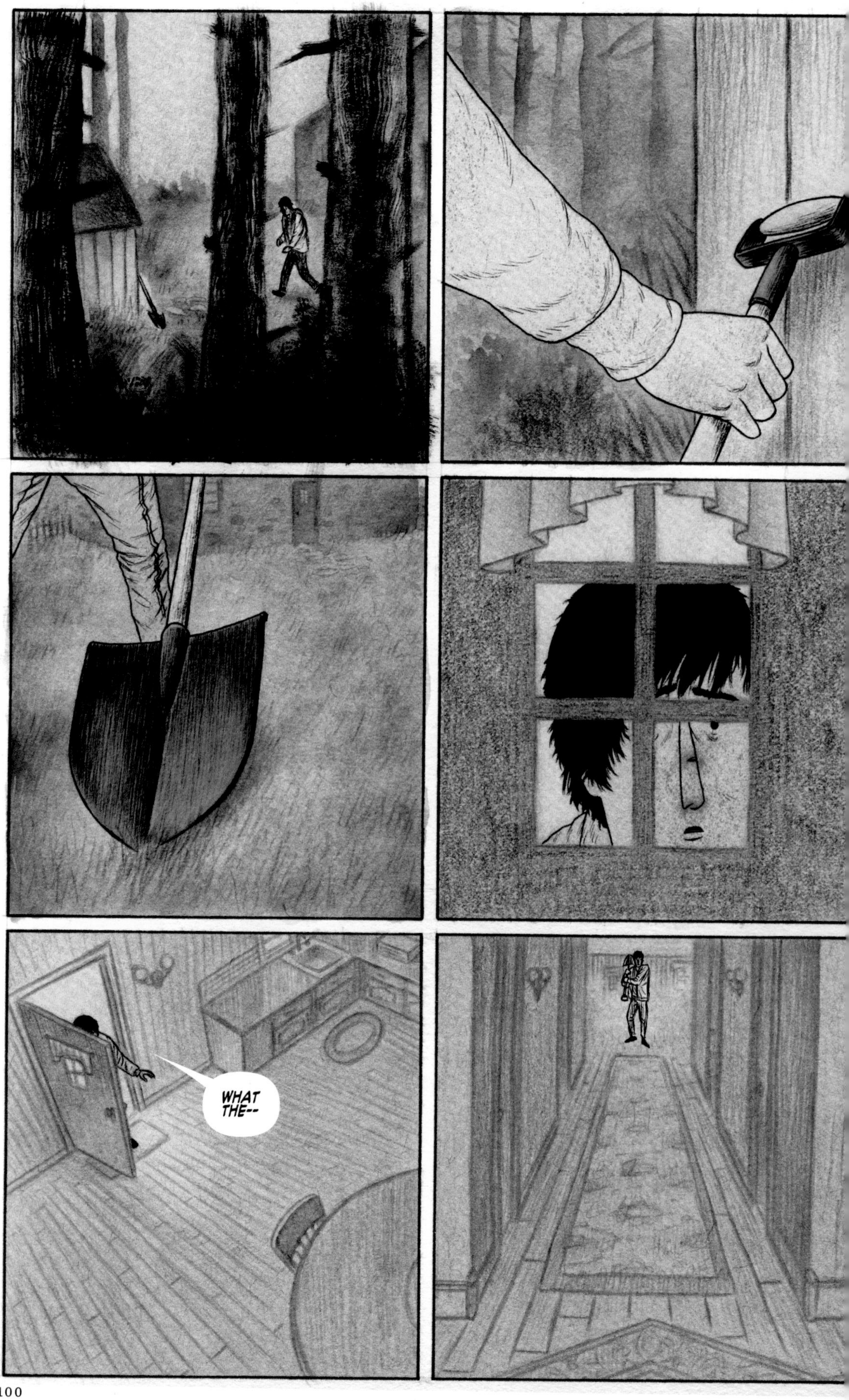
WHAT THE--

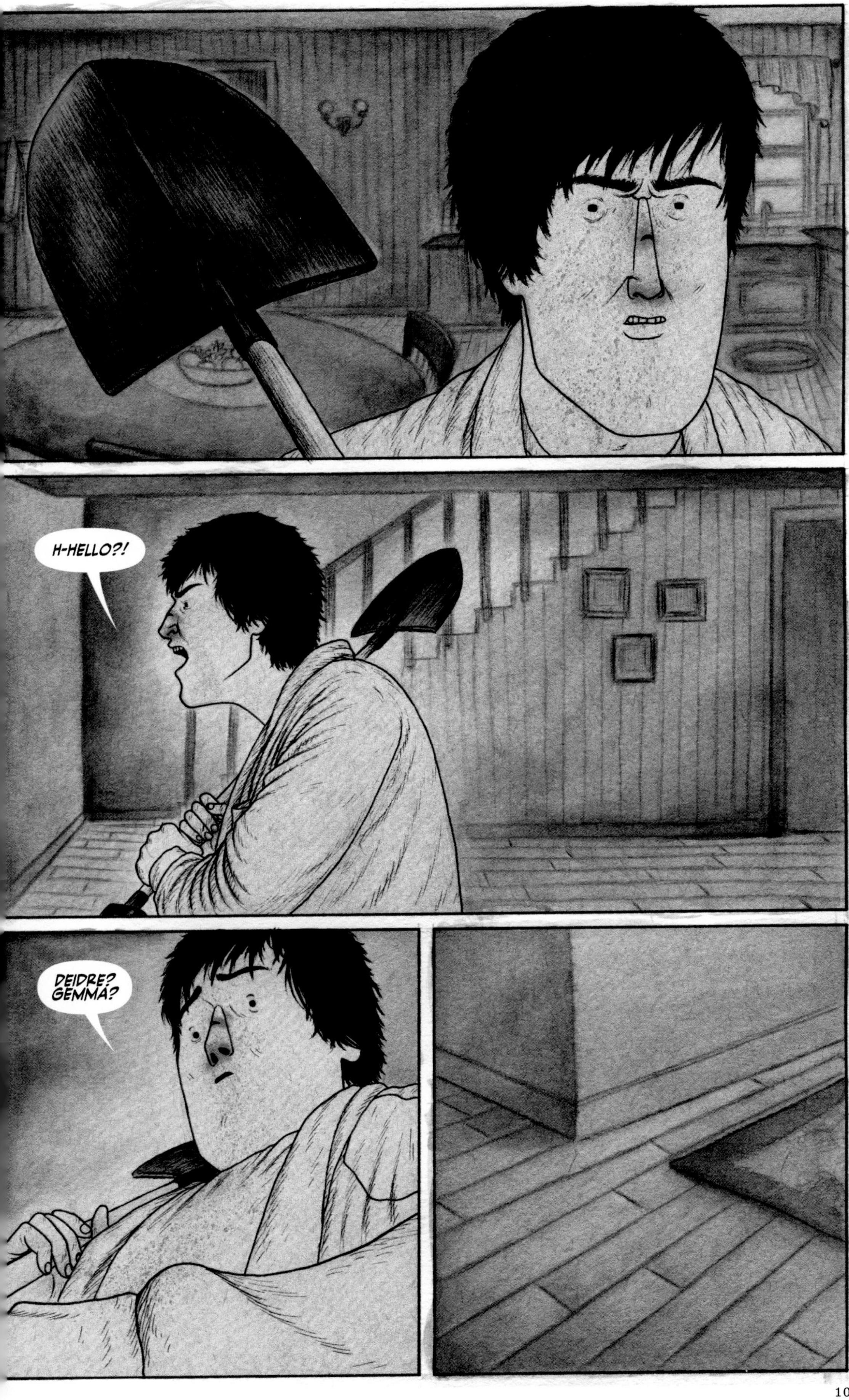
H-HELLO?!
DEIDRE?
GEMMA?

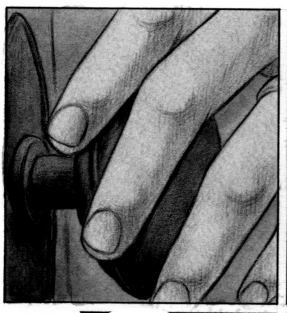

CULLY! I WAS SCARED SICK!

WHERE HAVE YOU BEEN?

WHAT?! WHAT'S HAPPENED, GEMMA?

WE NEED TO TALK, CULLY, IT'S A MIRACLE!

IT'S GONNA SOUND IMPOSSIBLE...

I DIDN'T LOSE THE BABY! I'M STILL PREGNANT, CULLY!

PUT THAT THING DOWN! YOU KNOW, YOU REALLY HAVE TO STOP DRINKING SO MUCH. YOU'VE BEEN ON A REAL BENDER.

I GET IT, IT'S BEEN HARD--BUT WE'RE OKAY NOW!

I JUST KNOW IT'S IN THERE, **CULLY**, THEY MUST HAVE MADE A MISTAKE. I SHOULD GET CHECKED--I KNOW IT'S IN THERE!

GEM--

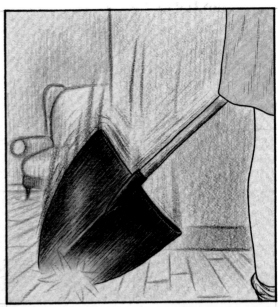

THE BABY--THE BABY IS OKAY? HOW--HOW DO YOU KNOW?

I FEEL IT **IN ME.** I KNOW IT SEEMS IMPOSSIBLE, BUT IT'S TRUE!

I'M SORRY I'VE BEEN SO STRANGE, I WAS DEPRESSED.

I JUST LOVE YOU.

I--I LOVE YOU--DEIDRE, YOU WERE--

DEIDRE WENT INTO TOWN, SHE'S GONNA MAKE US A PROPER SCOTTISH ROAST!

I'M **EATING FOR TWO** AGAIN!

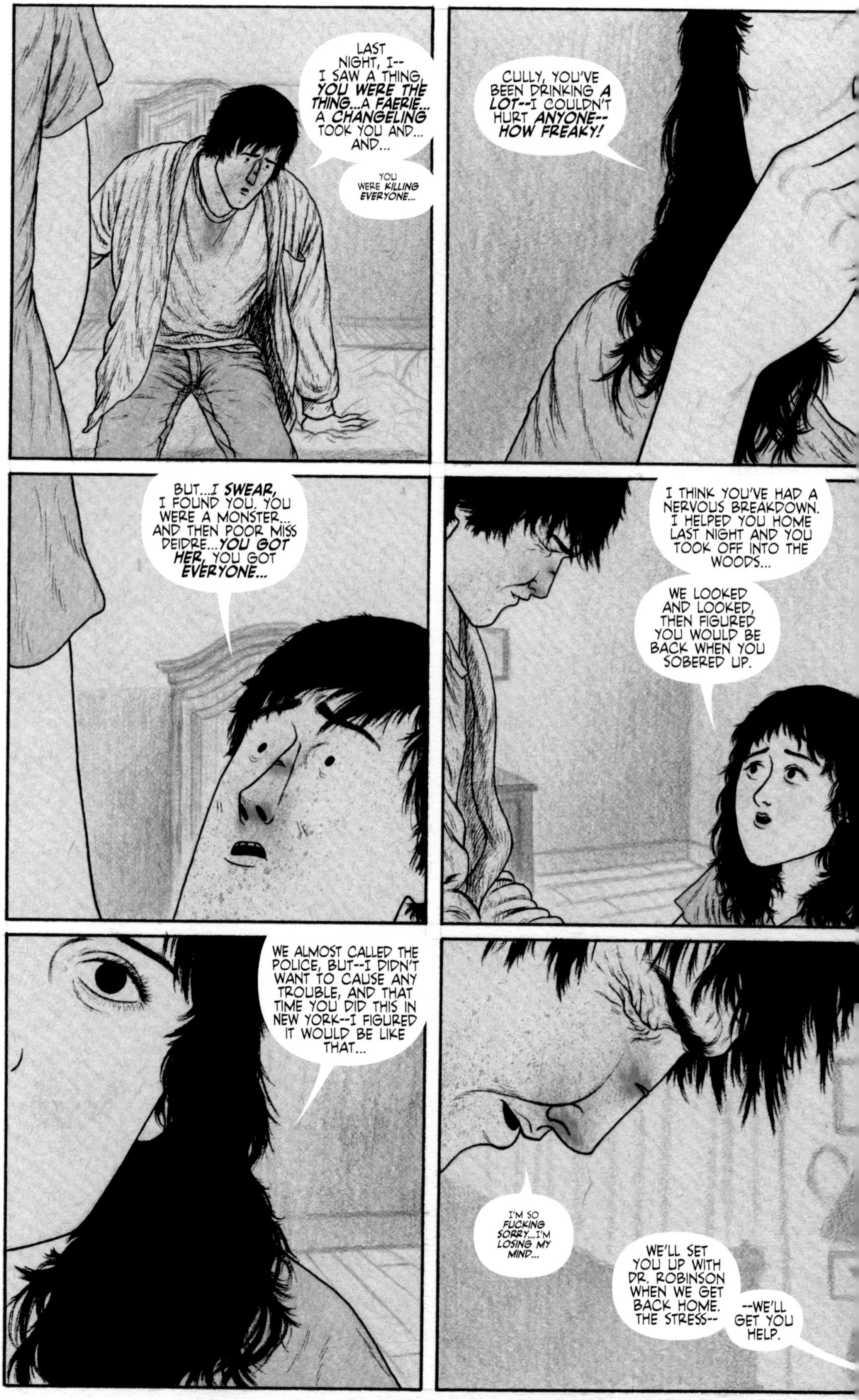
LAST NIGHT, I-- I SAW A THING, YOU WERE THE THING...A FAERIE... A CHANGELING TOOK YOU AND... AND...
YOU WERE KILLING EVERYONE...
CULLY, YOU'VE BEEN DRINKING A LOT--I COULDN'T HURT ANYONE-- HOW FREAKY!
BUT...I SWEAR, I FOUND YOU. YOU WERE A MONSTER... AND THEN POOR MISS DEIDRE...YOU GOT HER, YOU GOT EVERYONE...
I THINK YOU'VE HAD A NERVOUS BREAKDOWN. I HELPED YOU HOME LAST NIGHT AND YOU TOOK OFF INTO THE WOODS...
WE LOOKED AND LOOKED, THEN FIGURED YOU WOULD BE BACK WHEN YOU SOBERED UP.
WE ALMOST CALLED THE POLICE, BUT--I DIDN'T WANT TO CAUSE ANY TROUBLE, AND THAT TIME YOU DID THIS IN NEW YORK--I FIGURED IT WOULD BE LIKE THAT...
I'M SO FUCKING SORRY...I'M LOSING MY MIND...
WE'LL SET YOU UP WITH DR. ROBINSON WHEN WE GET BACK HOME. THE STRESS--
--WE'LL GET YOU HELP.

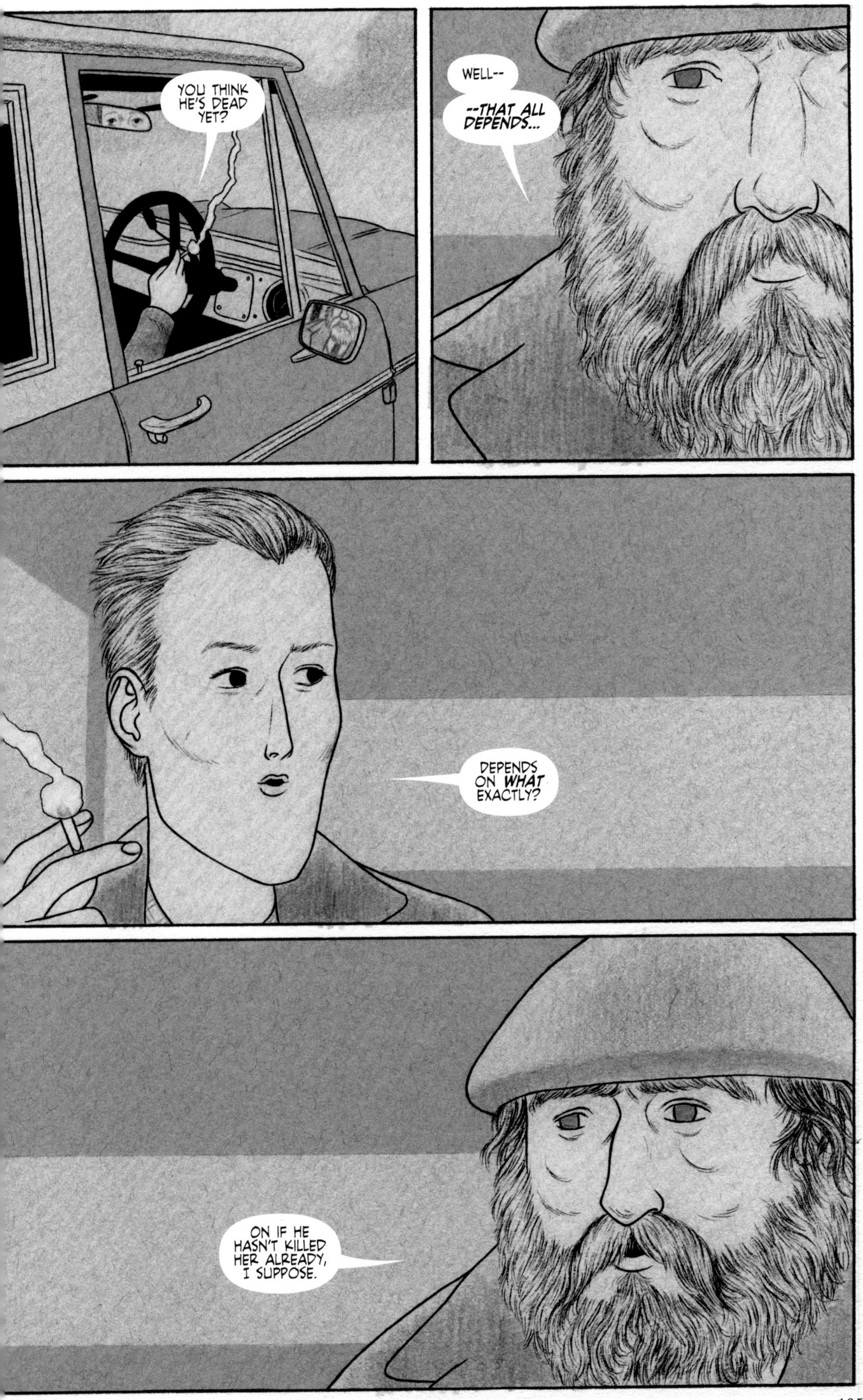
YOU THINK HE'S DEAD YET?
WELL--
--THAT ALL DEPENDS...
DEPENDS ON WHAT EXACTLY?
ON IF HE HASN'T KILLED HER ALREADY, I SUPPOSE.

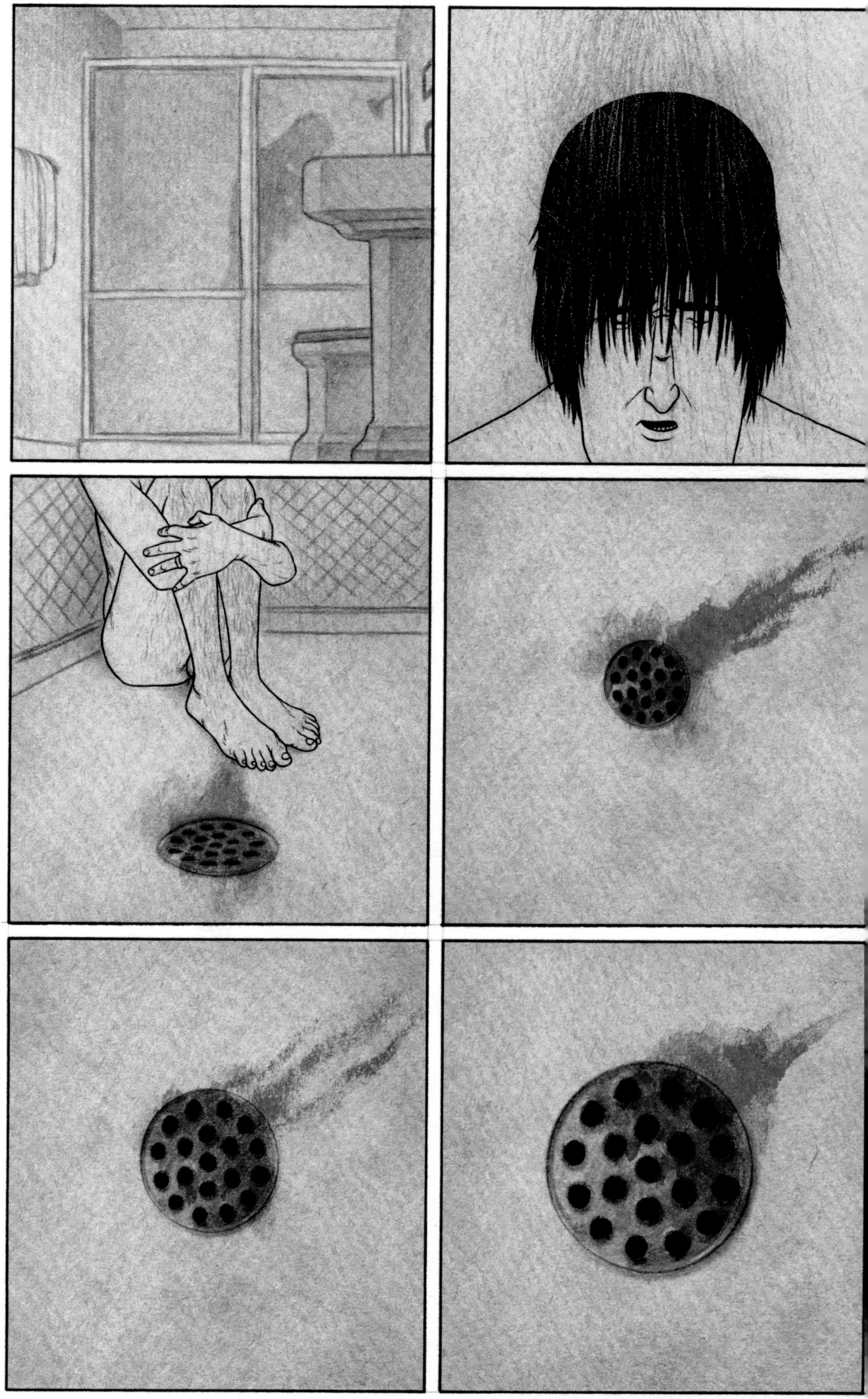

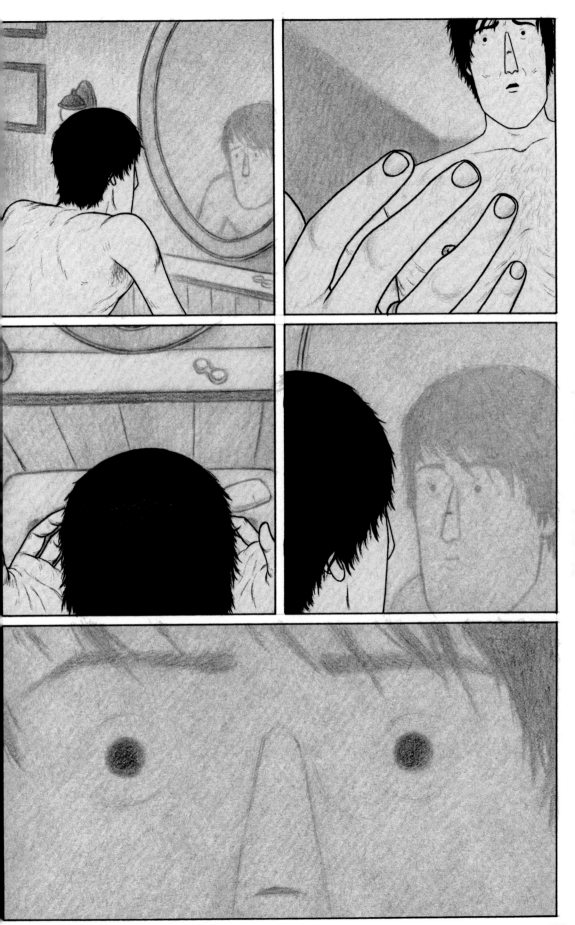

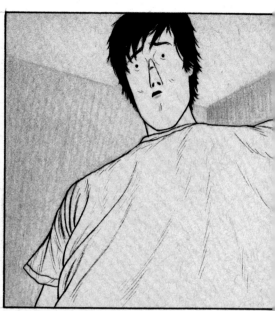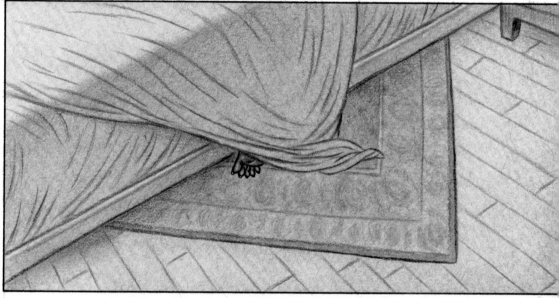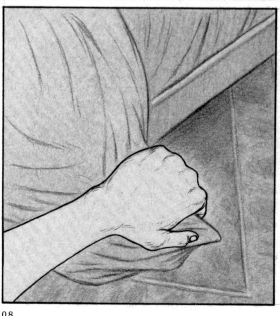

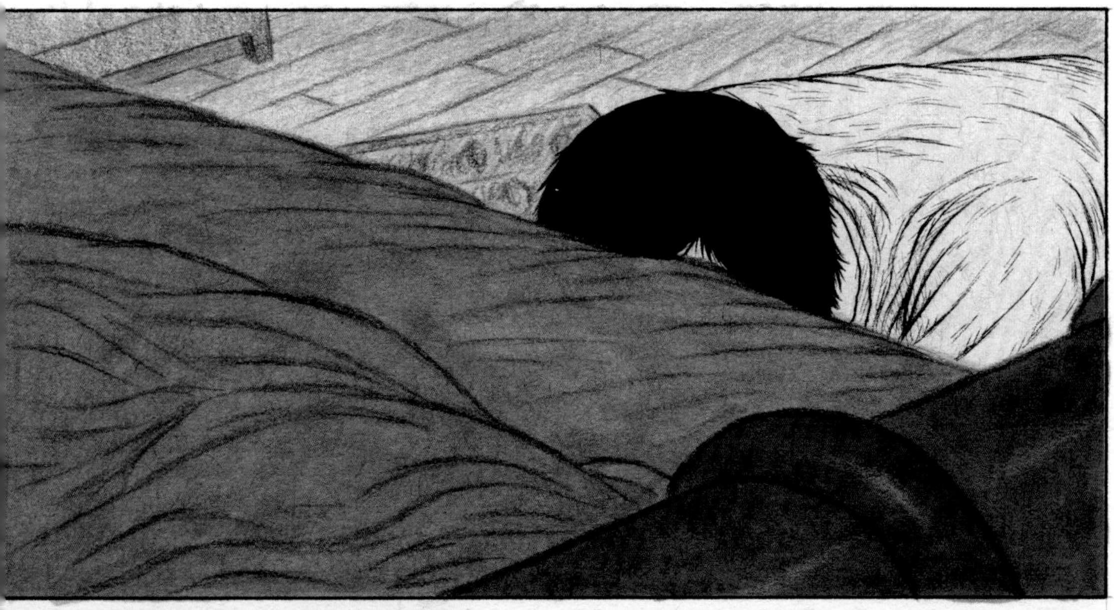
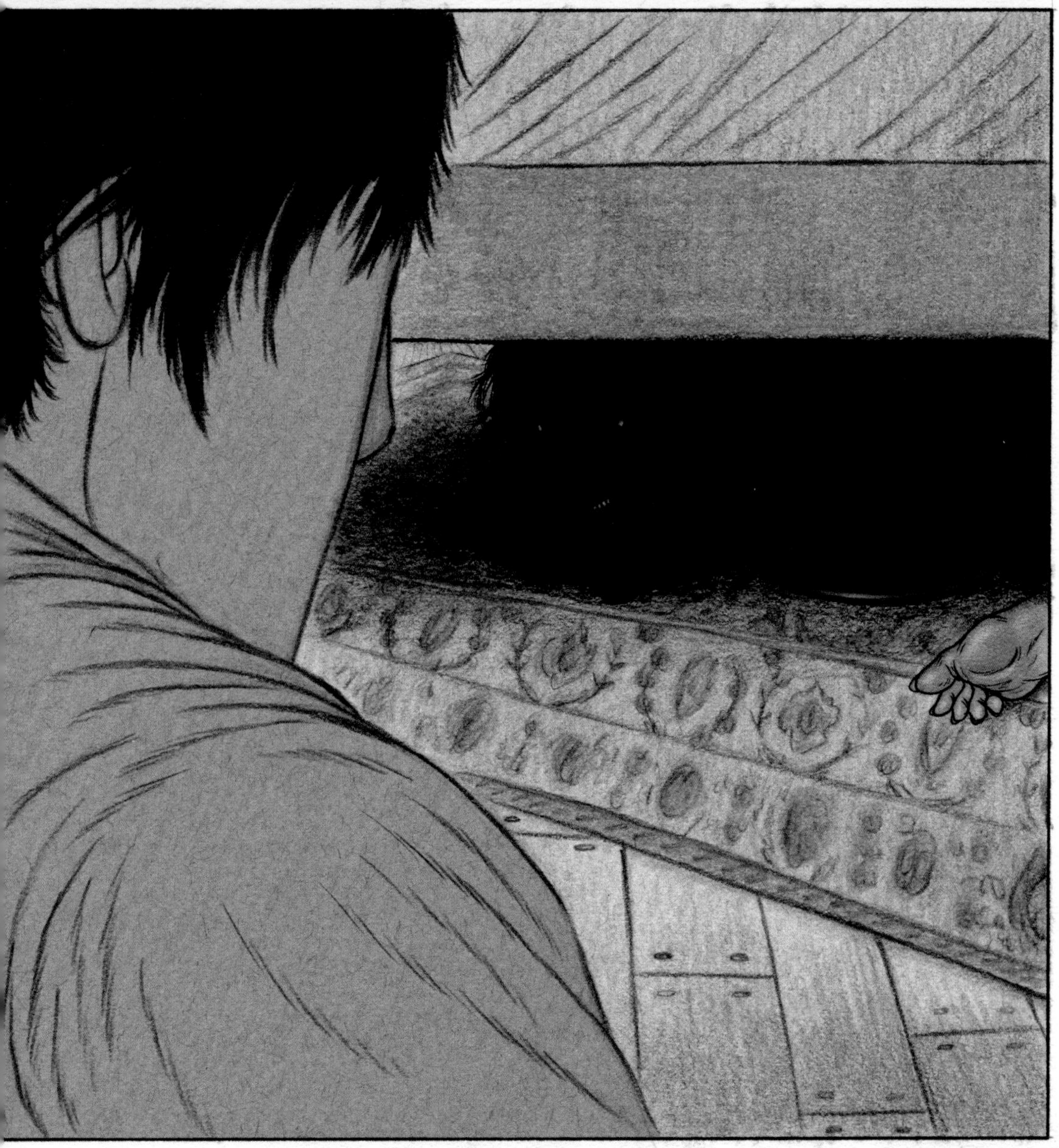

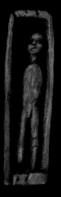

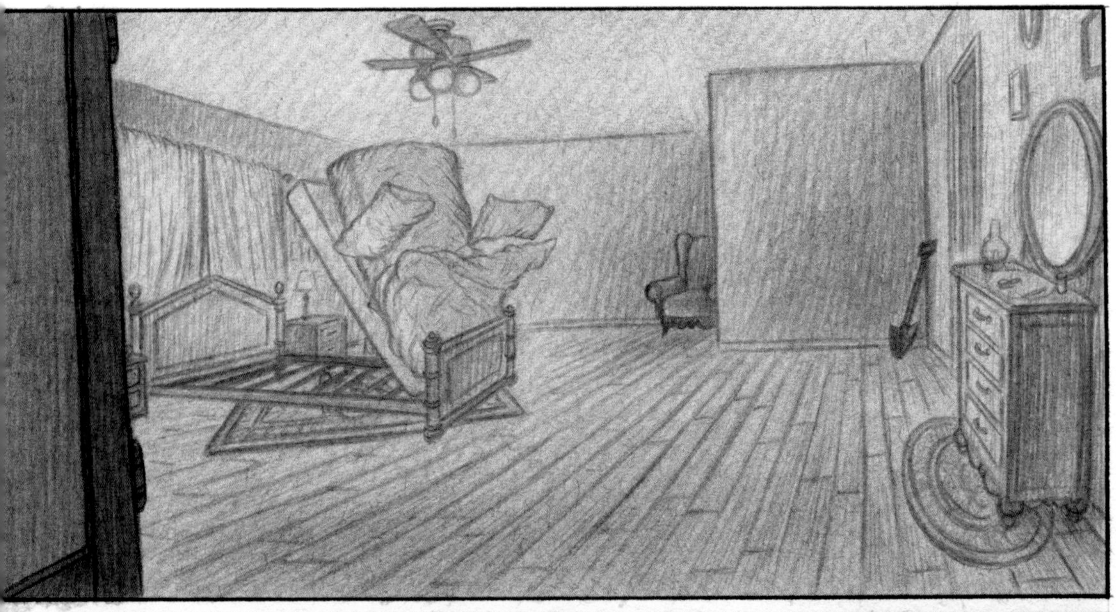

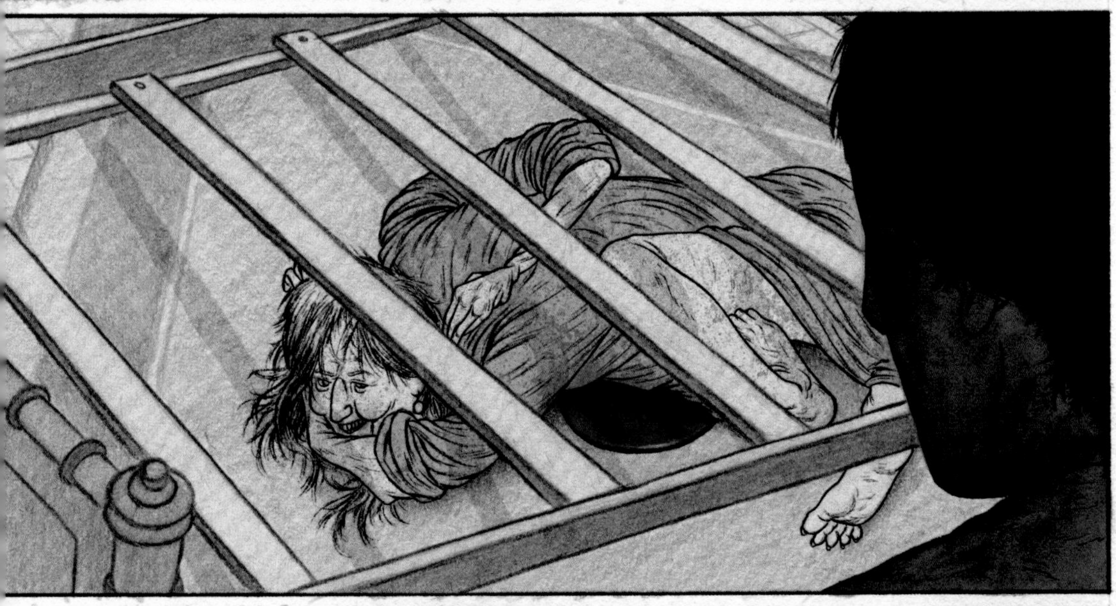

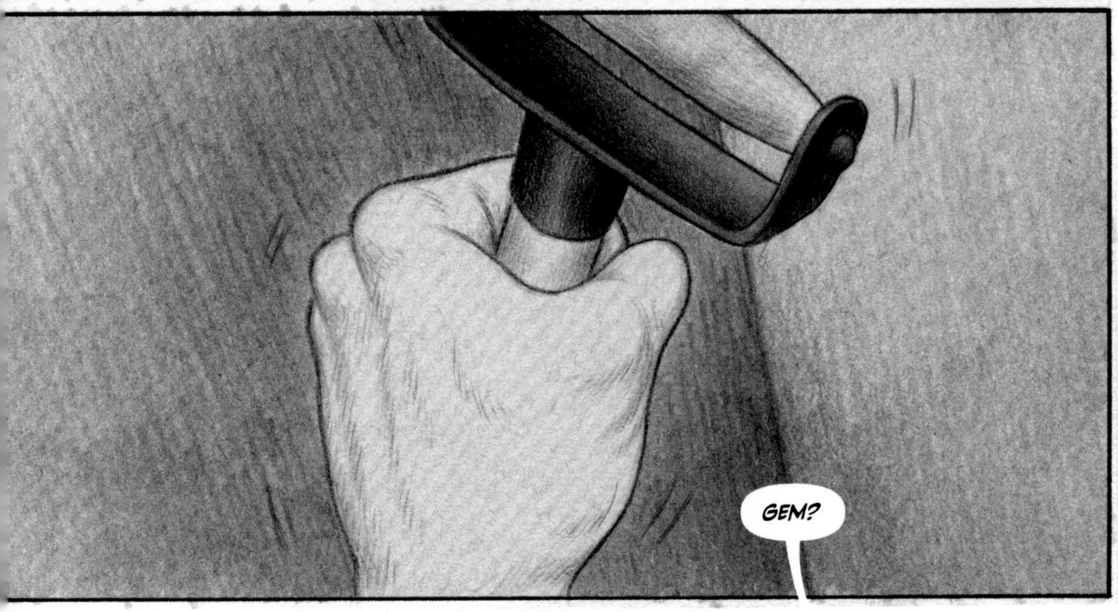
GEM?

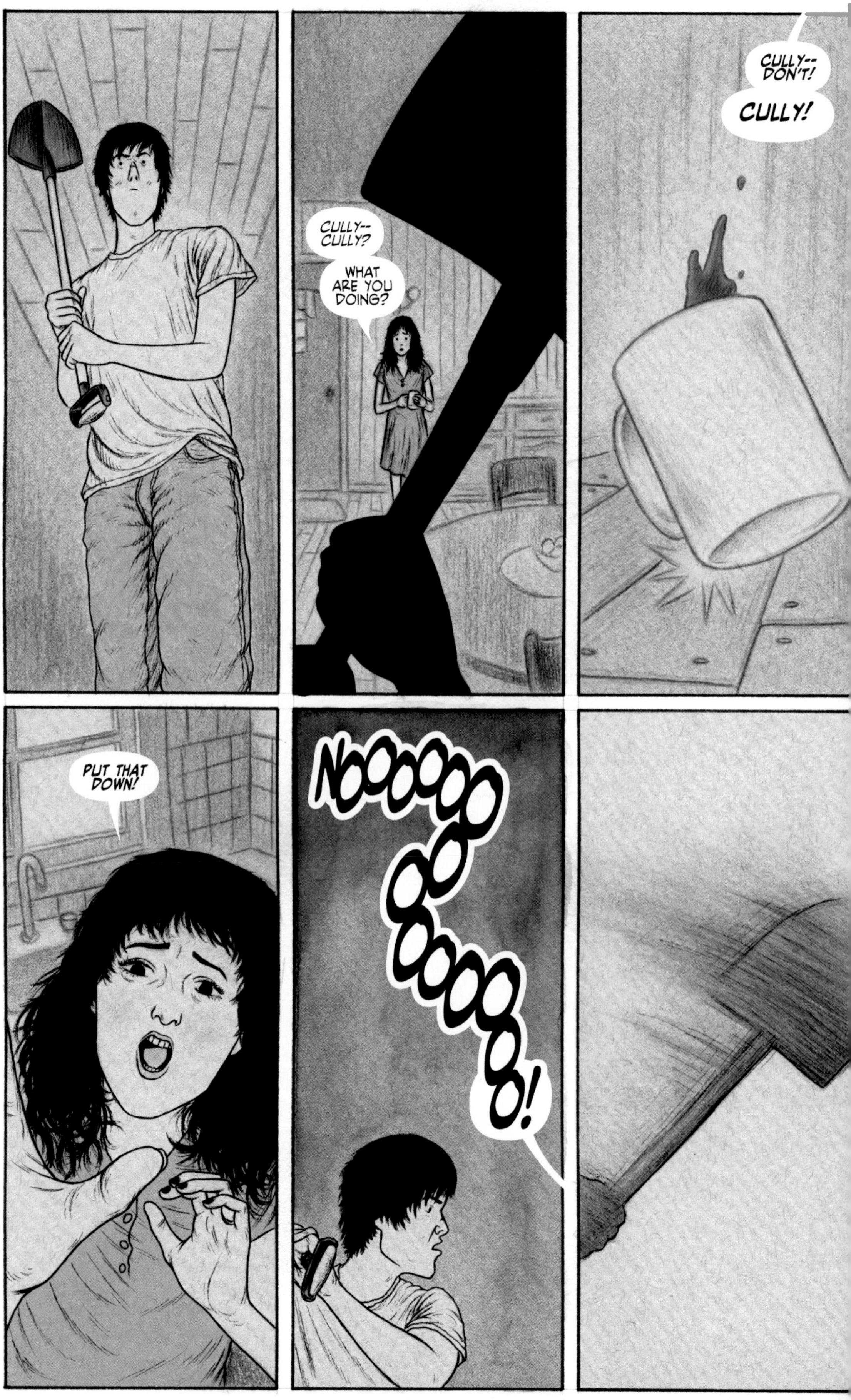
CULLY--
CULLY?
WHAT ARE YOU DOING?
CULLY--
DON'T!
CULLY!
PUT THAT DOWN!
NOOOOOOOOOOOOOOOOOOO!

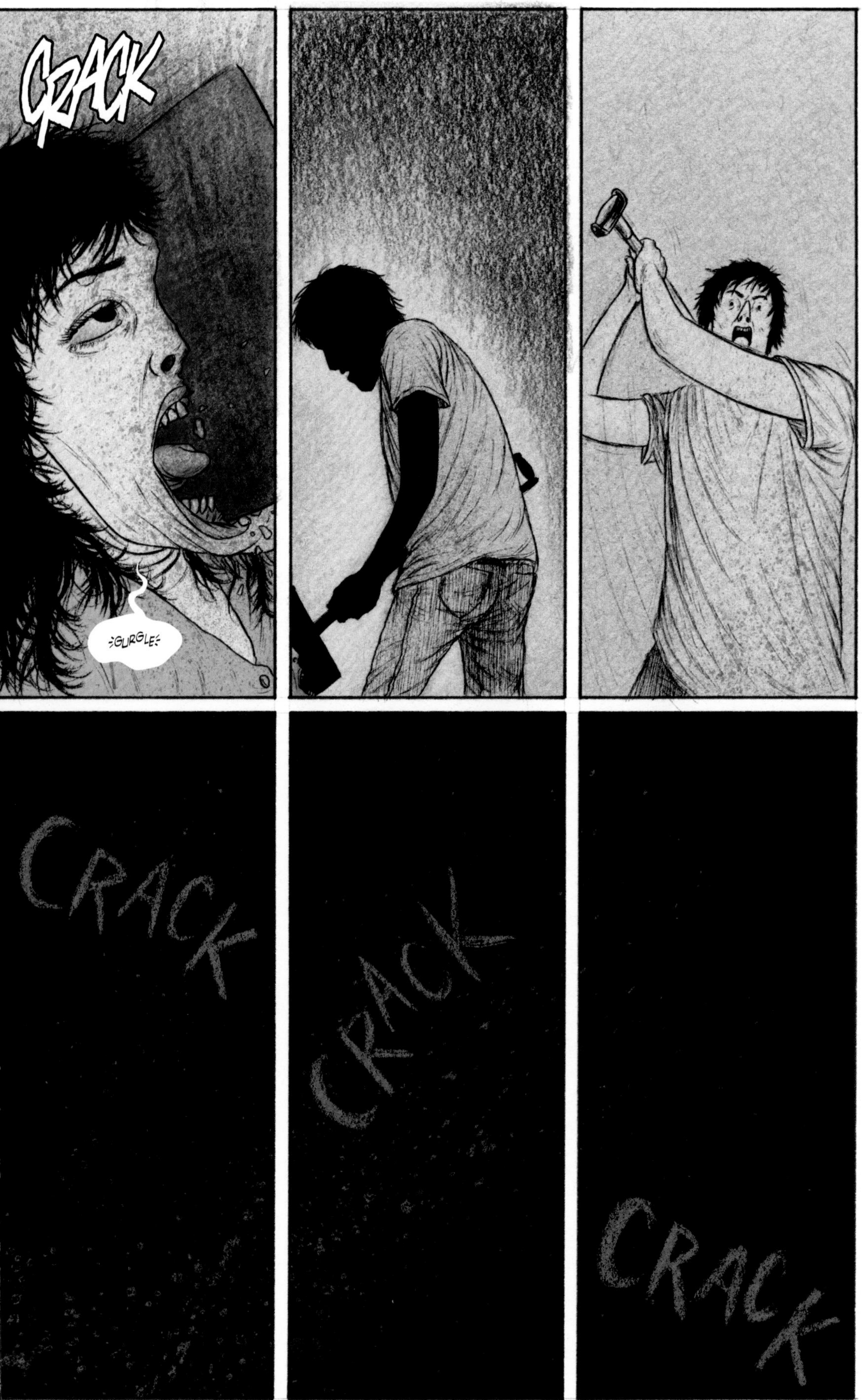
CRACK
GURGLE
CRACK
CRACK
CRACK

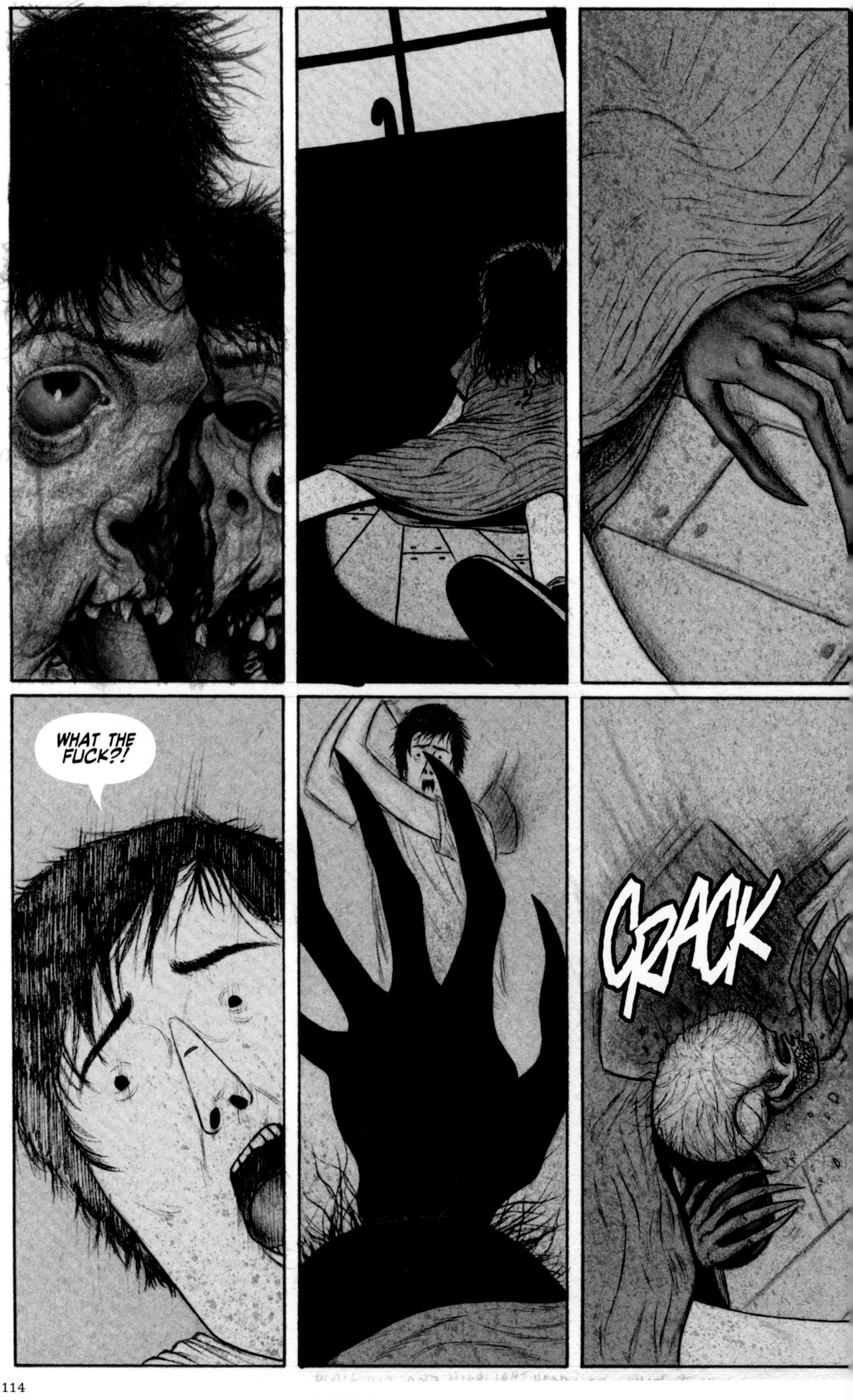
WHAT THE FUCK?!
CRACK

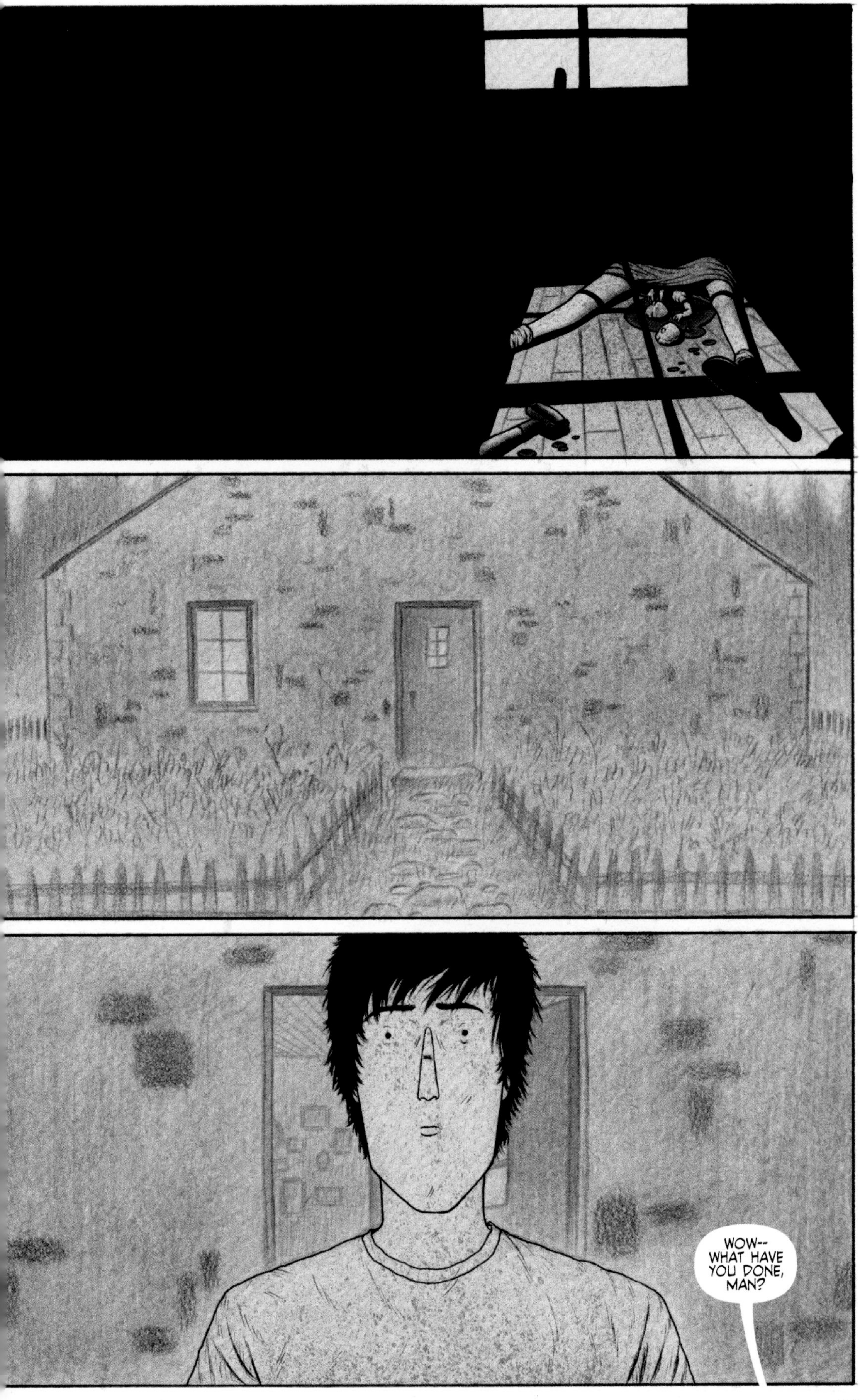
WOW-- WHAT HAVE YOU DONE, MAN?

JESUS CHRIST...HE KILLED HER... HE FUCKING DID IT, DIDN'T HE?
GOD--IT SURE APPEARS THAT WAY...*THIS IS BAD.*
THIS ISN'T PART OF THE PLAN, IS IT?
THERE IS NO PLAN. WE JUST DON'T WANT TO MAKE THIS WORSE. IT'S ALWAYS A BIGGER MESS WHEN WE TRY TO STOP IT.
HARD TO IMAGINE THAT.
OH, NOW HE'S ON THE MOVE?
KEEP SOME DISTANCE, *BUT FOLLOW HIM.*
GOD HAVE MERCY ON US ALL.

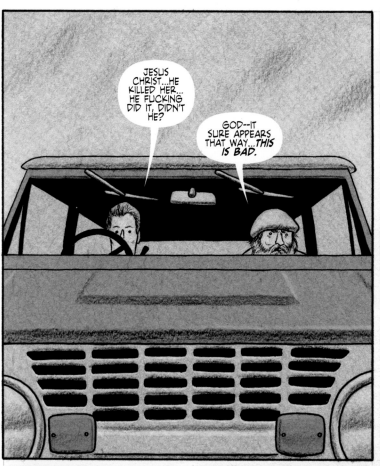

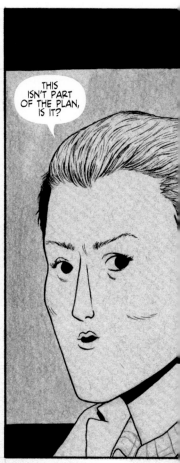

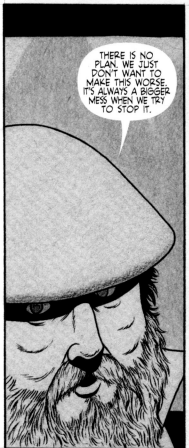

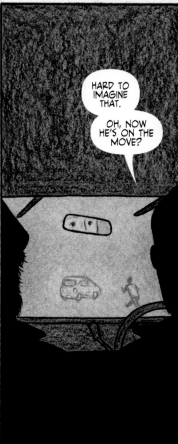

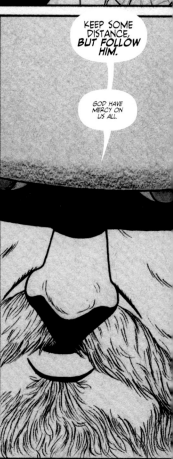

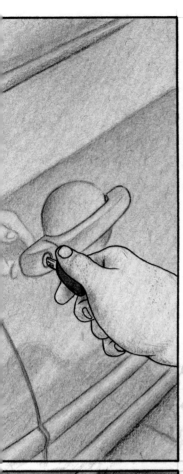

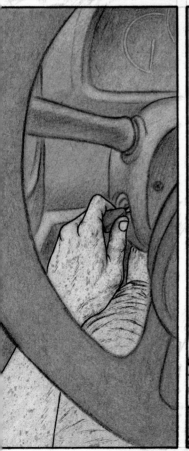

AHHHHHHH!!

WHY! WHY! WHY!

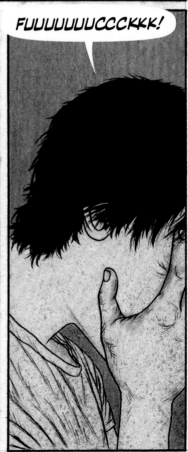

FUUUUUUUCCCKKK!

117

YOU GO BACK.

YOU GO BACK THERE. FIND YOUR ANSWERS.

UP ON THAT HILL, UP ON STORR. I KNOW IT'S A BIT OF A DRIVE, BUT IT'LL GIVE YOU A MOMENT TO GET YOUR HEAD TOGETHER.

YOU **DO** WANNA GET TO THE BOTTOM OF THIS, DON'T YA, CULLY?

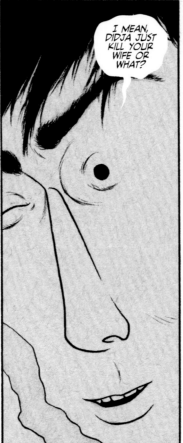

I MEAN, DIDJA JUST KILL YOUR WIFE OR WHAT?

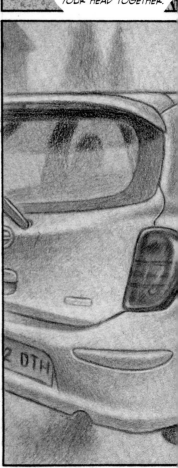

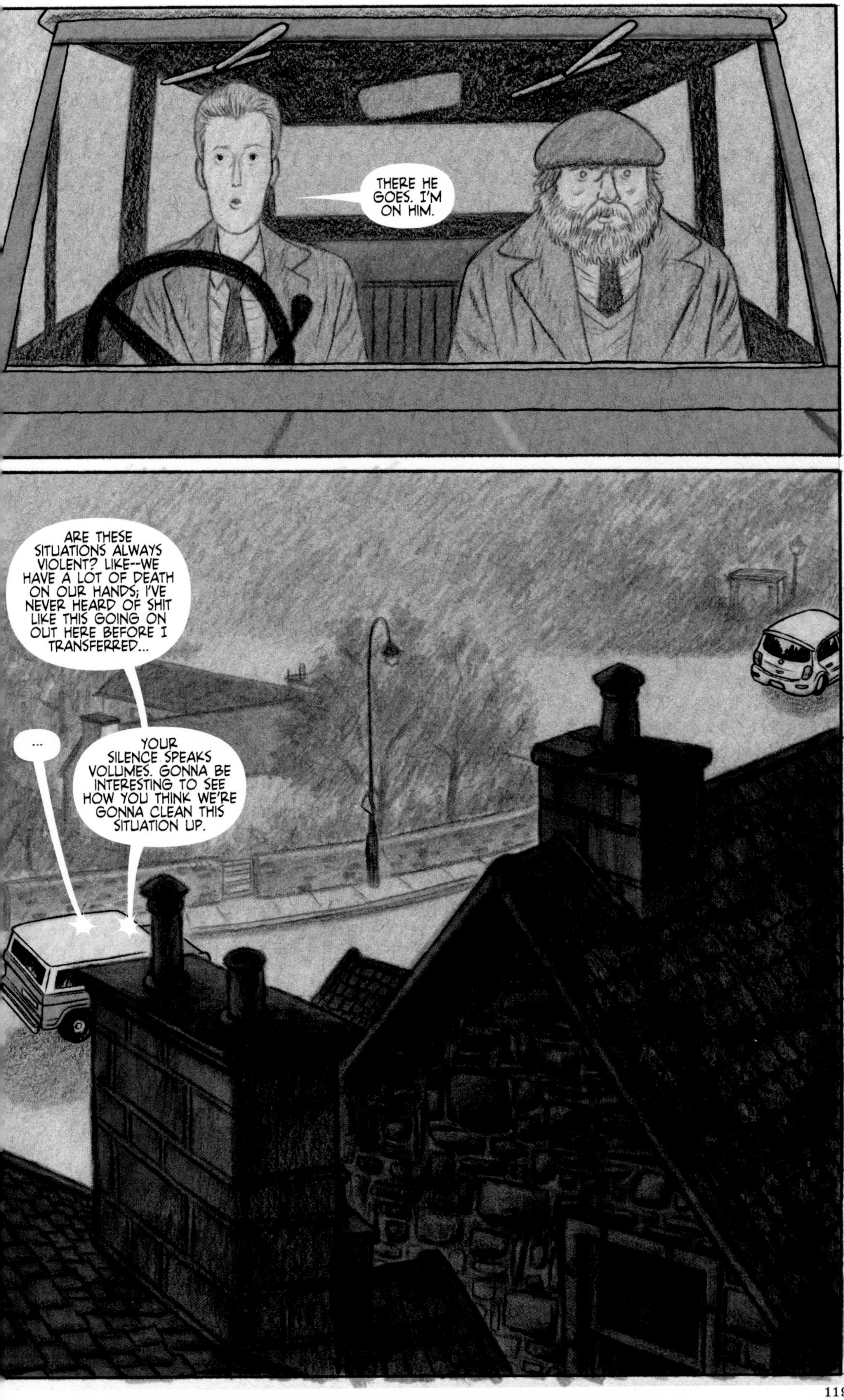
THERE HE GOES. I'M ON HIM.
ARE THESE SITUATIONS ALWAYS VIOLENT? LIKE--WE HAVE A LOT OF DEATH ON OUR HANDS; I'VE NEVER HEARD OF SHIT LIKE THIS GOING ON OUT HERE BEFORE I TRANSFERRED...
...
YOUR SILENCE SPEAKS VOLUMES. GONNA BE INTERESTING TO SEE HOW YOU THINK WE'RE GONNA CLEAN THIS SITUATION UP.

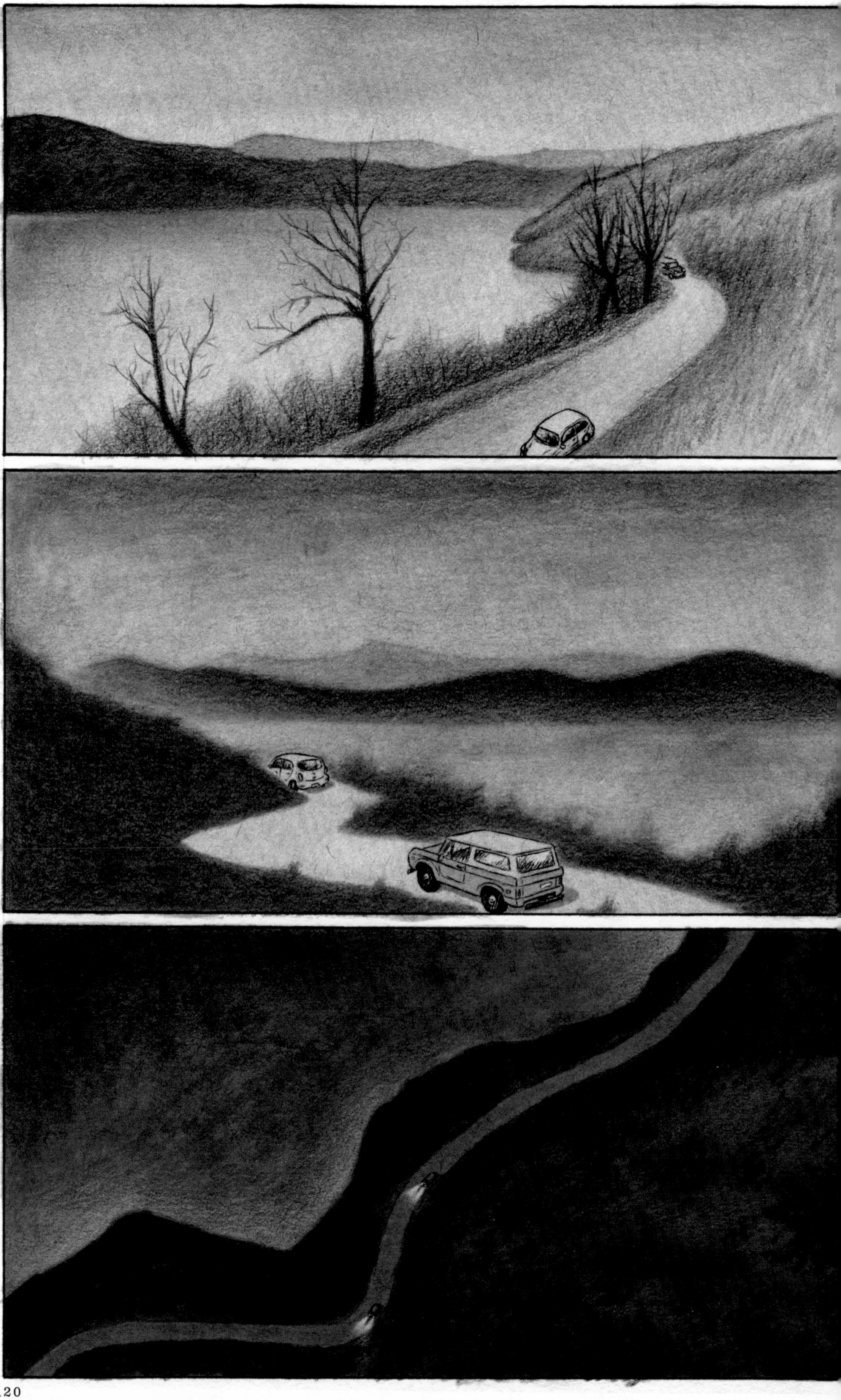

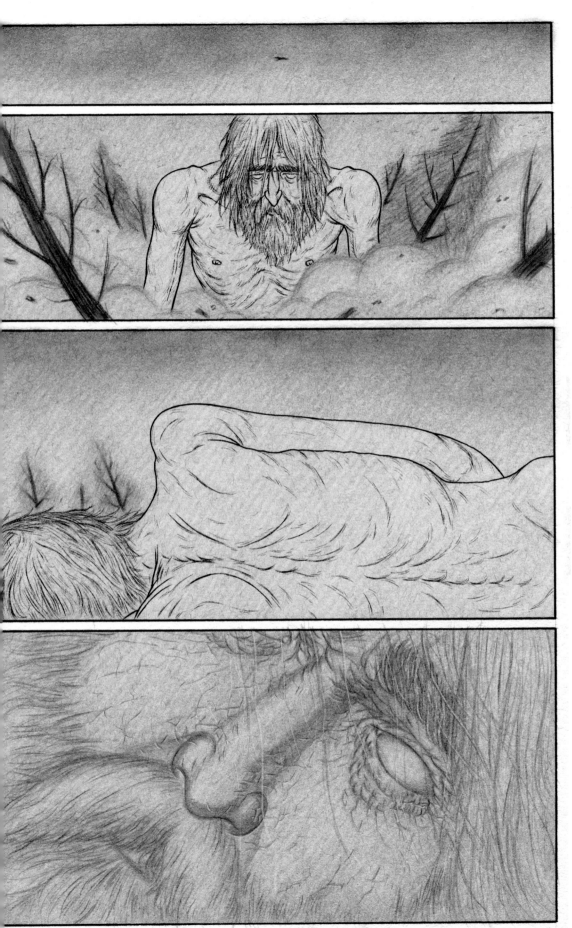

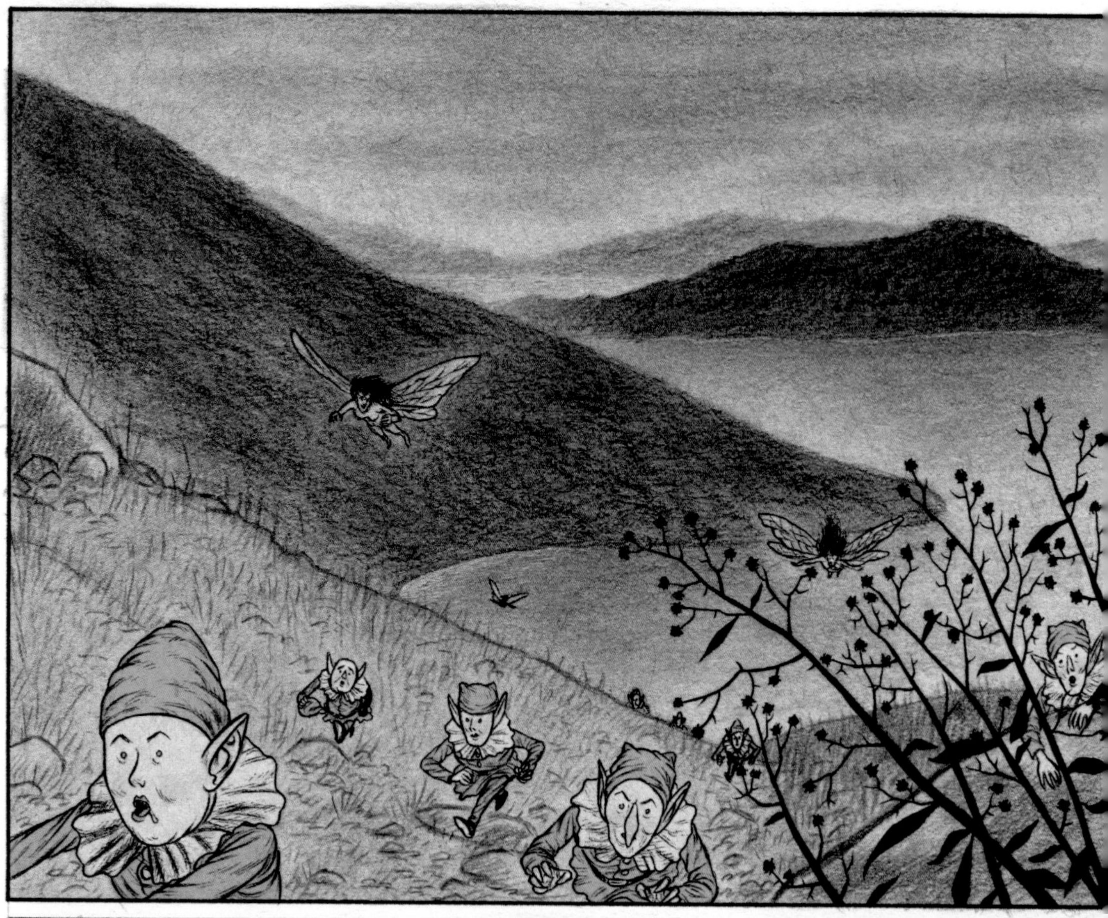

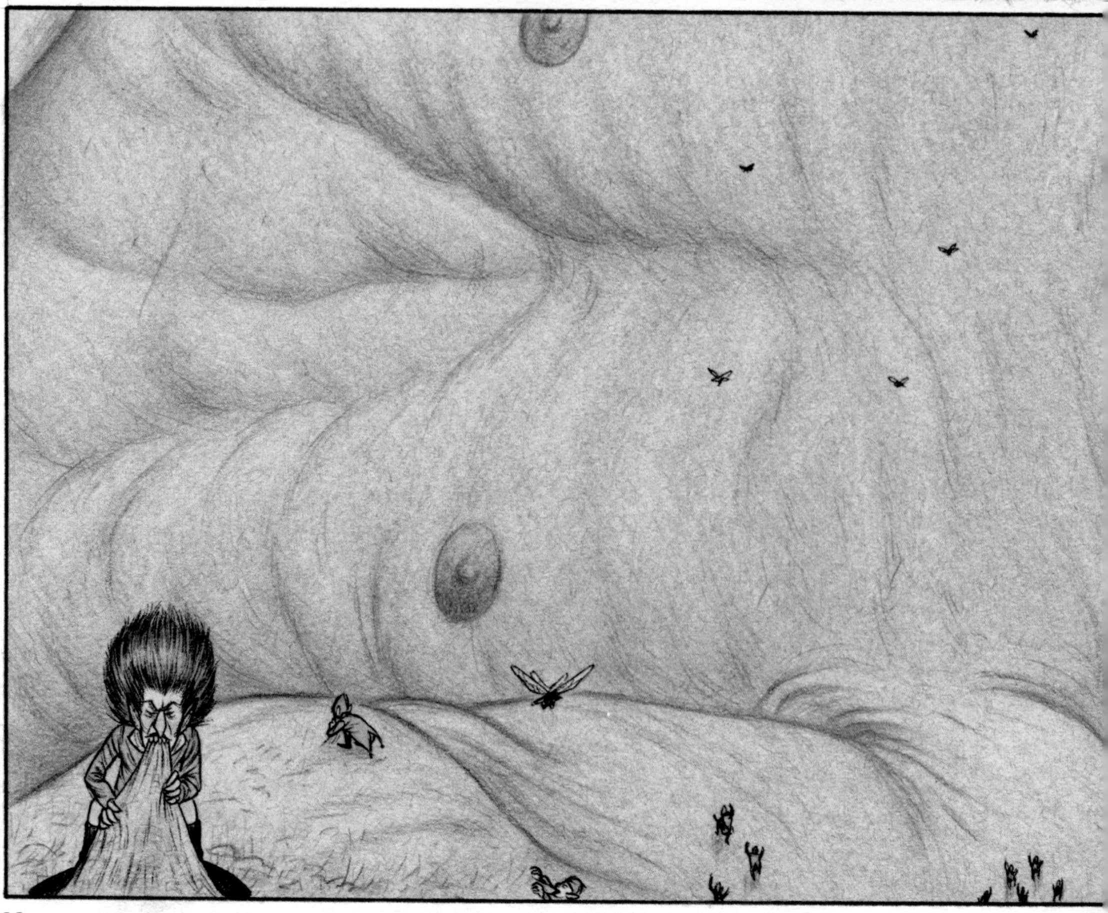

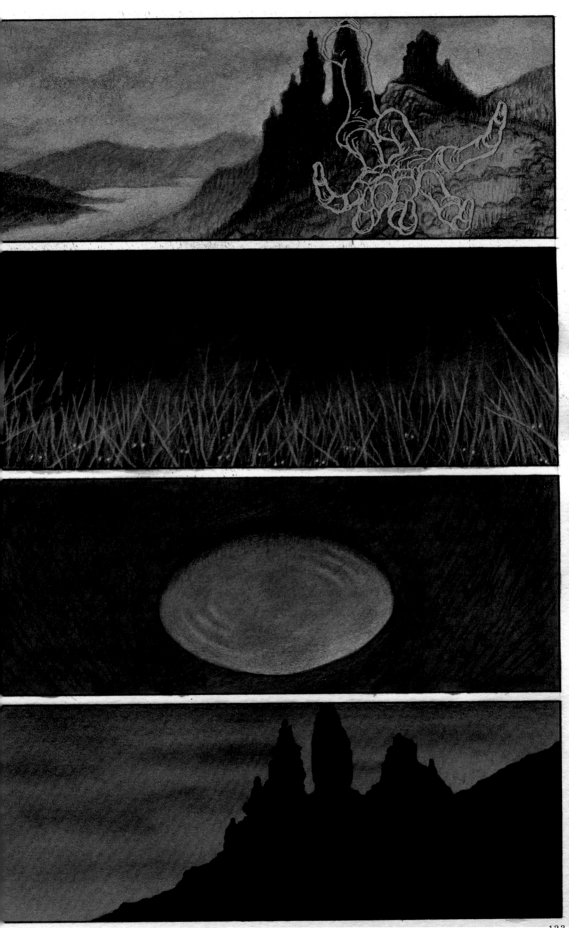

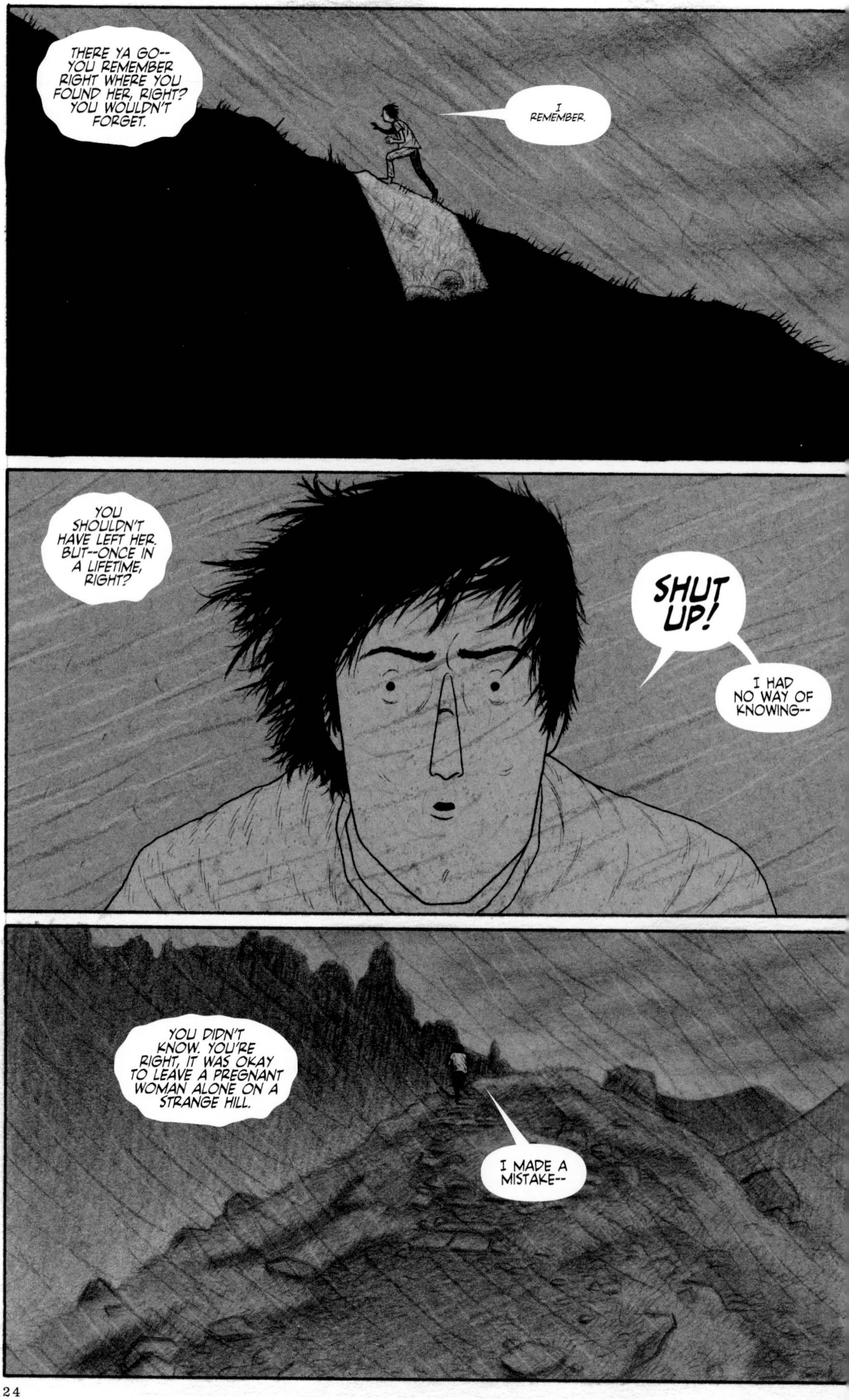
THERE YA GO-- YOU REMEMBER RIGHT WHERE YOU FOUND HER, RIGHT? YOU WOULDN'T FORGET.
I REMEMBER.
YOU SHOULDN'T HAVE LEFT HER. BUT--ONCE IN A LIFETIME, RIGHT?
SHUT UP!
I HAD NO WAY OF KNOWING--
YOU DIDN'T KNOW. YOU'RE RIGHT, IT WAS OKAY TO LEAVE A PREGNANT WOMAN ALONE ON A STRANGE HILL.
I MADE A MISTAKE--

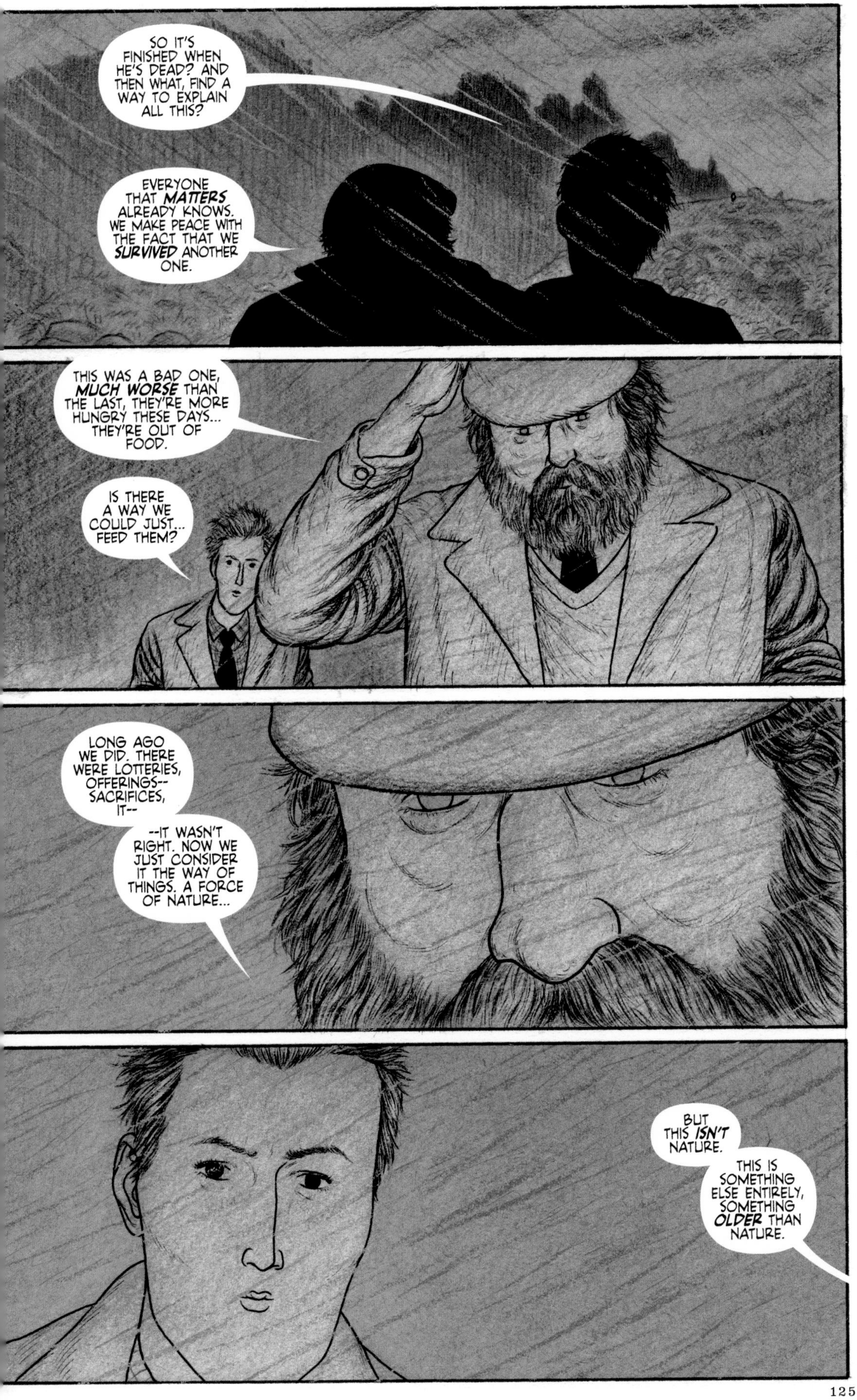
SO IT'S FINISHED WHEN HE'S DEAD? AND THEN WHAT, FIND A WAY TO EXPLAIN ALL THIS?
EVERYONE THAT MATTERS ALREADY KNOWS. WE MAKE PEACE WITH THE FACT THAT WE SURVIVED ANOTHER ONE.
THIS WAS A BAD ONE, MUCH WORSE THAN THE LAST, THEY'RE MORE HUNGRY THESE DAYS... THEY'RE OUT OF FOOD.
IS THERE A WAY WE COULD JUST... FEED THEM?
LONG AGO WE DID. THERE WERE LOTTERIES, OFFERINGS-- SACRIFICES, IT--
--IT WASN'T RIGHT. NOW WE JUST CONSIDER IT THE WAY OF THINGS. A FORCE OF NATURE...
BUT THIS ISN'T NATURE.
THIS IS SOMETHING ELSE ENTIRELY, SOMETHING OLDER THAN NATURE.

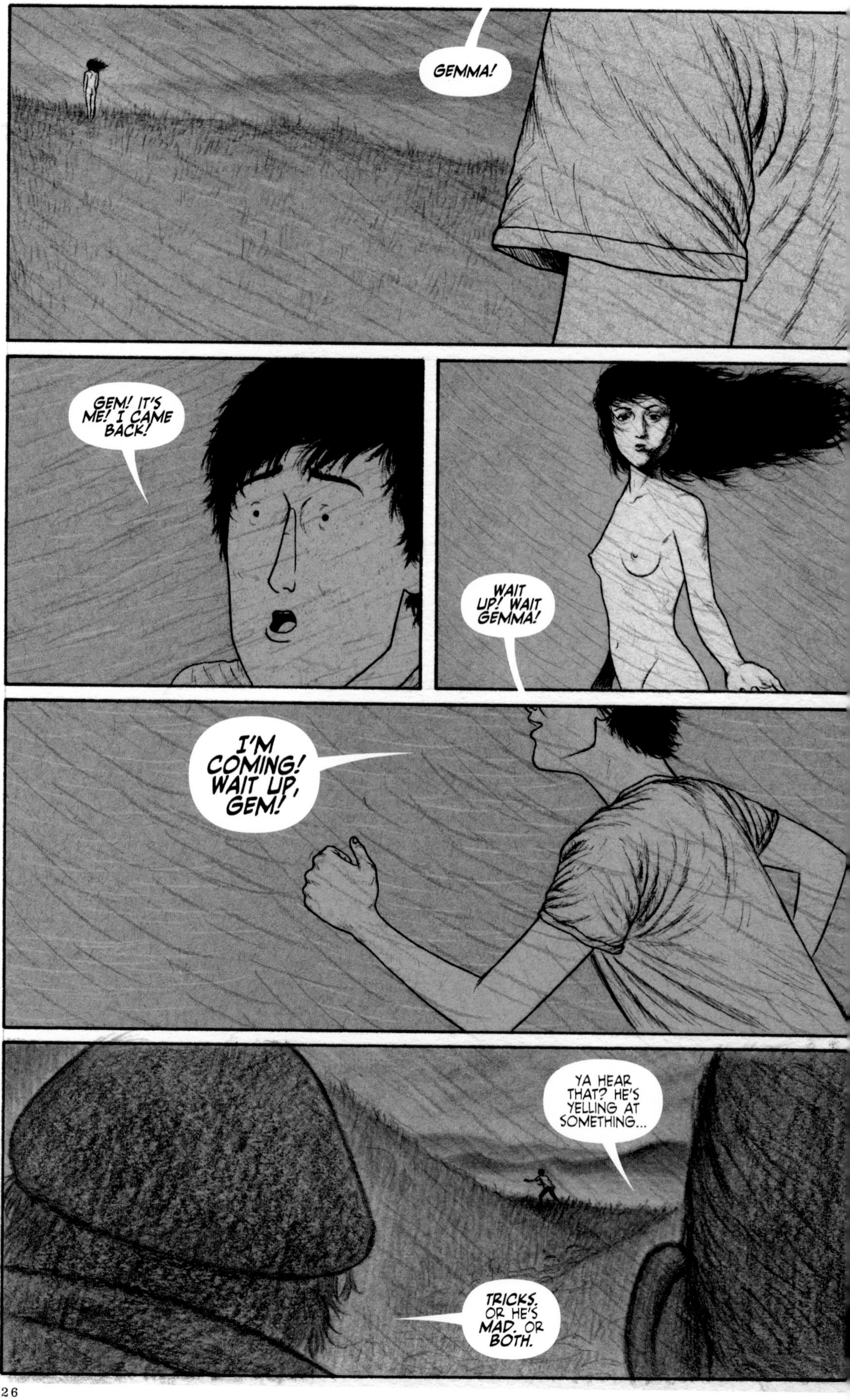
GEMMA!
GEM! IT'S ME! I CAME BACK!
WAIT UP! WAIT GEMMA!
I'M COMING! WAIT UP, GEM!
YA HEAR THAT? HE'S YELLING AT SOMETHING...
TRICKS. OR HE'S MAD. OR BOTH.

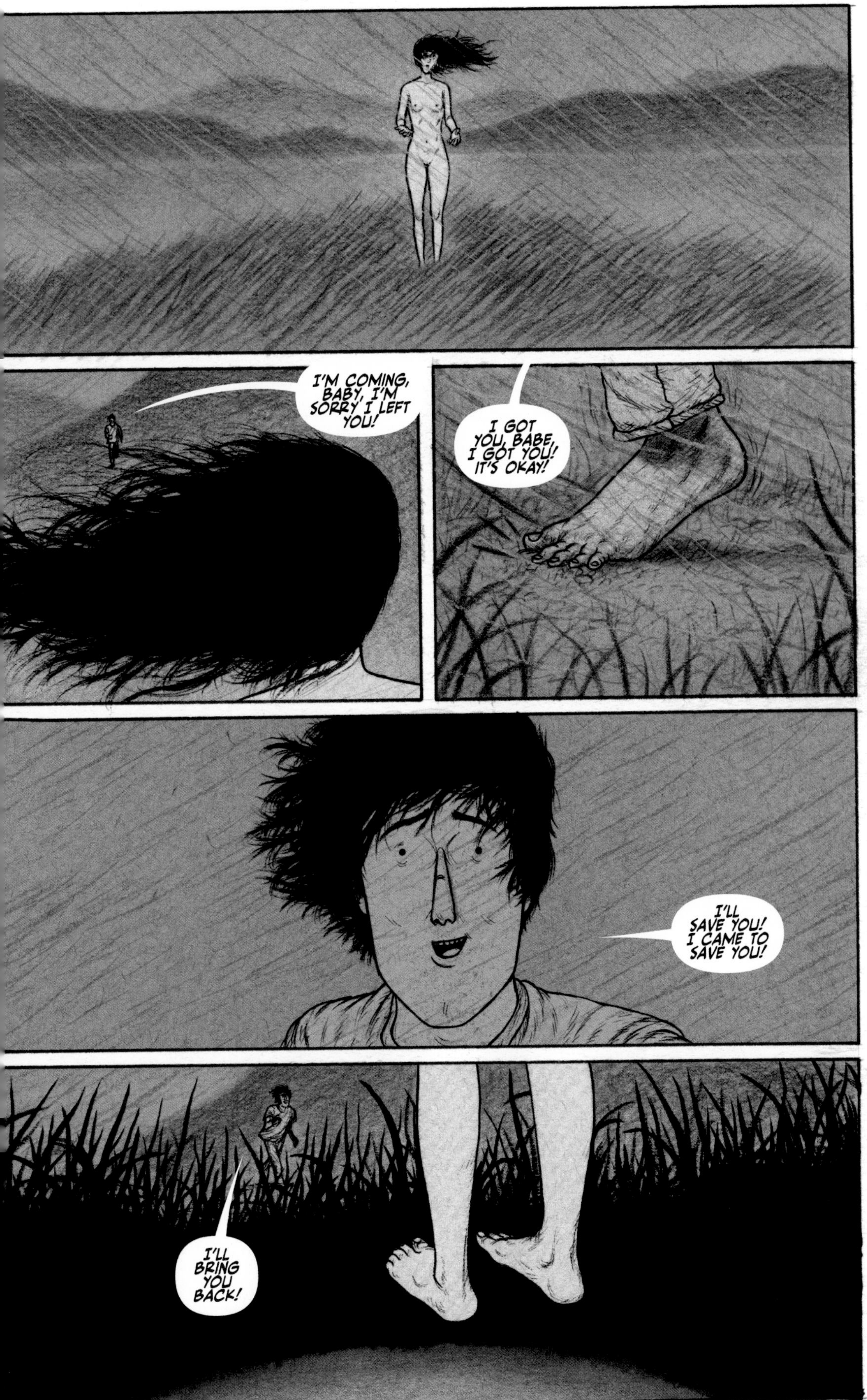
I'M COMING, BABY, I'M SORRY I LEFT YOU!
I GOT YOU, BABE, I GOT YOU! IT'S OKAY!
I'LL SAVE YOU! I CAME TO SAVE YOU!
I'LL BRING YOU BACK!

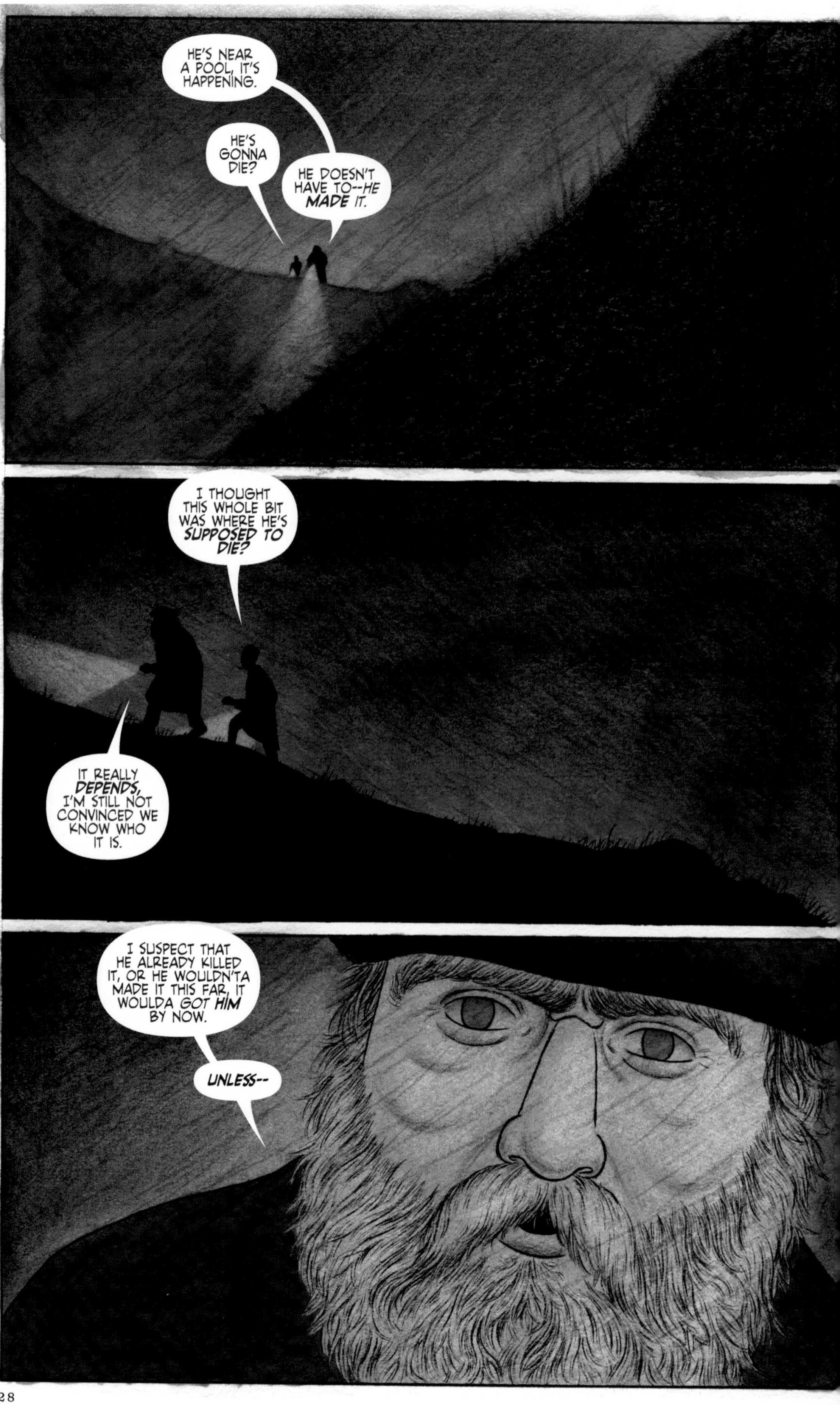

HE'S NEAR A POOL, IT'S HAPPENING.
HE'S GONNA DIE?
HE DOESN'T HAVE TO--*HE MADE* IT.
I THOUGHT THIS WHOLE BIT WAS WHERE HE'S *SUPPOSED TO DIE?*
IT REALLY *DEPENDS,* I'M STILL NOT CONVINCED WE KNOW WHO IT IS.
I SUSPECT THAT HE ALREADY KILLED IT, OR HE WOULDN'TA MADE IT THIS FAR, IT WOULDA *GOT HIM* BY NOW.
UNLESS--

GEM!
GEM!
NOOOOOOO!

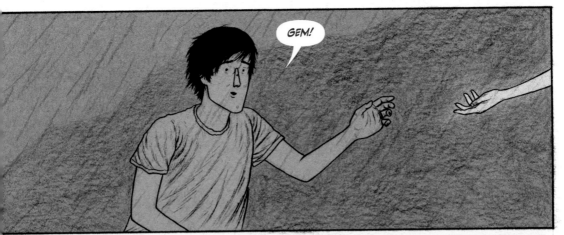

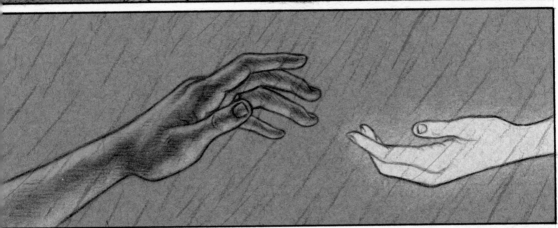

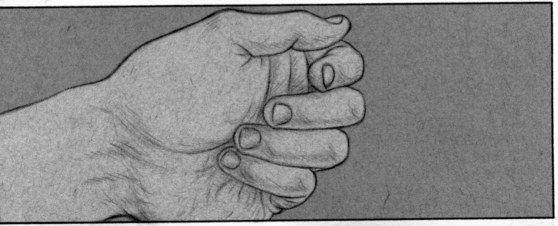

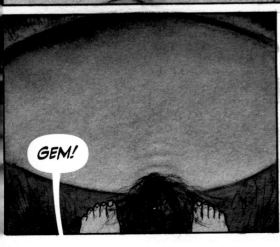

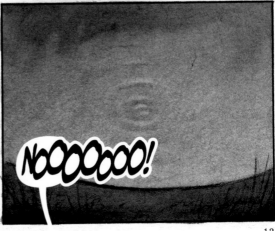

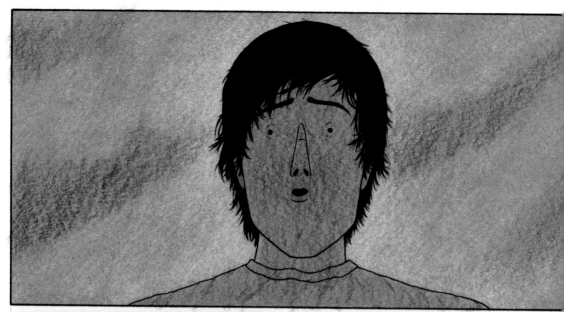

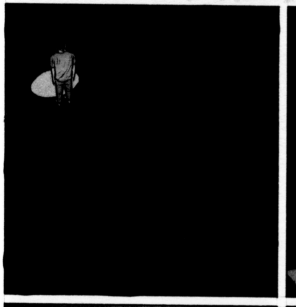

BACK AWAY FROM THAT POOL, MATE. YA DON'T NEED TA BE DOIN' THIS!

SHE'S IN THERE.

SHE'S *GONE*, MATE. YER SAFE NOW.

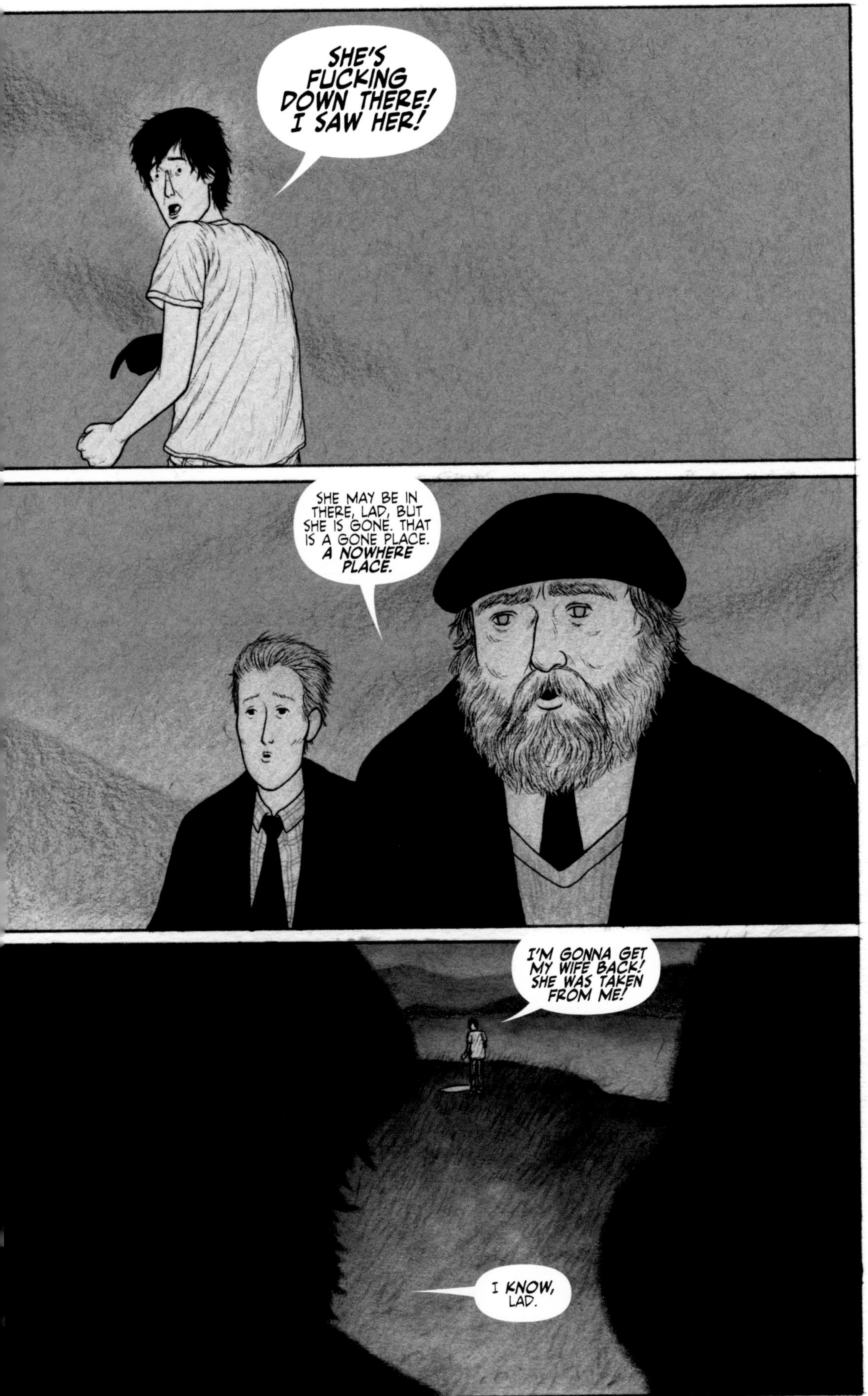
SHE'S FUCKING DOWN THERE! I SAW HER!
SHE MAY BE IN THERE, LAD, BUT SHE IS GONE. THAT IS A GONE PLACE. A NOWHERE PLACE.
I'M GONNA GET MY WIFE BACK! SHE WAS TAKEN FROM ME!
I KNOW, LAD.

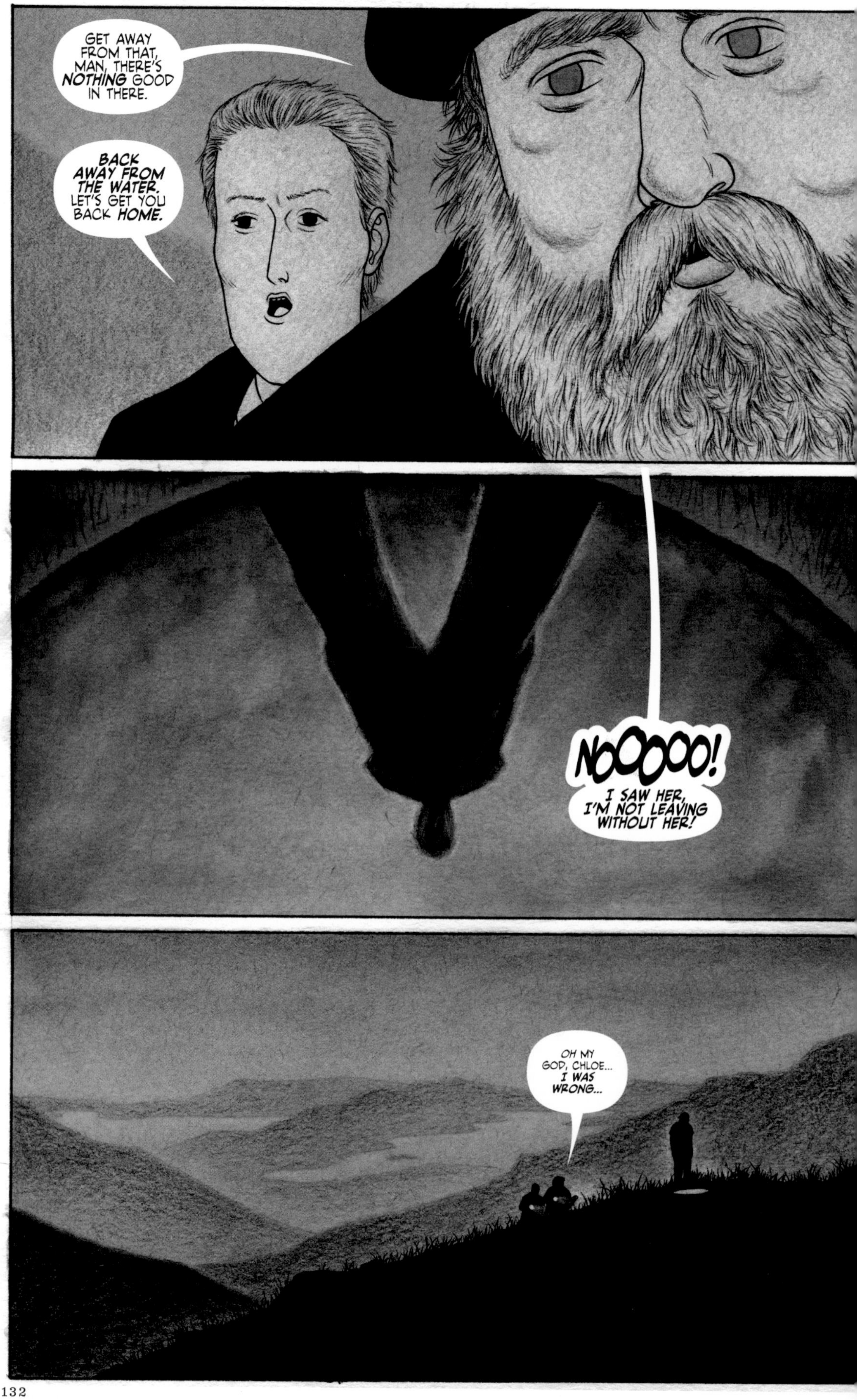
GET AWAY FROM THAT, MAN, THERE'S NOTHING GOOD IN THERE.
BACK AWAY FROM THE WATER. LET'S GET YOU BACK HOME.
NOOOOO!
I SAW HER, I'M NOT LEAVING WITHOUT HER!
OH MY GOD, CHLOE... I WAS WRONG...

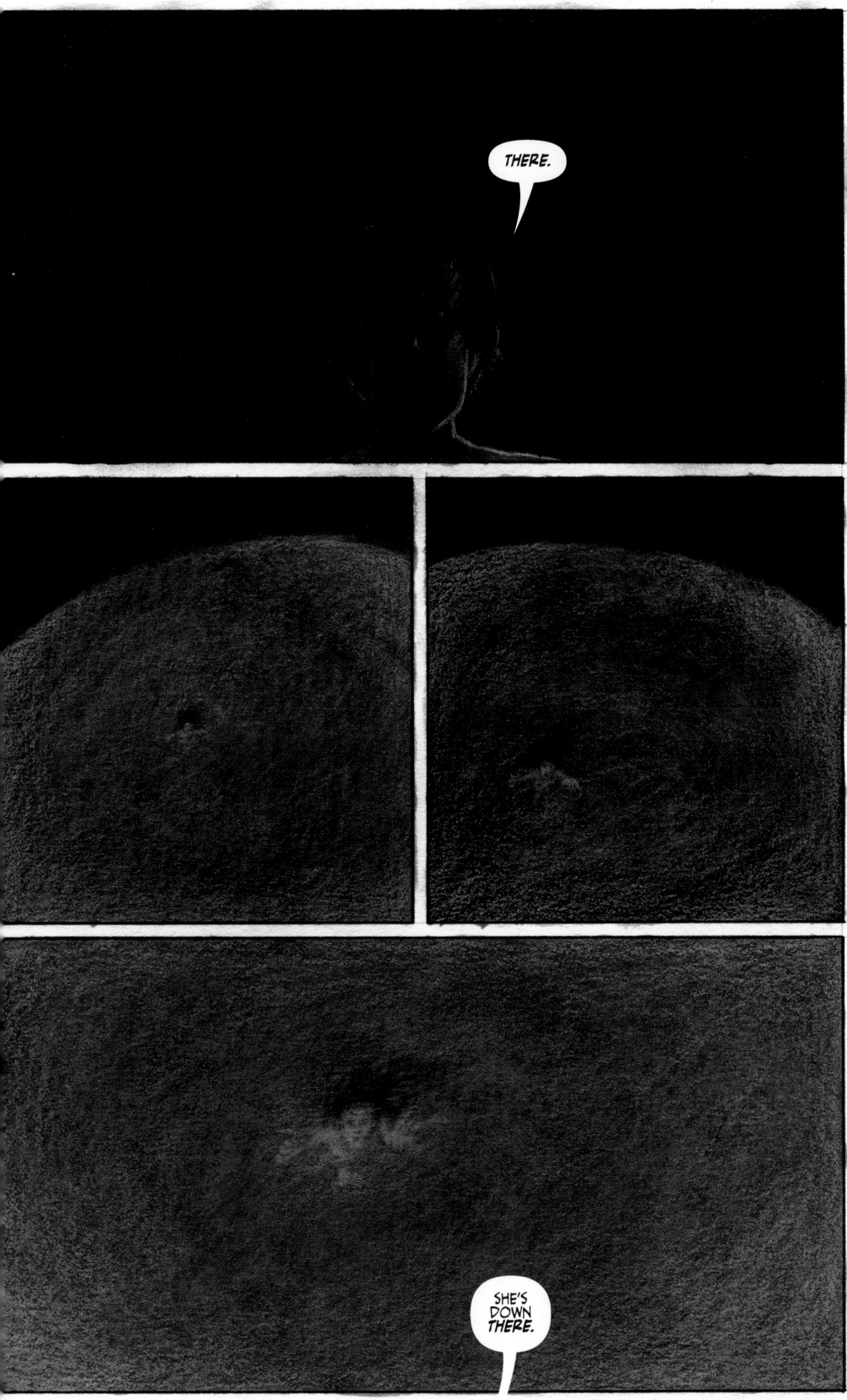
THERE.
SHE'S DOWN THERE.

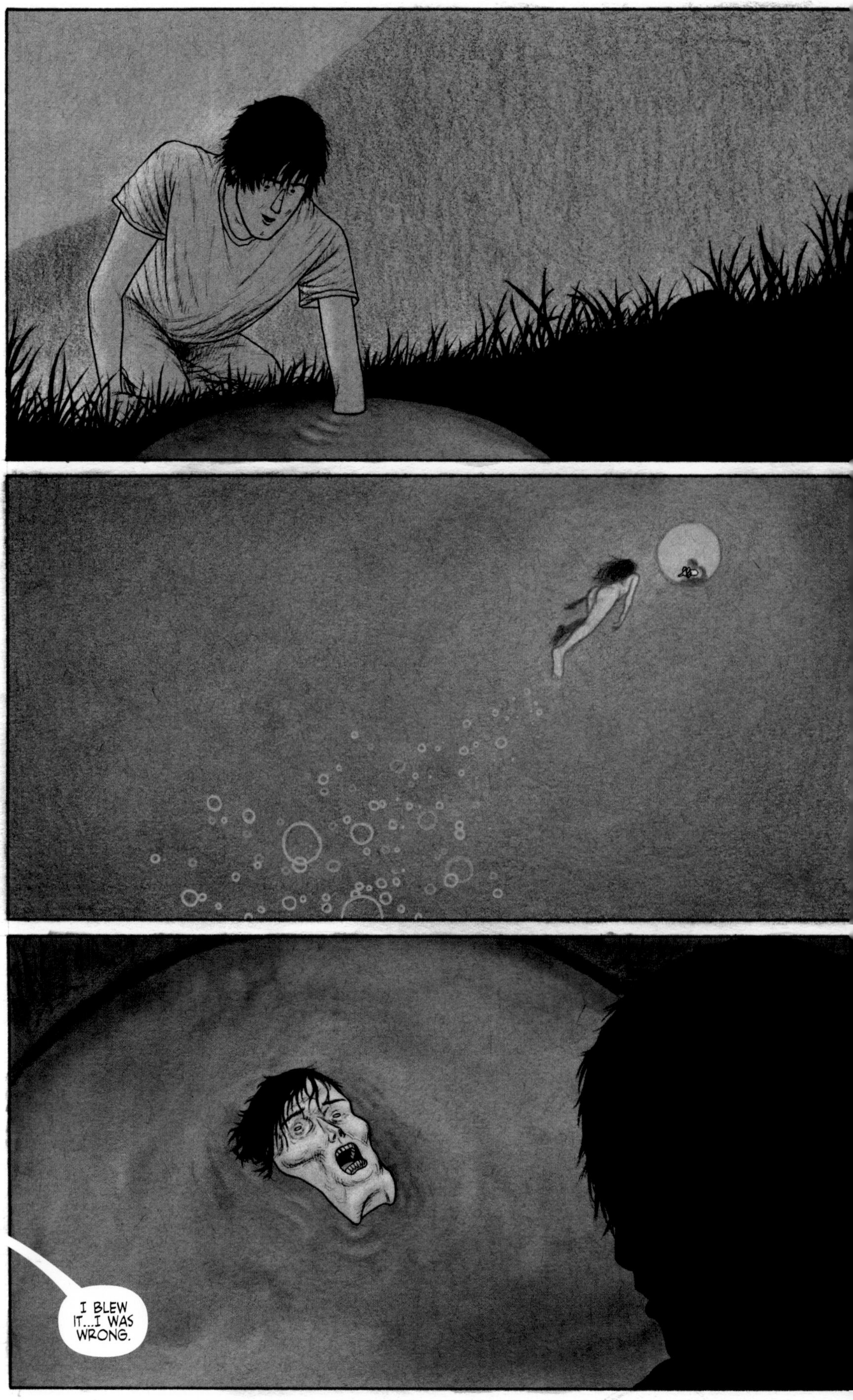
I BLEW IT...I WAS WRONG.

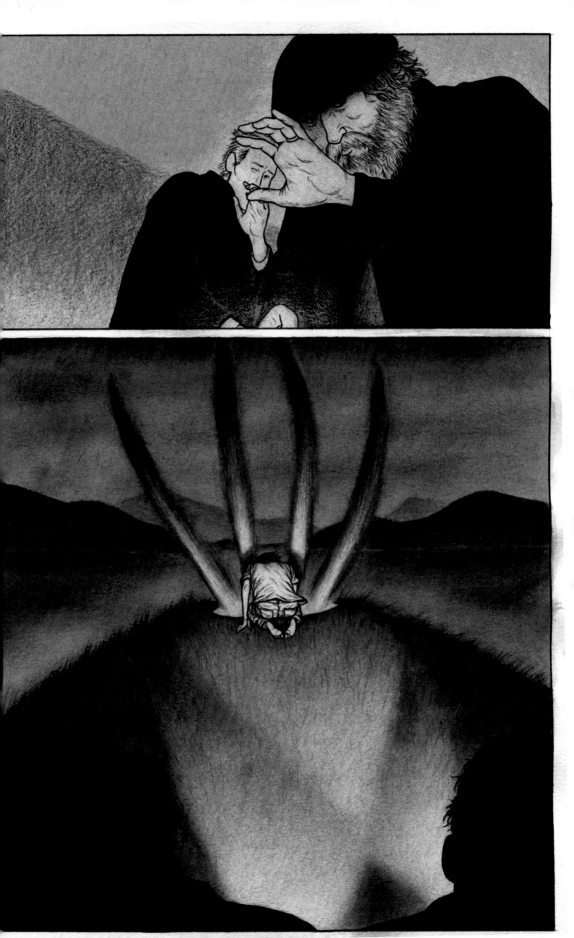

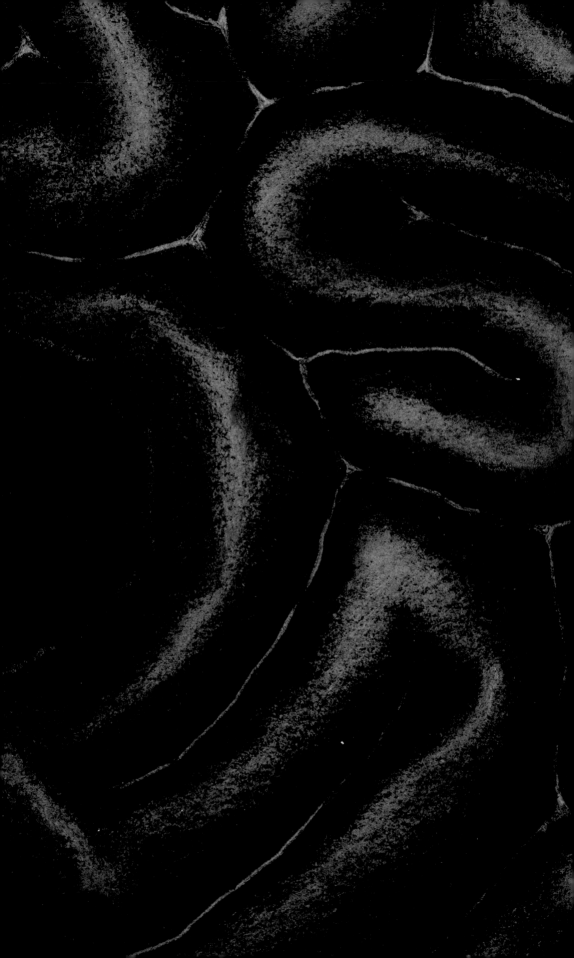

AFTERWORD

Double Walker is (naturally) a story of my personal fears.
Most great horror begins with the writer figuring out
what frightens them and it grows from there, in hopes
that the audience shares the same anxieties. I just knew
I wanted to explore identity, projection, and neurosis.
Having recently visited Storr, I became convinced that
something within me had changed. While this change
wasn't as dramatic as those experienced by Cully and
Gemma, in my meditations on this concept I came to
realize that it was my truth. Every moment serves to
irrevocably alter you. As we learn and grow, the "me"
of yesterday becomes a discarded husk; in this way we
become a strange new version of the thing left behind.

I can only hope that this iteration of me is better than the
ones that came before.

Thank you for taking the time to read this. Noah and I are
very proud to have done it again.

M.

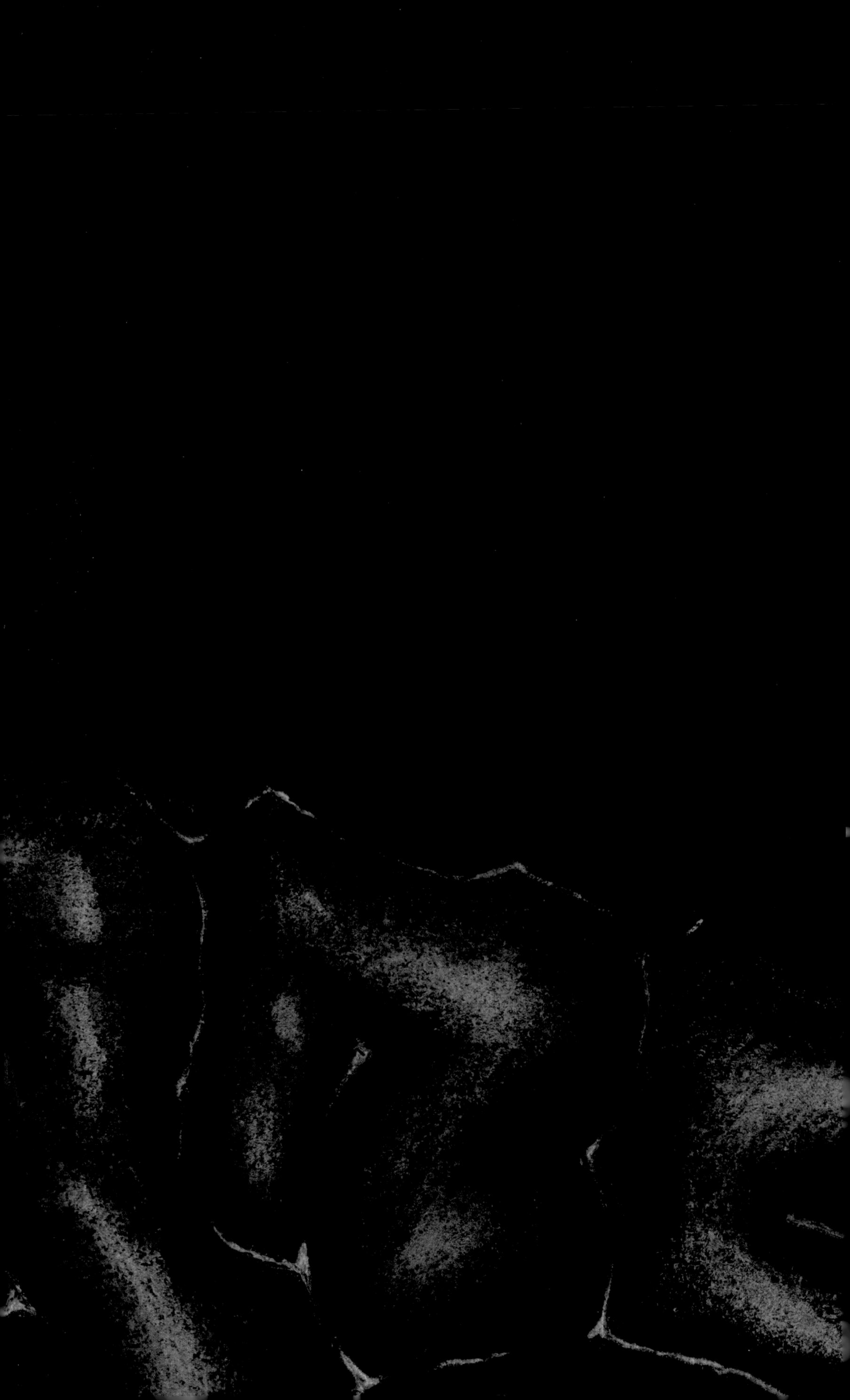

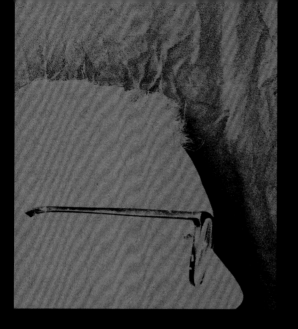

MICHAEL W. CONRAD is currently cowriting *Wonder Woman* and *Midnighter* for DC Comics. Michael continues to self-publish and document his existence through Mystery School Comics Group.

Tremor Dose, Michael's first collaboration with Noah Bailey, remains available through Comixology Originals.

Twitter/IG: @michaelwconrad
Web: www.mwconrad.com

Michael would like to thank Becky Cloonan for her support and partnership, Shelly Bond for being a great friend and mentor, and Noah Bailey for believing in what we do.

NOAH BAILEY is an illustrator and cartoonist from the Midwest.

Twitter: @boyishdeath
IG: @boyishdeathtribe

Noah would like to thank Michael for his magick. Becky for ALL of her help. Dad for his inexhaustible support and encouragement. Kyle, Tim, and Ryan for their friendship and brotherhood. Maggie for her love, patience, and kindness. Orson Welles, Charles Addams, Alex Toth, Gustaf Tenggren, and Richard Corben.

TAYLOR ESPOSITO is a comic book lettering professional, owner of Ghost Glyph Studios, and teacher at the legendary Kubert School. A former staff letterer at DC and production artist at Marvel.

Twitter: @taylorespo and @ghostglyph
IG: @ghostglyph

KYLE ARENDS is a graphic designer and musician living in Chicago.

For inquiries, please email kyle_arends@yahoo.com with the subject "I Promise This Isn't Spam."

COMIXOLOGY COMES TO DARK HORSE BOOKS!

AFTERLIFT
Chip Zdarsky, Jason Loo, Paris Alleyne, Aditya Bidikar
US $19.99/CAN $25.99
ISBN: 978-1-50672-440-9

BREAKLANDS
Justin Jordan, Tyasseta, Sarah Stern
US $19.99/CAN $25.99
ISBN: 978-1-50672-441-6

YOUTH
Curt Pires, Alex Diotto, Dee Cunniffe
US $19.99/CAN $25.99
ISBN: 978-1-50672-461-4

THE BLACK GHOST
Monica Gallagher, Alex Segura, Marco Finnegan, George Kambadai, Ellie Wright
US $19.99/CAN $25.99
ISBN: 978-1-50672-446-1

THE PRIDE OMNIBUS
Joe Glass, Cem Iroz, Hector Barros, Jacopo Camagni, Ryan Cody, Mark Dale, and others
US $29.99/CAN $39.99
ISBN: 978-1-50672-447-8

STONE STAR VOLUME 1: FIGHT OR FLIGHT
Jim Zub, Max Dunbar, Espen Grundetjern
US $19.99/CAN $25.99
ISBN: 978-1-50672-458-4

LOST ON PLANET EARTH
Magdalene Visaggio, Claudia Aguirre
US $19.99/CAN $25.99
ISBN: 978-1-50672-456-0

DELVER
MK Reed, Spike C. Trotman, Clive Hawken
US $19.99/CAN $25.99
ISBN: 978-1-50672-452-2

DRACULA: SON OF THE DRAGON
Mark Sable, Salgood Sam
US $19.99/CAN $25.99
ISBN: 978-1-50672-442-3

TREMOR DOSE
Michael Conrad, Noah Bailey
US $19.99/CAN $25.99
ISBN: 978-1-50672-460-7

THE DARK
Mark Sable, Kristian Donaldson, Lee Loughridge
US $19.99/CAN $25.99
ISBN: 978-1-50672-459-1

CREMA
Johnnie Christmas, Dante Luiz, Ryan Ferrier
US $19.99/CAN $25.99
ISBN: 978-1-50672-603-8

SNOW ANGELS VOLUME 1
Jeff Lemire, Jock
US $19.99/CAN $25.99
ISBN: 978-1-50672-648-9

SNOW ANGELS VOLUME 2
Jeff Lemire, Jock
US $19.99/CAN $25.99
ISBN: 978-1-50672-649-6

THE ALL-NIGHTER
Chip Zdarsky, Jason Loo, Paris Aditya
US $19.99/CAN $25.99
ISBN: 978-1-50672-804-9

ADORA AND THE DISTANCE
Marc Bernardin, Ariela Kristantina, Jessica Kholinne
US $14.99/CAN $19.99
ISBN: 978-1-50672-450-8

WE ONLY KILL EACH OTHER
Stephanie Phillips, Peter Krause, Ellie Wright
US $19.99/CAN $25.99
ISBN: 978-1-50672-808-7

THE STONE KING
Kel McDonald, Tyler Crook
US $19.99/CAN $25.99
ISBN: 978-1-50672-448-5

LIEBESTRASSE
Greg Lockard, Tim Fish, Hector Barros
US $19.99/CAN $25.99
ISBN: 978-1-50672-455-3

EDEN
Matt Arnold, Riccardo Burchielli
US $22.99/CAN $29.99
ISBN: 978-1-50673-090-5

ASTONISHING TIMES
Frank Barbiere with Arris Quinones, Ruairi Coleman, Lauren Affe, Taylor Esposito
US $22.99/CAN $29.99
ISBN: 978-1-50673-083-7

WE HAVE DEMONS
Scott Snyder, Greg Capullo
US $19.99/CAN $25.99
ISBN: 978-1-50672-833-9

EDGEWORLD
Chuck Austen, Patrick Olliffe
US $19.99/CAN $25.99
ISBN: 978-1-50672-834-6

ISBN 978-1-50672-808-7 / $19.99

ISBN 978-1-50672-833-9 / $19.99

ISBN 978-1-50672-447-8 / $29.99

AVAILABLE AT YOUR LOCAL COMICS SHOP OR BOOKSTORE
To find a comics shop near you, visit comicshoplocator.com For more information or to order direct, visit darkhorse.com

COMIXOLOGY ORIGINALS

DARK HORSE BOOKS

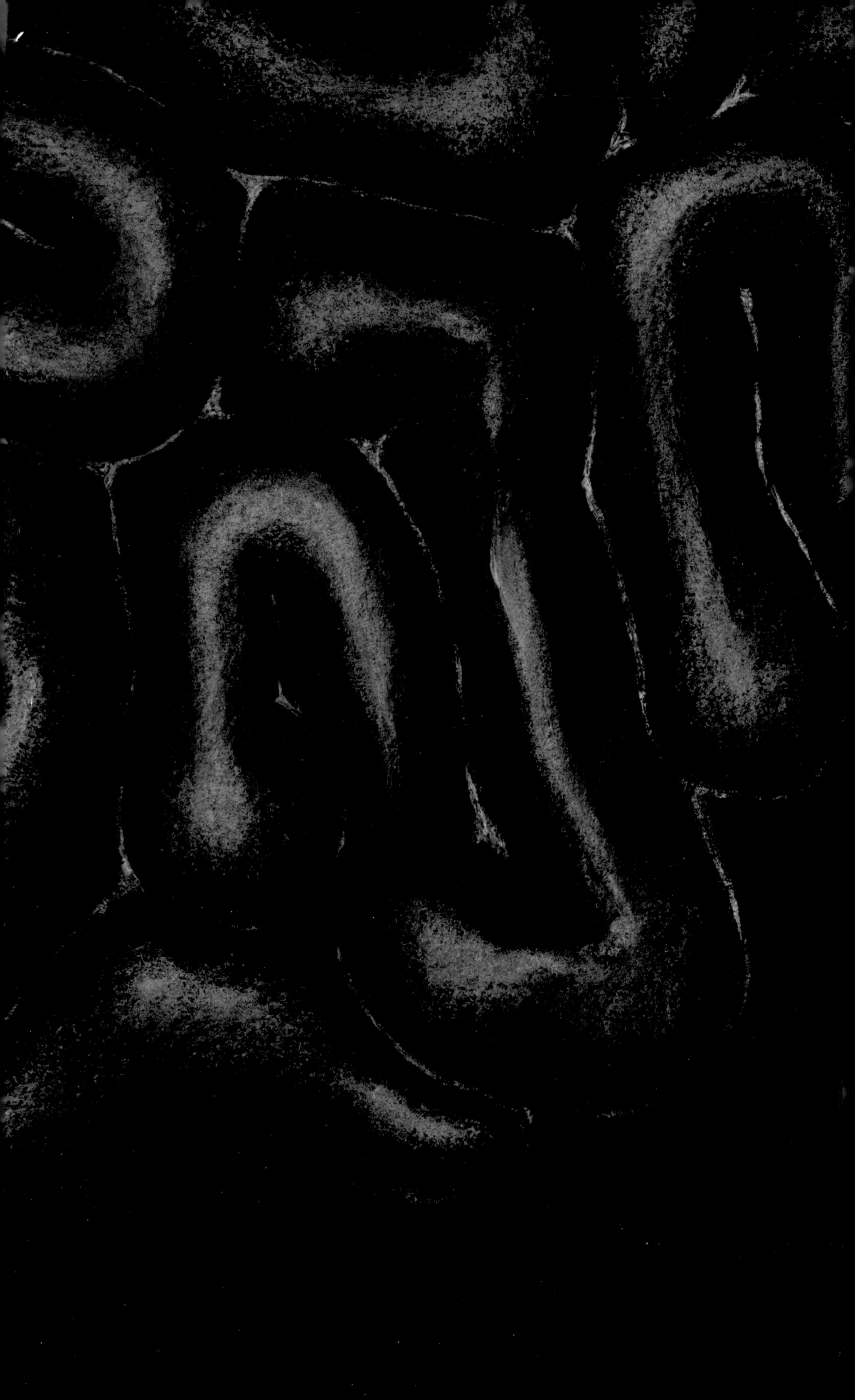